INTERDISCIPLINARY CONVERSATIONS

INTERDISCIPLINARY CONVERSATIONS

Challenging Habits of Thought

Myra H. Strober

Stanford University Press
Stanford, California

Stanford University Press
Stanford, California

Printed in the United States of America on acid-free, archival-quality paper

Library of Congress Cataloging-in-Publication Data

Strober, Myra H.
  Interdisciplinary conversations : challenging habits of thought / Myra H. Strober.
    p.   cm.
  Includes bibliographical references and index.
  ISBN 978-0-8047-7231-0 (cloth : alk. paper)
  1. Interdisciplinary research—Case studies.   2. Communication in learning and scholarship—Case studies.   3. Communication in science—Case studies.   I. Title.
Q180.55.I48S77   2010
001.4—dc22

                                                          2010010837

Contents

To my husband, Jay Jackman, with love and gratitude

I INTERDISCIPLINARITY IN PERSPECTIVE

1 Why Study Interdisciplinary Conversations?

SOME YEARS AGO, A COLLEAGUE AND I HAD A RESEARCH project that combined history and economics to explain how and why elementary school teaching became a woman's occupation in the United States. Midway through the project, at a team meeting, his research assistants and mine both presented analyses. His students were excited. They had found several diaries, which they used to understand teachers' reasons for entering the profession. They brought the diaries to the meeting and handled them lovingly. But my students were dismissive. Trained as quantitative researchers who use large data sets, they felt the diaries were unreliable and biased sources, representative only of those teachers who happened to write diaries.

Later in the meeting, the tables were turned. My students had large piles of computer output, complex statistical regressions on economic and educational data from several states. The history students argued that the quality of these nineteenth-century data was poor and said they didn't trust them. And besides, the regressions explained only 50 percent of the variance. Could you really think you'd explained something when half the explanation was still unknown?[1]

My historian colleague and I explained (again) that by using both quantitative and qualitative methods we were developing a richer understanding of the feminization process, that while we agreed that both methodologies had flaws, each contributed something of value to solving the puzzle. It was a hard sell.[2]

The questions raised by this story are at the heart of this book. What makes interdisciplinary conversations so difficult? What makes them fruitful?

The debate about barriers to interdisciplinarity is currently highly polarized. Columbia religion professor Mark C. Taylor maintains that disciplinary departments fatally impede interdisciplinarity. His solution? Abolish departments.[3] Sharply countering this view, sociologist Jerry Jacobs of the University of Pennsylvania contends that universities are doing a fine job in accommodating the flow of ideas across disciplines and need put in place little more than what already exists.[4]

Taylor and Jacobs are both wrong. We should *not* abolish departments and the disciplinary training they provide. But to nurture interdisciplinarity, faculty and administrators could go much further than they currently do.

The extraordinary complexity of knowledge in today's world creates a paradox. Its sheer volume and intricacy demand disciplinary specialization, even subspecialization. Innovative research and scholarship increasingly require immersion in the details of one's disciplinary dialogue, and departments are ideal settings for helping faculty to do this. However, departments limit the ability of academics to tackle problems that transcend disciplinary boundaries. The difficult task for faculty and administrators is to retain the benefits of disciplinary specialization while at the same time fostering interdisciplinary collaboration.

Most discussions about barriers to interdisciplinarity are about funding, the academic reward system, and the difficulties of evaluating research from multiple disciplines. This book is about different barriers, barriers that are rarely recognized let alone discussed: disciplinary habits of mind, disciplinary cultures, and interpersonal dynamics. It is also about what faculty members and administrators can do to overcome these barriers to create productive interdisciplinary conversations.

Objectives of the Book

The book analyzes six complex and sometimes stormy faculty seminars at three research universities that sought to use the seminars to foster conversations across disciplines. The account provides a sober reality check for those interested in doing, encouraging, and funding interdisciplinary work.

In 1990, in the conclusion to her landmark book *Interdisciplinarity: History,*

Theory, and Practice, Julie Thompson Klein noted our limited understanding of interdisciplinary work and the need for "compiling narratives in order to understand how interdisciplinary work is actually done."[5] In the two decades since her book was published, there have been only a handful of such hands-on studies.[6] In its 2005 report on facilitating interdisciplinarity, the National Academy of Sciences repeated what Klein said earlier: "Social-science research has not yet fully elucidated the complex social and intellectual processes that make for successful IDR [interdisciplinary research]. A deeper understanding of these processes will further enhance the prospects for creation and management of successful IDR projects."[7] This book adds to our understanding of the processes by which faculty talk to one another across disciplines.

However, despite the rich data provided about interdisciplinary interactions, this study is limited, as are all case studies, by the relatively small number of faculty interviewed, the small number of seminars studied, and reliance on self-reports. Moreover, all six seminars took place at three private research universities in the United States, not necessarily representative even of private American research universities, let alone of other types of institutions in the United States or elsewhere.

Yet all faculty everywhere are captives of their disciplinary cultures and habits, which, while they permit focus and access to deep knowledge, constrain interactions with colleagues from other fields. This close reading of the pleasures and pitfalls of interdisciplinary exchange will resonate with faculty and administrators at all types of institutions worldwide.

In this book, I do not test a theory. Rather, I engage in an exploratory investigation of events in interdisciplinary conversations, an attempt to explain those events, and an analysis of the factors that appear to make the conversations more enjoyable and productive. I also examine the follow-up activities necessary for participants and institutions to garner the full benefits of interdisciplinary conversations.

At a time when more and more clarion calls for interdisciplinarity are being issued, this book furthers our collective understanding of the dynamics, rewards, and challenges of conversations across disciplines. Although it deals with interdisciplinarity more broadly than studies of team science, it has the same objective as those studies: to examine collaborations across disciplines in order to understand the "circumstances that facilitate or hinder . . . effectiveness."[8]

Faculty who participated in the six seminars said they were excited by the possibility of conversing regularly with scholars from other disciplines; they initially thought that because they would be talking to colleagues with the same level of education, employed in the same job at the same university, they could easily converse with one another on intellectual matters. But it turns out that talking across disciplines is as difficult as talking to someone from another culture.[9]

Differences in language are the least of the problems; translations may be tedious and not entirely accurate, but they are relatively easy to accomplish. What is much more difficult is coming to understand the way colleagues from different disciplines *think*—their assumptions; concepts; categories; methods of discerning, evaluating, and reporting "truth"; and styles of arguing—their disciplinary cultures and habits of mind. The difficulty my students and those of my historian colleague had with interdisciplinary work was not that they did not understand one another's language; it was that they did not accept one another's fundamental beliefs about how to ascertain knowledge.

Moreover, the students working on my research project and many of the faculty in this study were neither open-minded nor patient. As academics, they had been taught to put skepticism and criticism first. Despite their expressed interest in learning across disciplines, they were not willing to fully enter into another cognitive world, suspending judgment until they obtained some mastery of strange ideas and methods. When new ideas and ways of thinking did not fit fairly easily into their own cognitive structures, they shut them out. This tendency was mitigated only when the seminar leader explicitly structured the series of conversations to focus on commonalities, contrasts, and synergies across ways of knowing.

Reading this book may well change your thinking about interdisciplinary work. You will learn that talking to colleagues across disciplines is not for the faint of heart, that it is more difficult than most people imagine. You will learn that engaging in interdisciplinary conversation is not always a positive experience, that unless participants are open-minded and dialogues well structured, the conversations can be boring, confusing, unpleasant, or downright hurtful. You will learn that interdisciplinarity doesn't always lead to new ideas; sometimes it simply rearranges the deck chairs. But you will also discover that interdisciplinary conversations have great potential and that there are several strategies and practices that increase the chances that they will be productive.

How you read this book may well depend on your own disciplinary background. If you are a historian, you may wonder why there is so much fuss about interdisciplinarity. Doesn't everyone use material from other disciplines in their work? If you are bewildered by postmodernism, or simply opposed to it, you may strongly identify with some opponents to it, as depicted in Chapter 4. If you believe that conversations should be allowed to unfold rather than be structured from the outset, you may be sympathetic to the style of leadership described in that same chapter. Whatever your reactions, they likely stem, at least in part, from your own disciplinary culture and habits of mind; watching your responses may well give you an immediate sense of what these concepts mean.

Interdisciplinarity at Research Universities

At the end of the 1990s, many research universities, private foundations, and government agencies began to increase their interest in interdisciplinarity. And since 2000, in part because of grants from foundations and government agencies, research universities are even more active in promoting interdisciplinary work; many of them have made interdisciplinarity a strategic goal.[10] For example, in 2004, Stanford made interdisciplinary research a strategic goal of its five-year plan, announcing three major interdisciplinary research initiatives in human health, the environment, and international relations.[11] Also in 2004, the University of Southern California launched a strategic plan calling for more interdisciplinarity, including promises to create "mechanisms that remove structural disincentives to such collective efforts.[12] In 2008, Purdue joined the chorus: "Through its new strategic plan, Purdue will set the pace for interdisciplinary synergies."[13]

The 2004 plea by Vartan Gregorian, then president of the Carnegie Corporation, was typical of many foundation executives and program officers:

> The complexity of the world requires us to have a better understanding of the relationships and connections between all fields that intersect and overlap— economics and sociology, law and psychology, business and history, physics and medicine, anthropology and political science.[14]

And a 2003 National Institute of Medicine report argued for more integration not only within the sciences but between the sciences and the behavioral and social sciences:

> Some parts of the scientific frontier require . . . the mobilization of interdisciplinary research teams. . . . Increasingly, investigators will need to integrate

knowledge.... And greater prominence must be given to research in the behavioral and social sciences.[15]

Two foundational beliefs motivate this increase in interest in interdisciplinarity: first, that finding effective solutions to complex problems requires collaboration by faculty from multiple disciplines; second, that faculty interchange across disciplines promotes creativity and hence increases the pace at which knowledge can move forward. In Chapter 2, we shall examine in greater depth the theory and evidence behind the idea that cognitive diversity is associated with creativity.

The Faculty Seminars and This Study

Atlantic Philanthropies was an early adopter of the idea that interdisciplinarity is advantageous for universities, and during my term there as the program officer for higher education from 1998 to 2000, the foundation made grants to three research universities to fund six interdisciplinary faculty seminars (two at each university).[16] To protect the anonymity of the faculty I interviewed, I call the universities Washington, Adams, and Jefferson.

Each seminar ran for one academic year, and the universities used their funding to hire postdoctoral fellows (postdocs), relieving most faculty participants of one course. Postdocs were also invited to participate in the seminars. The underlying rationale for the seminars came close to anthropologist Clifford Geertz's notion that interdisciplinary colloquia provide a means for faculty members from different disciplines to come together and teach one another about their fields:

> The hard dying hope that there can again be (assuming there ever was) an integrated high culture ... has to be abandoned in favor of the much more modest sort of ambition that scholars, artists, scientists, professionals, and (dare we hope?) administrators ... can begin to find something circumstantial to say to one another again ... one in which econometricians, epigraphers, cytochemists, and iconologists can give a credible account of themselves to one another.[17]

The aspirations for the conversations were modest: to provide an opportunity for faculty to talk to one another about their disciplinary perspectives on a variety of topics. The hope was that these conversations would lead participants to develop new interdisciplinary courses and perhaps, eventually, interdisciplinary research proposals. There were no products that the group as a whole was asked to create, except intellectual camaraderie and a sense of being a part of a university (as opposed to a department).[18]

The seminars differed by size, participation of high-level administrators, and leadership. They also differed in breadth of focus and the number of different fields from which faculty were drawn. (For details, see Appendix Table A-1.)

At Washington, the seminars were about the social sciences, and the vast majority of participants were from social science fields. The president and the provost, both of whom were humanists, were participants in both seminars. In the first year, the conversations were about the social sciences per se and were used not only to explore the social sciences, but also to convince the president and the provost that the social sciences at Washington should receive additional financial resources and that the university should fund an interdisciplinary social science research program.

In the second year, Washington's conversations were focused on inequality. This time, the seminar was attended not only by the president and the provost, but also by a vice-provost from the humanities. However, the conversations were not designed to persuade these administrators, but rather solely to examine the ways in which each of the social sciences understands and studies inequality.

At Adams, the conversations were about science studies in the first year and ethics in the second year. Adams administrators who wrote the grant proposal hoped that faculty conversations on these subjects would lead not only to collaborative courses, but also to the development of university programs in those areas. The Adams seminars were smaller than the others; they were the only ones not led by a faculty member and the only ones in which no administrators participated. In the science studies seminar, faculty from the sciences, social sciences, and humanities were all represented. In the ethics seminar, most attendees were from the humanities; and the ethics seminar was the only one of the six that included junior faculty.

The topic of Jefferson's first seminar was consilience, how various fields can be brought together; the topic of its second seminar was representation, how various fields represent reality. Jefferson's seminars had even more administrative participation than did Washington's. Also, the Jefferson seminars were the only ones that included faculty from the arts as well as those from the sciences, social sciences, and humanities. Administrators at Jefferson hoped the seminars would serve to introduce their star faculty from various fields to one another and that the conversations would serve to tie faculty more closely to the university.

After I left Atlantic Philanthropies and returned to Stanford, I continued my conversations with seminar leaders and visited one seminar session at each university. In effect, the seminars provided six fishbowls, and I wanted to understand what happened in them. In 2002, I applied for and received a grant from the Ford Foundation to interview a sample of faculty and write a book about the seminars. I know of no other such detailed study of interdisciplinary conversations among faculty at a research university.[19] (Details of the study are in the Appendix.)

What Makes Interdisciplinary Conversations Fruitful?

From the perspective of Atlantic Philanthropies and the administrators who wrote the grant proposals, the conversations would be deemed fruitful if they resulted in new interdisciplinary courses and perhaps, eventually, collaborative research projects. But faculty interviewees found their seminars productive in other ways. They recollected with great pleasure conversations that engaged them in serious intellectual play and reminded them of why they had become academics in the first place. They also reported satisfaction with new intellectual insights, enhanced intellectual self-esteem, and new relationships with colleagues from other fields.

The affective aspect of conversations figured prominently in assessments of the conversations' success.[20] Participants appreciated conversations that were infused with productive conflict, conversations that were neither uncivil nor dull. Although some were able to glean intellectual insights from conversations even when they were conflict-ridden, they did not judge such conversations to be fruitful overall.

In evaluating the success of the seminars, I use both the criterion in the original grant proposals—the creation of new interdisciplinary courses and research proposals—as well as criteria faculty used to assess their own experiences: providing opportunities for serious play, developing new intellectual insights, gaining enhanced intellectual self-esteem, and meeting new colleagues from other disciplines.

It is not necessarily a good thing to organize interdisciplinary conversations. They may become destructive, creating deep resentments and fostering distaste for interdisciplinary dialogue. Prerequisite to a series of fruitful conversations are a mix of intellectually diverse participants who practice open-mindedness and interpersonal civility and a leader who carefully structures the sessions toward a search for intellectual common ground.

Plan of the Book

This introductory chapter explains the book's focus, introduces the subject of interdisciplinarity at research universities, describes the study on which the book is based, and discusses measures of success. Chapter 2 examines the concept of interdisciplinarity and its rationale. What is interdisciplinarity? For that matter, what is a discipline? What are the arguments in favor of disciplinarity? What are the barriers to it?

The four chapters in Part 2 explain and analyze the details of what happened in the conversations. Using theoretical frameworks from such scholars as Clifford Geertz, Howard Margolis, Pierre Bourdieu, Elliot Eisner, Dell Hymes, Helen Schwartzman, and Peter Elbow, we will examine how cultural practices and habits of mind, as well as interpersonal dynamics, contributed to the difficult dialogues and at how and why some conversations avoided problems that surfaced in others.

Part 3 looks at what we have learned in this study. Chapter 7 argues that outstanding leadership is one of the most important ingredients for the success of interdisciplinary conversations. The chapter applies the work of several scholars of leadership to examine the techniques of the various seminar leaders and summarizes the skills that differentiate successful from less successful leadership.

Chapter 8 looks at the outcomes of the conversations. It introduces the concept of serious play to explain the intellectual enjoyment and insights that many faculty got from their interdisciplinary exchanges. It also examines the likely reasons why the goal of creating joint teaching and research projects was not met.

Chapter 9 reviews the barriers to interdisciplinarity, the social science explanations for these barriers, and the successful strategies used by some leaders to mitigate these barriers. It concludes with an analysis of the centrality of open-mindedness to successful interdisciplinary dialogue. Returning to Chapter 3's discussion of Peter Elbow's distinction between the doubting game and the believing game, I argue that the monopolistic hold of the doubting game in academia (and in business as well) seriously inhibits our ability to engage with ideas from other fields. In addition to having excellent leaders who know how to establish an atmosphere of trust among participants, maximizing the fruitfulness of interdisciplinary conversation requires that participants listen to one another nonjudgmentally, seeking to fully absorb unfamiliar ideas and methodologies before attempting to evaluate or criticize them.

2 The Calls for More Interdisciplinarity

IN THE OPENING YEARS OF THE TWENTY-FIRST CENTURY, the problems that confound us are complex. Whether the challenge involves creating more sustainable sources of energy, rebuilding a badly fractured global economic system, or promoting gender equity, the scholars and researchers working to solve perplexing problems at the cutting edge of their field must track developments in their discipline or subdiscipline in minute detail, lest they miss some recent new information. They must become not only specialists, but subspecialists.

At the same time, however, finding coherent solutions to these multifaceted problems requires that scholars and researchers collaborate with colleagues outside of their discipline.[1] Designing humane rules for containing health care costs requires input not only from physicians and economists but also from ethicists. Creating peaceful relationships with countries across the world requires insight not only from historians and political scientists, but also from agronomists and anthropologists. Collaboration across disciplines increases the likelihood that proposed solutions will be effective.

To the extent that interdisciplinarity enhances creativity, collaboration also increases the possibility that solutions will be innovative. As scholars and researchers consider questions from outside their own disciplines, learn other disciplines' methods of answering questions, and think about the possible significance of other disciplines' findings for their own work, they may begin to think about their own disciplines' knowledge in new ways.[2] Moreover, by consulting with scholars and researchers from other areas, they may avoid mistakes that arise from too narrow a view.

On the teaching side, the call for interdisciplinarity results from a dissatisfaction with the idea that undergraduate students, whose coursework exposes them to multiple disciplinary perspectives, are left to integrate them on their own. Although many departments help students to integrate knowledge *within* the discipline, for example, by requiring a capstone course in the major, they do not assist students to integrate knowledge *across* disciplines. Nor is there generally a place in the curriculum where students are systematically taught to recognize the limitations of any single discipline, although they may be fortunate enough to have a professor somewhere along the way who points these out.[3] Interdisciplinary courses are places where the limitations of various disciplinary perspectives can be discussed, even if only indirectly.

This chapter deals with three questions: What is interdisciplinarity? Why is it seen as desirable? What are the barriers to interdisciplinary work?

What Is Interdisciplinarity?

To define interdisciplinarity, I first discuss the definition of a discipline, including a brief history of the development of disciplines. To be interdisciplinary one must first be proficient in a discipline. The whole purpose of interdisciplinary collaboration is to draw on disciplinary expertise in several disciplines.

As will become obvious, the definitions of what a discipline is are both complex and variegated. I examine them in some detail because learning about their intricacies helps us to understand the difficulties of interdisciplinarity and the complexities involved in placing these manifold aspects of various disciplines side by side.

A second aspect of understanding interdisciplinarity is differentiating it from its close relatives: multidisciplinarity, cross-disciplinarity, and transdisciplinarity. Although I conclude that for the purposes of this book I will not distinguish among these cousins, it is important to understand the different degrees of possible integration of disciplines that each of these terms suggests.

What Is a Discipline?

Merriam-Webster's Collegiate Dictionary, 11th ed., defines *discipline* as "a field of study," and gives the Latin definition of the root, *discupulus,* as "pupil."

Quoting from the 1972 publication by the Organisation for Economic Co-operation and Development (OECD), Julie Thompson Klein defines a discipline as "tools, methods, procedures, exempla, concepts, and theories that account coherently for a set of objects or subjects."[4] However, these definitions are not helpful in distinguishing between disciplinarity and interdisciplinarity, since both are branches of learning and both may fit the OECD description. Moreover, disciplines are more than simply branches of learning. They provide not only "a conceptual structure," but also "an instructive community" and "a communication network," as well as a "cultural system" and a sense of personal identity.[5]

The history of academic disciplines (and the history of a search for their integration) goes back to ancient Greece and the philosophies of Plato and Aristotle.[6] Aristotle divided knowledge into three categories, in descending order of status: theoretical (including theology, mathematics, and physics), practical (including ethics and politics), and productive (including fine arts, poetics, and engineering), with philosophy considered the branch of knowledge that would bring all other knowledge together.[7] This idea of philosophy as an integrative field persisted until the nineteenth century.[8]

By medieval times, knowledge was divided into two main categories: the *trivium*, consisting of grammar, rhetoric, and dialectic; and the *quadrivium*, which included arithmetic, astronomy, geometry, and music. These were the basis for studying natural, moral, and mental philosophy.[9] But there was no disciplinary specialization for students; they were expected to study in all of these fields.

Disciplines were further differentiated at the new universities that were created during the eleventh century in Italy, at Salerno for medicine and at Bologna for law, and in the twelfth century in Paris, Oxford, and Cambridge, to provide education not only in medicine and law, but also in arts and theology.[10] During the next several centuries additional universities were formed throughout Europe. However, it was not until the scientific revolution of the sixteenth and seventeenth centuries that disciplines became more important. As scientists such as Copernicus, Galileo, Kepler, and Newton achieved success, the idea took hold that new knowledge could be gained by limiting the questions on which one worked.[11] The development of science academies in the seventeenth century, and especially the publications produced by those academies, further enhanced the idea that disciplinarity led to great accomplishments.[12] In the late seventeenth and eighteenth centuries, enlightenment thought aided the growth of disciplines both within and outside of science.

The idea that human beings could find answers to complex problems by means of their reason fostered the view that limiting scholars' fields of inquiry and systematizing knowledge into categories was indispensable to progress.[13]

The prototype for the research university that is familiar today was created in Germany in the late eighteenth century. Meant to provide a liberal (broad) education for students, as well as a faculty engaged in research, it was this type of university that became the model on which several American universities ultimately reorganized themselves a century or so later. But although the power of disciplinary knowledge continued to increase in the eighteenth century, with calls (from Auguste Comte, for example) for the nonsciences to become more "scientific,"[14] the plethora of disciplines with which we are now familiar did not emerge until the latter part of the nineteenth century.

In the United States, in the last two decades of the nineteenth century, twenty-five disciplinary associations were formed.[15] At the same time, major American universities led the way in restructuring into disciplinary departments, creating the undergraduate disciplinary major as well as discipline-based graduate programs.[16] These two developments, the growth of disciplinary societies outside universities and the growth of discipline-based departments with disciplinary majors and graduate programs within universities, greatly consolidated the power of disciplines and disciplinary knowledge.[17] Departments became the channels through which academic resources flowed, and they, combined with new journals, some of them published by departments and some by disciplinary societies, became the arbiters of academic quality.[18] Today, among the major research universities, only Carnegie Mellon and Rockefeller are not organized by departments.[19]

To decide whether a branch of knowledge is a discipline by using knowledge criteria alone is an unpromising task. For example, would the existence of a distinctive theory, paradigm, body of information, methodology, or scholarly journal allow us to agree on whether women's studies is a discipline, whether clinical psychology is a discipline or a subdiscipline, or whether statistics is a discipline or a branch of mathematics? Knowledge criteria do not result in agreement among academics on these matters, in part because knowledge is constantly changing, and in part because participants in the debate are not impartial arbiters. In other words, disciplines are both categories of knowledge and categories in academic institutions.[20]

Stephen Turner has a rather pragmatic definition of a discipline. A field is a discipline if it meets two conditions: (1) it has departmental status across a large number of institutions, and (2) it has a market for new doctorates. In other words, to be termed a discipline a field must have both "identity and exchange."[21] The identity comes from achieving departmental status. The exchange comes from having a market for new doctorates.[22]

In some respects this definition of disciplinarity is unsatisfactory, because it relies so heavily on the politics and economics of institutions and deals with matters of epistemology only indirectly. However, its emphasis on departments and doctoral training is useful for understanding interdisciplinarity. Interdisciplinarity is difficult because scholars and researchers who have been trained and socialized in one field have trouble talking to their counterparts trained and socialized in other fields. By defining disciplines as synonymous with departments, we ensure that the scholars who wear a particular disciplinary hat have been socialized in similar fashion and that their initiations and ongoing customs and culture are both different from those of other scholars and akin to those of academics with the same disciplinary label.[23]

Those who take what has been termed a genealogical approach to studying disciplines (following Friedrich Nietzsche and Michel Foucault) argue that attempts to define them must make reference to power as well as to knowledge. As Ellen Messer-Davidow, David Shumway, and David Sylvan put it, "Genealogy insists that knowledge and power are implicated in each other."[24] Timothy Lenoir, following both Foucault and Pierre Bourdieu, defines disciplines as "institutional formations for organizing schemes of perception, appreciation, and action, and for inculcating them as tools of cognition and communication."[25]

This multiplicity of definitions calls our attention to the extraordinary complexity of disciplines and the numerous dimensions along which they differ (degree of stability, degree of consensus, tightness of paradigm, openness to other ideas, and status).[26] Nonetheless, the term *interdisciplinarity* is perhaps even more difficult to pin down.

Interdisciplinarity and Its Cousins

Veronica Boix Mansilla defines *interdisciplinarity* as "a form of inquiry that integrates knowledge and modes of thinking from two or more disciplines . . . or established fields of study . . . to produce a cognitive or practical advancement (e.g. explain a phenomenon, create a product, develop a method, find a solution, raise a question) that would have been unlikely through single disciplinary means."[27] She notes that this definition has three salient features: its goal is the advancement of basic or applied knowledge, it uses disciplinary knowledge, and it is integrative.[28]

The definition put forth by the National Academy of Sciences is similar: "Interdisciplinary research is a mode of research by teams or individuals that integrates information, data, techniques, tools, perspectives, concepts, and/or theories from two or more disciplines or bodies of specialized knowledge to advance fundamental understanding or to solve problems whose solutions are beyond the scope of a single discipline or area of research practice."[29]

Interdisciplinarity, multidisciplinarity, cross-disciplinarity, and *transdisciplinarity* are all terms used to indicate that two or more disciplines are being used to solve a problem (or create a problem), explore a problem, comment on a text, or teach a class. *Multidisciplinarity* and *cross-disciplinarity* are synonyms and denote less integration of methodologies, theories, contents, and perspectives than does *interdisciplinarity.*

Transdisciplinarity denotes an even greater level of integration, although there is a wide range of possible definitions of the term.[30] In some cases it refers to the creation of a unity of all knowledge, such as when Jean Piaget talked of "a total system without any boundaries between disciplines,"[31] or when E. O. Wilson proposed a consilience of knowledge, a concept that we shall discuss further in Chapter 5.[32] In the biomedical context, transdisciplinarity means the "development of shared conceptual frameworks that integrate and transcend the multiple disciplinary perspectives represented among team members."[33] In some European literature, it is called Mode 2 knowledge and often includes cooperation between researchers and "stakeholders in society," the idea being that the work transcends sectors of interested parties.[34]

Using a culinary metaphor, a disciplinary dish consists of only one food—a potato, for example. If we add steamed carrots and sautéed peas to the potato, we have a multidisciplinary or cross-disciplinary dish. For the dish to be interdisciplinary, the vegetables have to be integrated, cooked together into a soup or tossed into a salad.[35] To become transdisciplinary, the individual ingredients would have to be no longer identifiable; for example, if all of the cooked ingredients for a soup were put through a blender, we would have a transdisciplinary soup.[36]

Unfortunately, culinary metaphors are inadequate to distinguish types of knowledge in the real world, where the degree of integration of disciplines in research and teaching spans a broad spectrum.[37] It is relatively easy to discern the two ends of the spectrum; for example, when faculty members lecture sequentially in a class, each laying out his or her disciplinary insights and leaving it to students to integrate (or fail to integrate) the various frameworks, we have a clear example of multidisciplinarity. At the other extreme, when two disciplines become a single discipline, as for example when biology and chemistry form biochemistry, we have a clear instance of transdisciplinarity.[38]

In between the extremes, however, it is not always obvious where we should draw the dividing lines between multidisciplinarity and interdisciplinarity or between interdisciplinarity and transdisciplinarity. For example, suppose scholars or researchers modify their understandings based on perspectives from another discipline (such as when economists use findings from psychology to revise their assumptions about the rationality of decision makers);[39] or they use protocols, equipment, or insights developed in another discipline(as when immunologists use laboratory techniques developed in genetics or chemists integrate ideas from biology or physics);[40] or they generate synergies (as when an economist and a literary theorist use Gary Becker's economic theory of marriage to examine the motivations of characters in Jane Austen's *Pride and Prejudice*).[41] It is not clear what name we should give to these various types of collaborations.

In their review article on interdisciplinarity, Jerry Jacobs and Scott Frickel align themselves with those who make "loose distinctions" between interdisciplinarity and multidisciplinarity.[42] And as Daniel Stokols and Shalini Misra and their colleagues observe with regard to medical science, in practice transdisciplinarity and interdisciplinarity are often treated as "basically equivalent" and the term *interdisciplinarity* is used.[43] I agree with the notion of loose distinctions. When I began this research, I made finer distinctions than I do now. At this point, I find the lines between multidisciplinarity, interdisciplinarity, and transdisciplinarity often hard to draw. As a result, in this book I use the term *interdisciplinarity* to refer to situations in which more than one discipline is involved, regardless of the degree of their integration.

In addition to terminology, there are two other questions in the literature on interdisciplinarity that are of interest for this study. The first concerns the centrality of integration to interdisciplinarity. Is more integration *better* than less? In teaching, there is evident value in assisting students to integrate perspectives from their various courses and giving them an understanding of the limitations of any single disciplinary lens.[44] But in creating new knowledge, it is not necessarily better to integrate perspectives. For example, Yvonne Rogers, Mike Scaife, and Antonio Rizzo argue that in cognitive science, a field that draws on researchers from philosophy, psychology, and artificial intelligence, important new developments have emerged even though the field has remained multidisciplinary rather than interdisciplinary and researchers continue to use methods and constructs from their own disciplines.[45]

The question of the centrality of integration to interdisciplinarity also comes up with respect to fields such as women's studies, racial and ethnic studies, and cultural studies, which are generally included under the interdisciplinary umbrella but have scholars who are not much interested in integrating scholarship; they are primarily involved in using other disciplinary perspectives to critique their own.[46] We need a broader definition of interdisciplinarity if we are to include these fields.

Lisa Lattuca suggests that a definition of interdisciplinarity that stresses *interactions* between disciplines rather than collaboration or integration is a more inclusive definition.[47] Since the groups studied here were focused on interaction rather than collaboration or integration, this is an important point.

David Sill makes a related point when he argues that integrating interdisciplinary work should be seen as a process rather than an outcome.[48] This observation is also important for this study because even though I may consider the new knowledge faculty obtained as an *outcome* of the seminar, it is quite likely that many of them viewed their seminar experience as a *process* in which they integrated other disciplinary perspectives into their own thought.

A second question concerns the role of single-faculty interdisciplinarity. Some researchers equate interdisciplinarity or multidisciplinarity with the involvement of multiple faculty.[49] But multiple players are not necessary for interdisciplinarity; a single faculty member can absorb material and insights from another discipline, by reading, discussion, or both, and integrate them into his or her courses or writing.[50] Indeed, as we shall see, most of the interdisciplinarity that emerged from the six seminars studied here was of that type.

Why Should We Care About Interdisciplinary Research and Teaching?

As noted in Chapter 1, there are two major premises underlying the push for interdisciplinarity: the solutions to some problems require insights from multiple disciplines, and the diversity of disciplinary knowledge, perspectives, and methods is a source of creativity.

Promoting interdisciplinary work is not new.[51] From the time of its founding at the turn of the twentieth century, the Rockefeller Institute was interested in interdisciplinary research in the biomedical sciences.[52] In the 1920s, the Social Science Research Council was created to promote more collaborative work across the social sciences, and the Laura Spellman Rockefeller Foundation was also interested in this goal.[53] In the 1930s, area studies came into being in some universities, and in the 1940s and 1950s, government agencies brought disciplines together to make progress on issues in agriculture and military applications of science. The Manhattan Project, which produced the atomic bomb, is probably the most frequently cited example of interdisciplinary work. In the 1960s and 1970s, interdisciplinary work was encouraged as a way to solve social problems.[54] In the 1970s, the OECD became interested in interdisciplinarity and issued an influential study on the subject, and two professional associations concerned with interdisciplinarity were formed, the U.S.-based Association for Integrative Studies and the International Association for the Study of Interdisciplinary Research.[55]

In the last twenty-five years of the twentieth century, there was also a huge growth in the number of interdisciplinary teaching programs in U.S. universities. In a sample of almost two thousand institutions of higher education, Steven Brint and his associates found that the number of such programs grew almost 250 percent during the period from 1975 to 2000, from 674 to 1,633. This growth was *not* due merely to increases in student enrollment, which grew only about 18 percent during that period.[56]

What is new in the current scene is the intensity of the call for interdisciplinarity and the increased funding available for it. Jacobs and Frickel point to numerous instances of a recent "heating up" of efforts, most of them "top-down," to promote interdisciplinarity.[57] These efforts have come from major research universities as well as from the National Institutes of Health, the National Science Foundation, the National Academy of Sciences, the MacArthur Foundation, the Andrew W. Mellon Foundation, the Robert Wood Johnson Foundation, and the American Association of Universities (the association of major research universities).[58]

In his 2005 interviews with 144 leaders at eighty-nine research universities and his review of sixty-nine strategic planning documents from research universities, Brint found that the vast majority sought to promote interdisciplinary research by offering start-up packages to selected faculty to head up interdisciplinary centers, providing seed money for new projects, and creating multidisciplinary graduate programs.

Creso Sá reports that the University of Wisconsin at Madison pioneered a cluster hiring program to foster interdisciplinarity, which has now been emulated at Rensselaer Polytechnic Institute, Florida State University, and Louisiana State University, but that some of the cluster faculty at the University of Wisconsin "have reported the usual perceptions of interdisciplinary work being undervalued at the time of evaluation and promotion."[59] Duke University and the University of California have both sought to make faculty promotion and evaluation procedures more favorable to interdisciplinary work.[60] Although these efforts have been greatest in the sciences, they have also been present in the humanities, arts, and social sciences.[61] However, the extent to which these efforts have been successful in creating more interdisciplinary work has not yet been reported.

There has also been an increase in interest in interdisciplinarity as a topic of study. In a wide variety of disciplinary journals between 1990 and 2007, there were nearly eight thousand articles that had the term *interdisciplinarity* in the article's title, the number of such articles rising steadily during that period.[62]

Interdisciplinarity Is a Complement to Disciplinarity, Not a Substitute

The merits of interdisciplinarity may have been oversold in the recent burst of interest in interdisciplinary work and its alleged ability to solve societal problems and promote the growth of knowledge.[63] And it may be that administrators' encouragement of interdisciplinarity is in part an effort to tap into new sources of funds.[64] Or they may be hoping to transfer some power away from departments and toward the central administration.[65] But in my experience, most administrators, governmental agencies, and philanthropies do not seek a wholesale reorganization of knowledge structures, but rather some changes at the margin, a shift in the balance between specialized disciplinary work and interdisciplinary collaboration. *Both* disciplinary specialization (and subspecialization) *and* interdisciplinary work are seen as critical to the continued advancement of knowledge.[66]

From a cognitive perspective, by definition, one cannot be interdisciplinary unless and until one has a thorough grasp of disciplinary knowledge.[67]

Julie Thompson Klein, one of the earliest and foremost scholars of interdisciplinarity makes a similar point: "The present condition underscores the importance of developing both disciplinary expertise and interdisciplinary capacity. Nothing less is capable of equipping members of interdisciplinary teams for the tasks and the problems they address."[68] Also, from a resource perspective, funds are limited and government agencies are seeking to support both disciplinary and interdisciplinary research.[69]

In the same way that individuals seek to balance their investment portfolios with a mixture of stocks and bonds, administrators and funding agencies want to rebalance universities' research portfolios such that they have a higher proportion of interdisciplinary work. Investing in research within a single field may be thought of as comparable to investing in bonds; it is a relatively safe investment, but with possibly less potential for solving the major problems of society. Investing in interdisciplinary research, on the other hand, is riskier; it requires a large initial investment (learning a new field or creating collaborative ventures with colleagues from other fields) that may not pay off at all. On the other hand, the payoff might be spectacular. The advice financial advisers give about the wisdom of a diversified investment strategy is apropos here. Universities need both disciplinarity and interdisciplinarity in their teaching and research portfolios.

James March's distinction between exploitation and exploration follows this line of reasoning.[70] March defines exploitation as activities that rely on existing knowledge; people who engage in them "exploit" what they already know. People who engage in activities involving exploration, on the other hand, move away from what they already know and seek new activities. Exploration is far riskier than exploitation.[71] Using a simple model, March shows that for the well-being of a company as a whole, its optimum project investment portfolio should have more exploration than it is likely to get if individual decision makers are left on their own.[72]

In many ways, Atlantic's decision to fund the seminars studied here was an effort to promote more exploration-type behavior among institutions and faculty. One of my interviewees, biochemist Victor, said that part of his enthusiasm about his seminar came from the willingness of both Atlantic and Jefferson to support a risky endeavor.

> What universities should be doing is . . . thinking of lunatic, insane, crazy, ridiculous ideas, because they have the luxury of doing so; in the business world,

you can't always do that because you may fail. Our job is to fail. We should be generating ten wacko, wild ideas a year . . . and if nine of them fail, we're doing our job.

Interdisciplinarity and Creativity

The idea that diversity fosters creativity has deep roots. Adam Smith argued that "when the mind is employed about a variety of objects it is somehow expanded and enlarged."[73] Seventy years later, John Stuart Mill was even more specific:

> It is hardly possible to overrate the value . . . of placing human beings in contact with persons dissimilar to themselves, and with modes of thought and action unlike those with which they are familiar. . . . Such communication has always been, and is particularly in the present age, one of the primary sources of progress.[74]

Leigh Thompson defines creativity as "the production of novel and useful ideas—the ability to form new concepts using existing knowledge." She identifies its constituents as fluency, flexibility, and originality. Fluency is "the ability to generate *many solutions*"; flexibility is "the ability to change approaches to a problem"; and originality is "the ability to generate unusual solutions."[75] Although creativity is an individual trait, groups can also be creative, capitalizing on, and perhaps even enhancing, the creativity of its members.[76]

The argument that scholars and researchers from multiple disciplines are more creative than those from a single discipline comes from the idea that thinking in terms of *categories* of ideas (as opposed to number of ideas) about a problem enhances creativity, so that when members of a team are diverse with respect to education, experience, perceptions, and point of view and are asked to chew on a problem, they come up with a greater number of categories, which increases their fluency, flexibility, and originality.[77]

Often the root of creativity is analogical reasoning, "the act of applying one concept or idea from a particular domain to another domain."[78] At the same time, one of the blocks to creativity may be failure to notice that information from one area of knowledge can be transferred to another. Experts are better than novices in recognizing the promise of transferring knowledge across domains within a discipline. The case for interdisciplinarity among experts is that because their collective expertise is more diverse than that of any individual expert, interdisciplinary groups have the potential to more readily apply concepts across knowledge realms.[79]

From an economic perspective, this argument translates to the notion that cultural diversity (or disciplinary diversity) will improve productivity and increase output or improve the quality of output. From a sociological perspective, the idea that bridging cultures leads to creativity was taken up recently by Ronald S. Burt, who demonstrated empirically that when individuals get input from more than one group, they learn more than one way of thinking and that gives them more opportunities to cull, translate, and integrate whatever information is most useful.[80]

In their study of scientists in biomedicine, Rogers Hollingsworth and Ellen Jane Hollingsworth found that institutes, such as the Rockefeller Institute and the California Institute of Technology (Cal Tech), that were "not differentiated into academic departments or other units that would fragment the production of knowledge," but instead provided researchers with a high degree of interaction in collegial groups that were diverse and interdisciplinary, were more likely to have scientists who were winners of their field's most prestigious prizes. In their words, "It is the diversity of disciplines and paradigms to which individuals are exposed in frequent and intense interactions that increases the tendency for breakthroughs."[81]

Related to the notion that diversity encourages creativity is the notion that fields are more fertile at their edges. In explaining the use of the name Hybrid Vigor for their interdisciplinary institute, Denise Caruso and Diana Rhoten clarify the metaphor.

> Hybrid Vigor was named to represent metaphorically (thus, by definition, imprecisely) the fecundity at the edges of a field, where cross-pollination between the wild and the cultivated can increased the overall health of crops.[82]

Whether or not agronomists have in fact corroborated the principle underlying this metaphor, it appears that there is a case to be made for it within the social sciences. In their book *Creative Marginality*, Mattei Dogan and Robert Pahre find that at the densely populated cores of social science disciplines too much agreement leads to scholars with "blinders," but that at the peripheries of fields, with many fewer players, there are often major innovations.[83]

In his book *The Difference: How the Power of Diversity Creates Better Groups, Firms, Schools, and Societies,* Scott Page presents theoretical and empirical work on the relationship between cognitive diversity and success in problem solving. His conclusion is that cognitive diversity—differences in "perspectives, heuristics, categorizations, and predictive models"—*can* improve "performance at problem solving," but that there is a high variance in outcome and many studies do not show such benefit.[84] He attributes this high variance to the fact that many people who engage in groups with cognitive diversity are inexperienced in such interactions. When the interactions work well, there is benefit; when they don't, there is none. In other words, the benefit is there to be reaped if the participants in the group can figure out how to do so.

Page's work brings us directly to the two main questions of this book. How and why do group interactions impede successful interdisciplinary exchange and what are the factors that appear to enhance successful interdisciplinary exchange? But before we analyze barriers to interdisciplinarity that stem from group interactions, we examine several institutional issues.

What Are the Barriers to Interdisciplinarity?

The push toward interdisciplinarity in academe by private foundations, government agencies, and administrators may be seen as an effort to get faculty to take greater risks in their decisions about what knowledge to pursue. Of course, numerous faculty already engage in exploration within their own disciplines, but the current call by administrators and others is for more interdisciplinary exploration. As Irwin Feller notes, there is a large gulf between universities' goals to strategically increase interdisciplinary work and the implementation of these goals. As he puts it, "strategic commitment is not implementation."[85] Or, as Andrew Abbott said about the history of interdisciplinarity: "Everybody always thinks it is a great thing, but nobody has figured out a way to make it work as a formalized, permanent structure."[86]

The world was not always this way. Historically, many of our most renowned scholars worked in multiple fields. Gottfried Leibniz made contributions in philosophy, history, and law as well as in mathematics. Johann Goethe not only created *Faust* and other literary masterpieces, but also worked in anatomy, botany, and law. And Karl Marx integrated material that would now fall into at least four of the social sciences—history, economics, sociology, and political science.

But in the contemporary context, at large research universities, if administrators, foundations, and government agencies want to see more faculty engage in interdisciplinary work, they need to lower the risk of doing so. Engaging in interdisciplinary projects has large up-front costs. For example, Lucy Shapiro reports that in starting Bio X, a large interdisciplinary institute at Stanford that combines biology, physics, engineering, and medicine, the four faculty founders needed to meet weekly for two years before they understood one another's work well enough to begin collaborative initiatives.[87]

Making seed funding and major grant funding for interdisciplinary projects more readily available may lower faculty risk to some extent, by reducing a faculty member's time spent searching for funds.[88] However, preparing a large multifaculty interdisciplinary proposal is more time-consuming than preparing a smaller proposal in one's own field, and the amount of money a single scholar receives from a large proposal where many faculty share the funding may be smaller than that obtained from a smaller proposal with fewer investigators. Moreover, if many teams are attracted by the large amounts made available for interdisciplinary research, the probability of obtaining funding from such requests for proposals may be diminished. In addition, coordinating with multiple faculty from several disciplines is often both time- and energy-consuming.[89] These negative aspects of seeking interdisciplinary funding may be particularly salient for junior faculty, who have only a short period of time to prove themselves before tenure and promotion decisions.[90]

A second set of risks of interdisciplinarity occurs at the evaluation stage of the project.[91] Not only may researchers find it difficult to find a journal wishing to publish work that crosses disciplinary lines, but to be deemed successful, the project, and hence the faculty involved, will need to be evaluated positively by colleagues in at least two different disciplines, each likely to use different criteria for originality or effectiveness.[92]

Hiring, promotion, salary, and grants generally favor those who specialize narrowly within their discipline;[93] and the evaluation system for tenure and promotion, in particular, presents a strong disincentive for young faculty to work outside of their discipline.[94] By conducting tenure and promotion reviews that value authorship of articles published in prestigious disciplinary journals, and by seeking evaluations from well-known scholars who work in a single discipline, research universities hamper young scholars whose work is interdisciplinary.[95] Many universities are now working to revise their evaluation and reward structures, but there is still much to do.[96] Eventually the revisions will need also to involve disciplinary organizations, scholarly journals, and ranking systems such as the National Research Council rankings of graduate education.[97]

Besides increasing funding for interdisciplinary work and revising university evaluation and reward structures as means of lowering the costs and risks of interdisciplinarity, there is a much less discussed third strategy: making it easier to talk to colleagues from other disciplines. This is the strategy highlighted in this book. It is a critical strategy, for even if foundation and governmental funding for interdisciplinary work were plentiful and institutional reward structures properly adjusted, disciplinary cultures and habits of mind would continue to result in high, sometimes prohibitively high, start-up and ongoing costs for interdisciplinary collaboration.[98]

It would be wrong to think that there is not already considerable cross-fertilization of ideas across disciplines at research institutions, particularly in numerous multidisciplinary teaching programs and research institutes that cross departmental lines.[99] And even when faculty do not consciously and specifically intend to be interdisciplinary, many of their ideas and methods have diffused widely across disciplines.[100]

Similarly, it would be wrong to think that faculty engage in interdisciplinarity only as a result of top-down initiatives. Lisa Lattuca's study of faculty who do interdisciplinary work clearly indicates that many come to this work "on their own," and not in response to calls from funding agencies or administrators.[101] And faculty who created the interdisciplinary fields of women's studies and various ethnic and race studies began their work *in spite of* college and university administrators and the efforts they made to thwart such work.[102]

Nonetheless, if we want to increase the proportion of interdisciplinary teaching and research at research universities, we will need to pay closer attention to dismantling the formidable barriers that remain, including the high cost of engaging in cross-disciplinary conversations.

Conclusion

This chapter presented multiple definitions of what a discipline is, as well as the term *interdisciplinarity*. As a working definition of a discipline, I use Turner's suggestion that we define a field as a discipline if it has departmental status at a large number of institutions so that there is a labor market for doctoral students educated in that field. With regard to interdisciplinarity, because in practice it is often difficult to distinguish between multidisciplinarity, interdisciplinarity, and transdisciplinarity (and because a single project can go through all of the various stages of integration), I use the term *interdisciplinarity* to apply to all teaching and research that relies on multiple disciplines, regardless of the level at which those disciplines are integrated.

The chapter also examined the arguments in favor of interdisciplinarity—enhancing the ability to solve problems that cross fields, and enhancing creativity and thereby the development of knowledge. In my view, it is foolish to say that interdisciplinary knowledge is per se better or worse than disciplinary knowledge, just as it is foolish to say that quantitative or qualitative knowledge is better or worse than the other. Different kinds of problems and questions require different kinds of research and knowledge.

But because seeking interdisciplinary knowledge is generally riskier than pursuing disciplinary knowledge, faculty need to be given incentives to undertake the additional risks, or the risks need to be reduced. Departmental reward structures favor disciplinary work and make interdisciplinary work risky, and the difficulties of evaluating interdisciplinary work adds to their riskiness. Moreover, the time-consuming and sometimes unpleasant task of communicating across disciplinary cultures adds an additional cost to interdisciplinary work.

The next section of the book, Chapters 3–6, details the processes of interdisciplinary conversation in the six seminars studied. By carefully examining these processes, faculty and administrators will learn what impedes productive dialogue, as well as how to overcome these impediments, thus lowering the costs (and thereby the risks) of interdisciplinary engagement.

II   LOOKING INTO THE FISHBOWLS

3 Difficult Dialogues: Talking Across Cultures

A T ONE POINT IN THE SCIENCE STUDIES SEMINAR AT ADAMS, participants witnessed an irresolvable blowup between a religious studies postdoctoral fellow and a professor of economics. In the Jefferson representation seminar there were three similar clashes of culture, although none openly exploded. What connects the Adams and Jefferson stories is that in each case scholars had difficulties bridging disciplinary cultures; in each case they had developed disciplinary habits of mind that severely hampered interdisciplinary conversation. They were blind to the rules they used to engage in scholarly dialogue and blindsided by the fact that others' rules were so different from theirs. They also failed to realize that their training had influenced not only how they conveyed information, but also what they perceived to begin with.

The Science Studies Seminar at Adams

Background
The proposal for funding for the Adams seminars was written by the dean of arts and sciences in collaboration with a vice-provost, both from the humanities. The university wished to build major new interdisciplinary programs in science studies and ethics and decided that the seminars would be in these areas as a means for faculty in these fields to get to know one another and jump-start the agenda for the development of new programs.

Unfortunately, however, there was some loss in the translation of these goals, because although the dean and vice-provost wrote the proposal and chose the seminar participants, neither played a leadership role in the seminars that the proposal outlined. Instead the dean and vice-provost offered the leadership of the seminar for both years to Nancy, whose partner the university was actively courting for a faculty position. However, they did not consider Nancy for a faculty appointment.[1]

The eight faculty in the science studies seminar, all chosen by the dean and vice-provost, were all tenured full professors—two scientists (a biologist and a mathematician), two social scientists (an economist and a psychologist), two humanists (one in religious studies and one in literature), and two with joint appointments (one in history and anthropology and one in philosophy and computer science). Two of the faculty, plus Nancy, were women. In addition, there were five postdoctoral fellows, one in biology, one in psychology, one in history, one in religious studies, and one in science and technology studies (see Appendix Table A-1).[2]

Key Players

I interviewed six faculty from the science studies seminar (see Appendix Table A-2). Those involved in my discussion of the flare-up between the economist and the religious studies postdoc are William, a professor of mathematics; Jack, a professor of economics; Larry, a professor of anthropology and history; and Nancy, the seminar leader.

William specialized in game theory and said he had applied to be in the seminar specifically to tap into his colleagues' knowledge about the phenomenon of cooperation in their own fields.

> Basically, the idea in Darwinian evolution is that cooperation should not evolve. . . . And yet, we do see some examples of cooperation in nature, and the question is, why does that happen? About twenty, thirty years ago, some evolutionary biologists had the idea of using this mathematical theory of games . . . to try to build a mathematical model to try to understand how this could happen by survival of the fittest. . . . And this is something that I've been playing with, with computer simulations. . . . But I really needed to understand a lot more the examples from biology, from society, and so forth, and I was hoping that I would be able to talk to people in other fields and learn how they would approach what I consider a fairly universal problem of cooperation.

As it turned out, there was not a great deal of cooperation in the seminar on the day William presented.

Economist Jack said that the provost's office encouraged him to apply for the seminar because it was known that he was interested in the office's goal of moving science studies forward. He emphasized that he joined the seminar *solely* because of his interest in the topic and not because of any broader interests in interdisciplinarity.

Unlike William and Jack, Larry was attracted to the seminar because of his own work integrating history and anthropology. Moreover, he had recently been reading in experimental psychology and was interested in how that body of knowledge fit into the science studies area.

Nancy was a young scholar with a Ph.D. in English. She had worked in women's studies, had taught in an interdisciplinary humanities program, and was probably more knowledgeable about interdisciplinarity as a subject of study than was any leader or participant in any of the six seminars.

The Quarrel

The flare-up began during a presentation that mathematician William was giving on game theory. Economist Jack, who was highly critical of the talk, said so forthrightly. But the way Jack gave his criticism was offensive to the young woman postdoc from religious studies, and she chastised him, telling him she thought he was insensitive. Jack responded by leaving the room. Despite some modest efforts over the next few days by the seminar leader, Nancy, to get Jack to rejoin the group, he never did.

Here is the account of the argument from anthropologist/historian Larry.

> Jack did a very serious critique of game theory, straight on. . . . And then, the postdoc . . . thought it was too harsh or too mean or not communal . . . not the kind of thing a Quaker would have done or something. I don't know. . . . But Jack was claiming that his . . . style . . . is what [economists] were trained to do. . . . And this person from religion, where you wouldn't do that, was appalled, shocked that someone would say "That's a stupid idea." I don't think Jack ever said "That's a stupid idea." . . . He said, "That argument doesn't flow," or something like that, and then he pursued it. And that's the game. . . . [But] that wasn't the game for this woman, and she laid into him for doing it in a very, I felt, a very aggressive way. . . . I think it came out of her views of the world. I think it was her religious background of having to build a community of people

who work together. . . . I don't think she was a Quaker, but [she thought] . . . we should come to consensus.

Jack's view of what happened was the same as Larry's. When I asked him why he left the seminar, he said he had questioned the mathematician in the way that he normally questions people in a seminar, but a postdoctoral fellow from religious studies was offended by what he'd said and told him off. He left and never came back.

Disciplinary Cultures and Habits of Mind

Examining this fight from the perspective of disciplinary cultures or disciplinary habits of mind explains a great deal about why interdisciplinary conversation can be so difficult. Clifford Geertz fleshed out the concept of disciplinary cultures in a 1983 article beginning with the notion that thinking, despite the fact that it is carried out by individuals, is a *cultural* phenomenon.

> Ideation, subtle or otherwise, is a cultural artifact . . . [and] cognition, emotion, motivation, perception, imagination, memory . . . whatever, [are] . . . social affairs.[3]

Geertz goes on to say that academics inhabit the world they imagine.

> To set out to deconstruct Yeats's imagery, absorb oneself in black holes, or measure the effect of schooling on economic achievement is not just to take up a technical task but to take on a cultural frame that defines a great part of one's life.[4]

Geertz noted that the first step in being able to explain one's cultural community to others is to notice that one is *in* a cultural community. The second step is to become, in effect, an ethnographer of one's own discipline, observing, describing, and measuring fundamental characteristics of one's invisible college (a term popularized by Thomas Kuhn), or intellectual village (a term introduced by Geertz). Geertz singled out the following for attention:

> language . . . the life-cycle . . . passage rites . . . age and sex role definitions, [and] intergenerational bonds[5]

Geertz devoted a great deal of his article to the importance of *where* one is inducted into one's discipline, that is, in which particular department one studies for the doctorate. He also noted the effect on disciplines of the fact that in some fields a scholar's best work is done early in a career (for example, mathematics) and in some fields the pinnacle of creativity comes with maturity (for example, history).[6]

Tony Becher and Paul Trowler define academic cultures as

sets of taken-for-granted values, attitudes and ways of behaving, which are articulated through and reinforced by recurrent practices."[7] These include "traditions, customs and practices, transmitted knowledge, beliefs, morals and rules of conduct, as well as their linguistic and symbolic forms of communication and the meanings they share.[8]

Becher likens academic disciplines to tribes

Men of the sociological tribe rarely visit the land of the physicists and have little idea what they do over there. If the sociologists were to step into the building occupied by the English department, they would encounter the cold stares if not the slingshots of the hostile natives.[9]

Becher and Trowler maintain that, like tribes, disciplines initiate their "young" into particular ways of thinking and behaving.[10] One can think of milestones in graduate training as akin to rituals in tribes and religious groups. Moreover, like tribes, disciplines continually reinforce their particular styles of thinking and behaving.

The literature on categories for distinguishing major differences among disciplines suggests distinctions based on numerous characteristics. Some of these include whether the discipline is hard or soft, pure or applied, paradigmatic or nonparadigmatic, studying life versus nonlife systems, and having a low or high degree of scholarly consensus.[11] John Holland's theory of differences among disciplines proposes six categories, four of which are useful for research universities: investigative, artistic, social, and enterprising.[12] We shall have more to say in Chapter 4 about Holland's theory when we examine whether faculty in certain disciplines can be said to display a particular disciplinary affect.

One important factor that shapes a discipline's culture is the degree of competitiveness among colleagues. Disciplines that require large amounts of funding to do their work (such as many of the sciences) tend to be more competitive than those where scholars can operate with merely a pencil and yellow pad in a café (such as mathematics), or in a carrel of a well-stocked library (such as most humanities). The people-to-problem ratio also affects disciplinary competitiveness, with higher ratios producing greater competition. And disciplines tend to be more competitive when there is widespread public interest in their findings and the time to publication is relatively short, such as in medical research.

Related to the concept of disciplinary culture is the idea of habits of mind, which was introduced by John Dewey in his 1916 book, *Democracy and Education,* and developed further by Howard Margolis.[13] Margolis uses the phrase to explain the difficulties academics face when attempting to shift paradigms within a discipline, but his analysis is easily applied to the difficulties of conversing across disciplines.

Margolis contends that physical habits have their mental counterpart in habits of mind and that the same instinctive and unthinking behavior that accompanies physical habits also is characteristic of habits of mind. Like physical habits, habits of mind are acquired through practice and are difficult to modify.

> Habits of mind ... [are] entrenched responses that ordinarily occur without conscious attention, and that even if noticed are hard to change.[14]

When habits of mind are inculcated in a cultural setting, such as a disciplinary community, no one in the community recognizes the behavior as a habit.

> A person is ordinarily conscious of a point of view. But unless specifically and effectively prompted, a person is ordinarily unconscious of habits and indeed is to a large extent completely unaware that she has various habits.[15]

> When everyone in a community shares a habit, it ordinarily becomes invisible, for what everyone does no one easily notices.[16]

Margolis points out that adopting new knowledge, which requires that we consider new cognitive patterns, is difficult because we have no history of recognizing those new patterns and are constrained by our habitual pattern recognition.

> If all cognition is reducible to sequences of pattern-recognition ... then what a person can do at any particular moment is constrained by the repertoire of recognizable patterns currently available. What I can make sense of at any particular moment (the intuitions that can occur to me) are constrained by the range of patterns I can recognize and by the habitual linkages among those patterns.[17]

This suggests, paradoxically, that someone *not* highly schooled in a particular discipline, say an undergraduate, will have an easier time learning material in that discipline than will a faculty member from a different discipline whose area of study is similar to that of the new discipline. I return to this matter in Chapter 9.

Just as disciplinary cultures include both subject matter and "tacit knowledge," so, too, do disciplinary habits of mind include both cognitive content and styles of thinking, presenting, interacting, and questioning.[18] Other authors have also pointed to the importance of habits of mind, although they use different terms to describe them: lenses, frames, orientations, cultural filters, paradigms, habits of expectation, mental models, and cognitive maps.[19]

Contrasting history and economics is instructive for understanding the notions of disciplinary cultures and disciplinary habits of mind.[20] In the course of their graduate work, doctoral students in history learn to be rather open-minded about paradigms, theories, and research methods.[21] Doctoral students in economics, on the other hand, learn to be relatively closed-minded about the ways in which other social sciences view human behavior or employ qualitative research methods. In their 1996 book, *Outside the Lines: Issues in Interdisciplinary Research*, Liora Salter and Alison Hearn argue that the more flexibility there is within a discipline, the more open practitioners of that discipline are to interdisciplinarity.

Writing for a book that examines doctoral training in a number of disciplines, William Cronon describes history as "open," not having a tight paradigm. Historians, Cronon argues, "strongly prefer multicausal explanations" and tolerate considerable ambiguity and disagreement among its practitioners.[22] The historians that Michèle Lamont interviewed for her study of evaluation in interdisciplinary settings made the point that the consensus among historians is not about a particular paradigm, but rather about the "careful archival work."[23] Craig Calhoun notes that historians, although they are narrow in that they work on a particular place at a particular time, are broad because within those constraints they take account of multiple factors—economic, political, social, and cultural.[24]

Not only do historians seem to be interested in other disciplines, but also, at least in the social sciences, other disciplines seem to be interested in history. Perhaps it is the absence of jargon in history that makes other social scientists read what historians write. In a 1982 study of the book-borrowing patterns of faculty and graduate students at the University of Pittsburg, Stephen Bulick found that history books were heavily used by social scientists in anthropology, geography, sociology, and political science. Interestingly, Bulick's finding did not extend to economics graduate students.[25] This is not surprising. Most economics graduate students are in the trenches learning economics only. If they read in other disciplines, it is in mathematics and statistics.

If history is on the open end of the disciplinary spectrum with regard to interest in other fields, economics is on the closed end. In her study of inter-disciplinarity, Lisa Lattuca noted that her informants at the liberal arts colleges and doctoral university in her sample pointed to economics as particularly resistant to interdisciplinary work.[26]

In his 1973 satire about the Econ tribe, economist Axel Leijonhufvud observed that engaging in conversation with other social scientists lowers one's status among the Econ.

> The low rank of the Develops [those who specialize in economic development] is due to the fact that this caste, in recent times, has not strictly enforced the taboos against association with the Polscis, Sociogs, and other tribes.[27]

Leijonhufvud also took notice of the confrontational nature of the Econs and used typical Econ jargon to describe it.

> Status relationships do not seem to form a simple hierarchical "pecking order," as one is used to expect. Thus, for example, one may find that A pecks B, B pecks C and *then C pecks A!* This non-transitivity of status may account for the continual strife among the Econ which makes their social life seem so singularly insufferable to the visitor. Almost all of the travelers' reports that we have comment on the Econ as a 'quarrelsome race' who talk ill of their fellow behind his back.[28]

The "pecking" of one another that Leijonhufvud described, along with his comment that others found the continual strife among the Econ "insufferable," may in large part explain what happened in the confrontation between economist Jack and the postdoc in religious studies in the science studies seminar. As Jack said, he was behaving as his training in economics had taught him to behave; he questioned the mathematician sharply (perhaps Leijonhufvud would say he "pecked" at him). This was his habit of mind.[29]

It may be that the fact that Jack was critiquing a mathematician added to his sense that he was in familiar territory, that the kind of behavior he used when critically assessing economic presentations was precisely the kind he should use for evaluating the game theory being presented by William. But it is more likely that Jack did not think consciously at all about his mode of critique. Over many years as an economist he had simply developed a habit of mind—sharp questioning of seminar presentations.

It is also likely that Jack never questioned the merits of his criticism of

William's work. Economists tend to have very high inter-rater reliability within the discipline about what they consider superior work and therefore are not exposed to a great many alternate perspectives about the merits of ideas. Moreover, having little or no contact with postmodern thought, they rarely note that work may be outstanding mostly in the eye of the beholder, that it is outstanding only because they have collectively deemed it such.[30]

For her part, the postdoc in religious studies had her own habits of mind—quite different from those of economists. Some of them were forged in graduate school, and some, as Larry suggested, may have come from her experience of living in a religious community, where the norm was most definitely *not* to peck at others in a confrontational environment but rather to develop a consensus in a mutually supportive environment.

The habits of mind of the two scholars were grossly mismatched. Absent an earlier discussion in the group about the existence of habits of mind and how to moderate them in an interdisciplinary conversation, a clash between the two was almost inevitable. And even with such a discussion, this particular clash might have been unavoidable.

Margolis argued that breaking habits of mind is exceedingly difficult.

Incompatible habits of mind block communication [and] easily evoke resentment[,] distaste[,] and frustration . . . [that] make breaking socially shared habits of mind harder than breaking with socially shared physical habits.[31]

While Margolis's observation might have predicted the conflict between Jack and the religious studies postdoc, Becher and Trowler's reflections on how economists handle conflict could have predicted Jack's decision to leave the seminar and never return. Becher and Trowler observe that among economists there is "systematic avoidance of overt controversy."[32] They quote an economist in their sample who says this about economists:

Disagreements sometimes become public, but it's more common simply not to communicate with people who hold a radically different viewpoint.[33]

In my experience, I have found Becher and Trowler to be right in this respect; mainstream economists do not generally communicate with people who hold radically different views, even within economics. Most mainstream economists know little if anything about less widely accepted economic theories or their empirical findings. When asked their opinion of a particular heterodox work, they generally respond by saying that they don't know anything about it, that the work is faddish, that fads come and go in economics, and that they can't really spend the time to delve into ephemeral trends which will inevitably die in the marketplace of ideas. Economists have great faith in the marketplace of ideas, rarely recognizing that the buyers of ideas in economics are none other than themselves, so that by their dismissive attitude toward new ideas they ensure the accuracy of their prediction.

Margolis argues that habits of mind cause us to dismiss novel intuitions within a discipline as "wrong." This seems particularly so in economics, although in recent years the field of behavioral economics, which has borrowed heavily from psychology, has had a powerful influence on some economists who no longer insist that people act rationally, always seeking to optimize their well-being.

Both Jack and the postdoc from religious studies were steeped in their own community's habits of mind. Neither recognized that they had these habits until they were confronted by the other's way of thinking. Unfortunately, when the two contrasting disciplinary cultures became clear, instead of producing a teachable moment about the power of disciplinary habits of mind, the disagreement led to two explosions of anger, the first from the postdoc and the second from Jack. Whatever substantive mathematical question Jack was raising about William's work was lost in the anger that followed the blowup. It is also interesting that although it was his work that was being criticized, William played no part in the altercation.

The Jefferson Seminar on Representation

Background

The representation seminar was the second seminar at Jefferson. The funding proposal for it, as well as the one for the first seminar, which was on consilience, was written by Jefferson's dean of arts and sciences, Joyce, a literary scholar, and its provost, Ed, a chemist. The leader of the representation seminar was Sam, a humanist who had been a participant in the first seminar and had just become an emeritus faculty member. It was Sam who chose representation as the seminar theme and explained that he wanted the seminar to explore how "reality" is represented in each discipline.

The seminar had fourteen tenured faculty: three scientists (professors of chemistry, computer science, and mathematics), four social scientists (professors of anthropology, economics, history, and sociology), five humanists (three professors from English and one each from film studies and literature), and two from the arts (a professor of music and an associate professor of fine arts). In addition, there was an artist-in-residence from the drama department. Five of the participants (slightly more than one-third) had been in the seminar the previous year. Of these, four were administrators or former administrators and one was the seminar leader. Half of the seminar faculty were women (see Appendix Table A-1).

The seminar also had nine postdoctoral fellows, more than any other seminar. Three were in the sciences (chemistry, computer science, and mathematics), two in the social sciences (sociology/anthropology and history), two in the humanities (English and American studies), and two in the arts (one in theater and one in fine arts).

Key Players

I interviewed eight members of the representation seminar (see Appendix Table A-2). The interviewees who play a part in the stories I am about to relate are mathematician Barry, studio artist Evelyn, dramatist Jane, and the seminar leader, Sam.

Mathematician Barry said he joined the seminar to learn new material and meet new colleagues. He was not particularly interested in the seminar's topic, how various disciplines represent knowledge. Artist Evelyn and dramatist Jane both said they joined the seminar because they felt isolated in their respective departments and thought the seminar could mitigate the sense of separation they had from the university as a whole. Neither was especially interested in the topic of interdisciplinarity. Sam, a professor of humanities, had had many years of experience with interdisciplinarity, including spending several years leading a multiuniversity interdisciplinary seminar.

Mathematics—The Importance of Language

Barry's participation in the representation seminar gave rise to two problems. First, seminar participants were unable to understand his presentation. Second, although he came to the seminar regularly, he never made comments or asked questions; the other participants said they were perplexed by his silence.

Several people commented on the difficulty of understanding Barry's talk. They did not have the background in mathematics to appreciate what Barry was saying, and Barry seemed to lack the skills (or motivation) to translate for them. Dramatist Jane responded to my question about whether she had experienced any difficult moments in the seminar by citing her inability to understand Barry.

> A mathematics professor who couldn't communicate . . . in English. He could communicate in numbers and formulas, and it took me several, well, I think it was several hours before I understood that what he was [doing], and I was dutifully writing down everything he wrote so I could try to understand it. . . . And when we asked questions, he would think for a long time and then say he couldn't answer it. . . . That was a . . . difficult period . . . two different languages . . . but . . . no means of communicating.

Not only did seminar participants have trouble understanding Barry; he had trouble understanding them. In our interview, he corroborated his lack of participation.

> I was much less an active participant than I had hoped, [than I] would have liked to have been.
>
> Q: Any particular reason?
>
> A: [Pause] I think it wasn't really my medium, my natural habitat, to be in a situation like that. I hadn't gotten used to that kind of interaction. It is quite different from the way mathematicians interact.

When I asked Barry how mathematicians interact, his answer made it clear that he behaved in the interdisciplinary seminar in precisely the way that mathematicians behave in mathematics seminars, where only the presenter talks and everyone else listens, with the utmost attention, hoping to be able to follow the argument. The only interruptions are for clarification. Only after the seminar is over, perhaps weeks or months later, when participants have had time to fully digest what they heard, might they engage in private conversation with the presenter.[34] Barry felt he could not participate in the representation seminar dialogue because he had not had time to absorb what he had heard.

Despite the fact that Barry had a clear understanding of why he didn't speak in the seminar (except when he presented), nobody else in the seminar did, as evidenced by their bewilderment about this when I interviewed them. Since no one had ever asked him the reasons for his nonparticipation, no one could help him to bridge the enormous gap between his style of thinking, presenting, and questioning and the dominant style in the seminar.

Still, although he did not participate in the discussions, Barry felt he had gotten a great deal out of the seminar. I asked him if he had it to do all over again whether he would participate. He said he would because it was so interesting and because he'd learned so much.

> Before, I really had very little sense of what, for example, a sociologist really works on and how they go about their work. . . . If I did it again, now I have a sense of that . . . so, I might appreciate it more and participate more, be a more active participant.

One could interpret Barry's answer to mean that if he attended another such seminar, he would have a better understanding of its culture; he would understand that one cannot think as deeply and as extendedly in a humanities seminar as one does in a mathematics seminar. Whether he could actually change his behavior is a separate question.

Barry's experience shows clearly that language issues that inhibit interdisciplinary conversations go much deeper than matters of vocabulary. Barry understood the readings and he understood his colleagues' comments on them. Indeed, he found many of their comments intriguing and spent the seminar time quietly pondering them. It was the sociolinguistic system that was the problem for Barry.

Dell Hymes argues that language is embedded in a sociolinguistic system that varies across speech communities, each of which has its own rules of speaking.[35] Unfortunately for ease of interdisciplinary conversation, the linguistic system of a discipline is taken for granted by its practitioners, who fail even to recognize that they operate in such a system, let alone understand its characteristics or realize that those characteristics differ significantly from those of their colleagues' speech communities. As a result, when faculty join an interdisciplinary group, they expect that the conversation will proceed according to the unrecognized and unacknowledged rules by which they play when talking to colleagues in the same discipline.

Hymes's careful analysis of the cultural norms of speaking in groups frames a series of questions that help to draw attention to some of the sociolinguistic difficulties in interdisciplinary settings: What are the norms of interaction? Is interrupting okay? How are turns for speaking arranged? What is said outright and what is said subtly?

I would add several additional questions to Hymes's list: How intensely may people be questioned? To what degree must participants assume a "friendly" (versus "hostile") demeanor and language toward one another and toward the presenter? Are people expected to make presentations using PowerPoint or slides, or is this seen as "too formal"? Are people expected to have video clips in their PowerPoint presentations, or is that seen as "excessive"? Is it expected that presenters will show the actual statistical results used to reach their conclusions or is a verbal summary of main findings viewed as sufficient? Are people expected to write out their presentations and read them verbatim or to speak extemporaneously from a few notes? There are also questions concerning evidence and truth claims: What constitutes a good argument? What evidence is required to reject or confirm a hypothesis?

In general, in the six seminars I investigated, the sociolinguistic system in place was chosen (without consciousness) by the leader of the seminar simply because he or she was familiar with it. There was never discussion about the ground rules of the sociolinguistic system. And in my interviews, it was only those who came from speech communities with vastly different rules who pointed out the difficulties they had adapting to the seminar style.

Studio Art—Ways of Seeing

Both Evelyn from studio art and Jane from drama had difficulties with the unstated assumptions of the discipline of literary criticism, the dominant language community of the representation seminar. When I asked Evelyn what the session was like when she presented, she said she felt that she had been shoehorned into a format that didn't work for her.

> I showed slides of my work, from my student work all the way to my current work. . . . I hate showing slides. Things go by, people don't even notice what's in the paintings. They can't even see them. . . . At the beginning of the seminar . . . I said we could do a studio visit. . . . And it was, oh, thank you, but I don't know if we'll have time for that. No, we all have to sit around that table, and I had to . . . I had to have Xeroxes for people to read. . . . I was pigeonholed into the humanities format.

Evelyn felt that although the seminar was said to be interdisciplinary, the format made it a humanities seminar.

> It was a humanities seminar, and . . . for those of us who are not in humanities, we were strangers to this format; it was very uncomfortable. . . . That's why I think I was so reticent. I don't know how to talk around a round table. I don't

do that in my classrooms. . . . Work goes up on the wall; we all sit together and look at it.

Elliot Eisner's work on representation is helpful in explaining Evelyn's frustration. Eisner argues that the way in which we have been trained to represent reality in our work influences not only how we convey information publicly but also *what information we see to begin with*. This is very much in keeping with Margolis's notions of habits of mind quoted earlier:

> If all cognition is reducible to sequences of pattern-recognition . . . then what a person can do at any particular moment is constrained by the repertoire of recognizable patterns currently available.[36]

Eisner gives an example of a painter, a composer, and a sociologist all visiting a small town in Kansas. The medium through which each will communicate publicly when their visit is done shapes what each sees while there. In the case of the sociologist, for example, how she views and understands the town is determined by the sociological constructs that are a part of her training. As Eisner puts it,

> The kinds of nets we know how to weave determine the kinds of nets we cast. These nets, in turn, determine the kinds of fish we catch.[37]

Just as our brains require us to focus in order to perceive, public communication of experience requires that we choose one form of representation and thereby exclude others. Ignoring certain aspects of reality in order to concentrate on others is a natural consequence of understanding and communication. But whose understanding? Whose communication?

Using Eisner's framework, one can view multidisciplinary discussion not only as learning a new culture, but also learning a new way of perceiving. In an interdisciplinary seminar, information and connections that one normally disregards are suddenly presented and required to be digested. It is a difficult assignment.

Drama—The Doubting Game and the Believing Game

Dramatist Jane's main difficulty with the seminar was the immediately critical stance that the seminar leader and many participants took to the texts that were assigned.[38] Jane preferred, instead, to start discussions in a more positive frame of mind and "try on" ideas.[39]

> We read *Consilience* as our first book. . . . I thought it was exciting to be taken on a journey . . . follow the thread . . . and try on his [E. O. Wilson's] ideas. That's . . . my way of analysis.

Jane's desire to try on ideas is reminiscent of Samuel Taylor Coleridge's suggestion that to appreciate poetry one has to engage in "the willing suspension of disbelief."[40] It is perhaps not surprising that someone trained in drama has developed a habit of mind that involves routinely suspending disbelief.

But Jane was surprised that her colleagues did not think as she did.

> I was initially quite shocked at how some of the more . . . traditional academics responded, not only to *Consilience,* but to the work in general, by being extremely critical, which, initially, I saw as destructive.

Jane said that eventually she came to understand that it was through critiquing that her humanities colleagues evaluated Wilson's work, but for her, beginning with critique was simply not an effective way of working with new ideas.

> I came to understand over time that it was their true process of ascertaining the value of the ideas in the book; whereas . . . I start with a positive attitude and I try the ideas on and see what I can find. . . . I'm given a script, I dive in, I see what's there, rather than going, "it's bad," because then I could never connect to the work and do it justice.

As a result of the difference between Jane's way of reading material (trying it on) and the way most others in the seminar read (critiquing from the start), she felt cut off from her colleagues. And while she realized that the two different approaches stemmed from two different disciplinary socialization processes, that rational understanding did not make her feel any better. What finally did give her some comfort was the realization that she probably had a lot more fun using her method than they had using theirs.

> I would say that [their method of reading texts] isolated me in the seminar in a rather extreme way. I did come to terms with the fact that this was not of cruel or evil intent, though it would never be my way of approaching the analysis. . . . My training has been . . . to engage in . . . [the text] and try to go with it

rather than to withdraw and judge it. . . . You know, they saw things I didn't see, [but] I think I had more fun than they did.

Part of Jane's method of "trying on" the text required getting involved emotionally, and her second complaint about the literary approach to texts was that it took the emotion out of the material and substituted a scholarly distancing. Jane felt that that distancing made meaningful dialogue impossible.

> The overwhelming method of responding to anything [on the part of seminar members] was so impersonal and academic that it seemed to preclude any real exchange.

Jane felt that in her role as director or actress, analyzing texts the way she had been trained, first trying on ideas and engaging emotionally and only later stepping back and analyzing, was the only way that she could make the play as strong as possible for an audience.

> My training has been not to distance myself but to engage myself in whatever the imaginary role is . . . to engage in it and try to go with it rather than to withdraw and judge it. . . . I might step back in order to understand structure and structural flaws that I will have to handle as a producer of a piece of material. So if I find out, for example, that a play's . . . beginning, middle, and end isn't as strongly etched out as I think it will need to be . . . for the audience to receive the story that is intended . . . then I have to find out what the weaknesses are . . . in order to help it, rather than in order to say it's no good. . . . Saying it's no good only inhibits my ability to give . . . my everything to it, to make it happen.

Despite her ongoing frustration, however, Jane said she would participate again.

> I was frustrated . . . throughout the seminar; that does not mean that I didn't have a good time and I didn't learn things. It was an active frustration, not a giving-up sort of frustration.

To explain the difference in habits of mind between dramatists and literary scholars, it is useful to examine Peter Elbow's distinction between two academic games, which he calls the doubting game and the believing game. The point of the doubting game, which is played much more frequently than the believing game (indeed, Elbow argues that the doubting game's monopoly over scholarly discourse goes all the way back to Descartes), is to find error by finding fault. Thus, the doubting game begins with critique. Only if an interpretation withstands critique is it accepted.

In the believing game, however, error in interpretation is uncovered by precisely the opposite approach; each player initially believes *all* interpretations and through intense imagination proceeds to try on each of them. To play the believing game, one must strive to "get inside the head" of interpretations that seem foreign, and particularly give those opportunities to succeed.[41] Eventually, by sufficiently entering into the heart and soul of an interpretation, the player of the believing game is able either to determine that the interpretation is true or to reject it because something else seems truer.

Elbow argues that the doubting game is misapplied to matters of interpretation, that "there are no rules for showing that an assertion of meaning is false."[42] As a result, the way in which arguments about interpretation are won in a doubting game is through power and "rhetorical skill";[43] those who have minority interpretations are silenced, and therefore the richness of multiple interpretations, all of which may be true, may remain unrealized.

The two games are not, of course, mutually exclusive. In fact, Elbow recommends that both be used. His brief, however, is for the believing game because of the domination of the doubting game and most academics' lack of familiarity with and hostility toward the believing game.

In the representation seminar, the seminar leader and other members of the seminar from the departments of English and other literatures were used to playing the doubting game and sought (successfully) to play it in the seminar; the drama professor, on the other hand, was used to playing the believing game. Because she was a lone proponent of that game, she had insufficient leverage to have it emerge as the victorious practice. Instead, she remained frustrated.

Conclusion

By analyzing the altercation in the science studies seminar between an economist and a young scholar from religious studies, as well as the discomfort that a mathematician, studio artist, and dramatist experienced in seminars run by humanists, we begin to understand the power of disciplinary habits of mind and disciplinary cultures in impeding conversation across disciplines. The descriptions of economists' culture by Leijonhufvud and by Becher and Trowler combined with Geertz's analysis of the power of academic tribes' cultural norms and Margolis's examination of habits of minds go a long way toward explaining how economics met head on with religious studies. And Becher and Trowler's observation that economists tend to deal with conflict by avoiding it helps to explain why economist Jack left the seminar rather than try to work out his differences with the religious studies postdoc. It may also be that because his intellectual adversary was not a permanent faculty member but rather a postdoc, Jack was less motivated to work out the conflict than if she had been someone with high status in the institution.

In explaining why mathematician Barry had so much difficulty integrating into the seminar, it was advantageous to look at Hymes's detailed understanding of language systems in all their complexities. Barry's ways of absorbing cognitive material, as well as his ways of presenting it, were so far from the styles of others in the seminar that there developed an unbridgeable gulf. It is startling that nobody talked about this gulf during the seminar or made any effort to help mitigate it.

Eisner's understanding of the significance of differences across disciplines in "ways of seeing" was particularly informative in grasping how an artist's habits of mind can be so different from those of a humanist scholar. In Evelyn's view, the humanities format for showing her art that was imposed without much conscious thought by the seminar leader inhibited her colleagues' perceptions of her work.

In the case of Jane, the dramatist, whose disciplinary habit was to "try on" ideas rather than critique them, it was useful to explore Elbow's contrast between the doubting game, the game generally played in academia, and the believing game, in which scholars and researchers come to an assessment of the quality of work by first believing in it. The openness to ideas that the believing game engenders may well be essential to interdisciplinary conversation. By the same token, being stuck in the doubting game seems to severely inhibit such conversation, as we shall see in the next chapter.

4 Being in One's Comfort Zone: The Case of Ethics

I N THE ETHICS SEMINAR AT ADAMS A MAJOR ALTERCATION
occurred between Peter, an eminent professor of analytic philosophy, and Nabila, an assistant professor of English and women's studies. Peter
was offended by the postmodern presentations given by Nabila and others,
who were unable to satisfy his demands for clarity. On the other side of the
divide, Nabila and others found Peter's views about ethics narrow and un-
helpful. And so the battle was joined.

Daniel Yankelovich used the term "gated communities of the mind"
to describe the subcultures that account for academics' inability to talk to
one another across fields. The dynamics in the ethics seminar exemplify
what happens when members of those gated communities encounter one
another.

> I have listened for hours to economists and psychologists, historians and sociol-
> ogists, biologists and scholars in the humanities argue with each other without
> either penetrating the subculture of the other. It is almost as if these subcultures
> were gated communities of the mind.[1]

Neither side in the ethics seminar could understand the other's way of seeing.
The habits of mind and disciplinary norms on both sides of the conflict were
so orthogonal that participants were unable to communicate constructively.
And neither side trusted the other. Each side's adherents relied only on those
with whom they felt comfortable, with whom they had a "comfort zone." This

concept of a comfort zone was raised by several of those interviewed and will be explored further as we proceed.

Background on the Ethics Seminar

The seminar on ethics was the only one of the six seminars whose participants included junior faculty: three assistant professors, one each in languages, English, and law. There were also two associate professors, one in history and one in religious studies. Of the four full professors, there was one each in medicine, philosophy, political science, and religious studies. In addition, Nancy, the seminar leader, was from English. Forty percent of the faculty were women. There were also three postdocs, one each in political science, philosophy, and English (see Appendix Table A-1).[2]

Key Players

I interviewed nine participants in the ethics seminar. Except for the seminar leader, Nancy, who surprised me when she said she really had no interest in ethics as a subject of study, all of the interviewees said they joined the seminar, at least in part, because of its theme.

In addition to Peter and Nabila, another key player in the major clash examined in this chapter was Ahsan, an associate professor of religious studies. George, an assistant professor of law, was an important player in a second set of issues on which he disagreed with Peter.

Peter said his attraction to the seminar was twofold—the topic and the opportunity to choose a postdoc to participate with him.

> I was quite interested in the general topic that was proposed, ethics, both because I've been writing a lot on the natural selection approach to the evolution of ethics and because I'm interested in policy questions surrounding genomics. . . . And . . . I was very interested in what colleagues of mine from outside philosophy would have to say about this general subject of ethics. And the inducements associated with participating seemed to me particularly attractive . . . to have a postdoc that I could choose to participate in the program and sort of leaven his . . . life in the department was probably the most attractive feature.[3]

Although Peter saw himself as an interdisciplinary thinker, well known for the connections he makes between philosophy and biology, others in the seminar found him to be very much a traditional analytic philosopher and not at all interested in incorporating ideas from their disciplines into his thinking. As we will have several occasions to note, being interdisciplinary with regard to two fields does not necessarily imply an interest in being interdisciplinary more generally.

Nabila defined her field as postcolonial, feminist, and psychoanalytic studies. At the time she was asked to join the ethics seminar, she was co-leading a seminar on feminism and transnationalism. She had also team-taught several courses with faculty from other disciplines. She said she joined the seminar particularly because of her interest in ethics.

Ahsan, the associate professor of religious studies, joined the seminar both because of the topic and to gain some time off from teaching to work on a manuscript.

The secondary players in the ethics exchanges were Liz, an assistant professor of languages; Sarah, a professor of political science; Ari, an associate professor of history, and James, a professor of medicine.

Liz worked across the fields of literature and art history and described herself as someone for whom "interdisciplinary questions assert themselves even before a particular project begins." She joined the seminar because questions about ethics had become central to her work and because she thought the seminar had the potential for disrupting the usual hierarchy between junior and senior faculty.

Sarah, a political theorist, had done a great deal of work on liberal ethical theories. Like Ahsan, she joined the seminar because of her interest in the topic of ethics and also to gain some time off from teaching to work on a manuscript. Historian Ari was interested in the seminar's topic because he wanted to deepen his understanding of theories of ethics. James, a physician specializing in medical ethics, joined to learn about how different disciplines viewed the "cutting edge in ethics."

What Was in Dispute? Postmodernism Versus a Liberal/Rationalist Philosophy

I asked Peter what the seminar meant for him.

[It] led [me] to a profound pessimism about the humanities. . . . I had thought that the culture wars were over and that everybody had seen that the emperor of postmodernism was naked, but I was completely mistaken. My colleagues in

English and cultural studies and literature, who participated in the seminar, cast me into despair about the level of intellectual seriousness and willingness to be intelligible. . . . I was just appalled. . . . Their . . . sheer ignorance of . . . their own disciplines . . . of the theories and ideologies that they were trying to help themselves to, of the subject matter with which they are traditionally supposed to be concerned, and about the meaning of the word *ethics*. I thought this was a word in ordinary English use, but they didn't know what it was. . . . When [my postdoc] or Ari or James or I presented our material, it was intelligible to the others and resulted in give-and-take, a debate, a discussion about the substance of the theses we were defending or attacking. . . . When they [the postmodernists] talked, we couldn't understand what they were saying, and we kept asking them to explain, to translate, and they were completely incapable of doing so. And . . . when they threw about labels with which we were familiar, whether it was Freud or Kant or . . . Adam Smith, we couldn't identify what they were attributing to these people. You had three or four people in that room who were appealing to psychoanalytic theory but couldn't tell you the first thing about Freud's doctrines. . . . If you subjected them to . . . a Jeopardy-style series of questions about what is the libido, name the three parts of the psyche according to Freud, they wouldn't be able to answer. . . . They didn't even understand the theory which they felt was central to their line of research. . . . Not to mention the fact that this is a theory so completely discredited by scientific research over the last hundred years that the idea that it should actually help us understand anything is laughable in itself. . . . And if you asked them to explain Foucault or Derrida, that was even worse. . . . They . . . had the lingo, but they didn't understand the lingo.

I asked Peter how he defined ethics.

Ethics . . . has two components: one is [normative ethics,] the study of what we ought or ought not do, or what is permissible to do, what's valuable, good in itself. And the second is the study of the meaning and grounds of ethical claims . . . metaethics. Normative ethics [is] what I thought all these people would think ethics was about. What we should do, what we shouldn't do, what's morally right, and what's morally wrong. . . . What *did* they think it was? Lord preserve me, I have no idea what they thought it was. Ideology or ethnic differences or confronting retrograde establishment prerogatives?

Peter thought the seminar divided into two groups. "His" group included Ari, James, and himself. He said he thought that Sarah, the political scientist, was in his group from an intellectual perspective, but he was angry at her for failing to "discharge her responsibilities as an intellectual to insist that these people speak plainly and intelligently."[4] All those Peter identified as being in "his" group were Caucasian and, except for his postdoc, senior faculty. The people Peter saw in the opposing group—Nabila, Ahsan, George, Liz, and two postdocs—were all young or midlevel scholars, and many were people of color or from colonial backgrounds. Interestingly, although Nancy, the leader of the seminar, saw herself closely aligned intellectually and age-wise with this younger group, Peter did not put her in either group and said he admired her greatly. One member of the seminar who did not take sides in this post-modern/rationalist debate was a senior professor of religion. But Peter fought with him for other reasons—Peter was not fond of religion.

Seminar participants agreed that Nabila was the chief spokesperson for the postmodern view and that at least for the first part of the year the fights in the seminar were most frequently between her and Peter. Not only did Peter and Nabila have different views on ethics, but their styles of speaking were quite different. I have edited both of their responses for ease of reading, but even with the editing Peter's answers are crisp and definitive while Nabila's are more nonlinear and tentative, the responses of a young scholar clarifying her ideas even as she explained them.

Here is Nabila's definition of ethics.

> I . . . think of ethics as a reading practice. . . . It . . . informs my reading of texts . . . and, I think to some extent, my whole way of seeing the world.

> Q: So, do you see . . . ethics as helping to make difficult, practical decisions?

> A: No. I actually think in some ways it's about the *subject* of difficulty rather than having to make difficult decisions. . . . It's more that ethics is something that is engaged with when one is open to a form of otherness that one can't really understand but has to . . . try to do the work of understanding and engaging with that otherness.

She gave a long example, and I could see her struggling to explain what she meant. It was only at the end that her definition became clearer.

> In the very first seminar . . . the planning seminar for the rest of the year . . . Nancy brought up at the beginning of the meeting some of the difficul-ties that they had had last year in terms of interdisciplinary interaction. And Peter had said . . . that it's ridiculous to have these kinds of tensions over inter-

disciplinarity . . . as long as we can all move towards simple terms that we can define concisely and move to . . . a form of language that we all find common, we will be fine. And I said, well, isn't that all about the erasure of difference? Isn't it . . . relegating difference to the realm of the private . . . so the differences are not out there for discussion and engagement? . . . I said, it seems to me that what we actually need is an engagement with the idea of ethics that is about a recognition . . . of the impossibility of understanding, even as there is a struggle to do so. So, it seems to me that the ethical relation to the other is actually about the recognition of absolute otherness. . . . In some ways, ethics becomes—well, you asked for a definition—I suppose ethics becomes a kind of engagement with the difficulty of difference and the complexity of difference.

Nabila saw the difference between Peter and herself in political terms:

The difference between a kind of intellectual liberalism and more of a kind of left-identified response to the question of interdisciplinarity.

Sarah also thought the seminar was divided along political lines.

This seminar was highly problematic. . . . People were just working from different paradigms that divided the group pretty much in half. . . . The humanists in the room were mostly working from a certain paradigm that I don't even know exactly what to call it. It was colonialist or something like that. And the others in the room were not nearly as united in their theoretical perspective, but all were more-or-less defenders of some kind or other of liberal, rationalist perspective that the people on the other side think they've gotten beyond.

But the disagreement between Peter and Nabila was not only about the definition of ethics and political difference. More fundamentally, it was about the purpose of engaging in interdisciplinary discussion about ethics. Peter wanted agreement on universals. Nabila wanted celebration of difference. Peter practiced a discipline whose culture puts a premium on clarity and precision and seeks to propose carefully thought-out solutions to complex problems. Nabila was trained to value multiple interpretations and to believe that agreement across points of view is neither possible nor desirable. Peter's discipline seeks to solve problems. Nabila's seeks to "problematize," to create problems.[5]

Even though Peter considered Sarah a member of "his" team in the debates, Sarah said she disagreed with Peter "because he takes such an extreme position around ethics being a product of evolution and [argues that] we can't really take seriously questions about right and wrong." However, she found her disagreement with Peter was productive, forcing her to do some deep thinking.

> Peter, actually, was quite stimulating to me. . . . I have to figure out why I think [he's] . . . wrong, because [he] . . . has to be wrong; otherwise, everything I'm doing is worthless. But Peter is very, very smart, and I learned a lot from listening.

Sarah thought the seminar worked better when participants were not talking about "the big fundamentals" but rather about particular issues.

> We . . . got to the big fundamentals way too often, way too readily. . . . We did much better when we tried to talk about particular issues. . . . We did better when we were reading and responding to each other's work, because it would be about something specific, but when we just picked books that we thought were interesting . . . they tended to be these very abstract, theoretical kind of pieces, and people could only expose their most fundamental difficulties with one another without getting anywhere.

Translation of Concepts

One of the particularly difficult issues in the seminar was translation of concepts. Nancy had anticipated this in the first session when she brought up the issue. Peter's statement above noted his impatience with "the other group" being unable to define concepts to his satisfaction. One of the times he found the definition wanting was when he asked Nabila to define what she meant by historicity. Nancy commented on the difficulty of defining a term when one's usual experience is that the definition of that term is unnecessary because the people one normally talks to understand what it means.

> At one point . . . someone used the word *historicity,* and someone from outside their discipline . . . said, "*Historicity*—what is this term, what does it mean?" . . . The problem with translation of *historicity* is it's used . . . as a shorthand. . . . We all know what historicity is. It does levels of work for us, but it wasn't going to work for him. And he said, "You start doing work on that term and tell me what it means to you. Why are you using it?" It turned into kind of a calling on the carpet of the person. It was a little unfair. She had to define historicity, and she didn't do a particularly good job.

I asked Nancy for her definition of *historicity.*

I would say . . . historicity is a way of calling into question the naturalness of the past, of this idea that stuff happened in the past in this particular way and that there's an inherent truth to it. So that historicity is the indication that we know we're talking about stuff that's under construction by us.

In explaining the difficulty of translating the concept of historicity, Nancy introduced the concept of an intellectual comfort zone.

How could she make it make some sense to this guy that she needed the short-hand [the term *historicity,* when he] was outside of her intellectual comfort zone? . . . She wasn't able to convince him that her terminology was necessary or useful. In the end, he was still snorting and saying "buzzwords, jargon."

Sarah, a professor of political science, also pointed to language as a particularly difficult aspect of the seminars.

There were lots of moments when I just simply couldn't understand what certain people in the seminar were saying. . . . The language that comes out of the French philosophic stuff just needs to be deciphered for people who . . . don't live and work in it.

The Comfort Zone and Trust

Nancy explained how she herself sometimes shut down in the seminar, both physically and mentally, when she heard ideas that were outside her own comfort zone.

Some things I'm more comfortable with, some things I roll my eyes at when I . . . judge people to be . . . unconscious about grand narratives about truth with a capital T, when I hear them talking about biological truths of the body. All these things, I start to get real closed up inside to what they're saying. It might make me unable to listen to other parts of their arguments that might have . . . value to me.

On those occasions, she said, she sought out people she knew agreed with her way of thinking.

What I found myself doing sometimes is searching the room and making eye contact with the other literary poststructuralist types, and we're just like, oh, here we are again. We're suffering through this assault on what we think is a more adequate approach to truth.

Nancy thought those on the "other side" of the seminar divide did the same thing.

> And on the other side, too, I think that was happening. . . . One scholar wanted to read Derrida this semester . . . and Spivak as well, and we did. . . . But the people who were not going to be predisposed to being convinced by old Spivak ended up still being unconvinced and probably searching the room and rolling their eyes at Spivak and her indeterminacy and her hard language and her refusal to say anything simply.

Ahsan also used the term *comfort zone*. He first used it to describe a collaboration he had with a historian who was not in the seminar.

> There is an intellectual comfort zone that I have [with him]. . . . He can criticize me and I can criticize back. I can tell him, "I don't agree with you," and he wouldn't take it personally. And, boy, he would tell me, you know, what you are doing, this is absolutely wrong, don't do it this way. . . . And so, it's a comfort zone one develops . . . and a trust. . . . I think the key word is trust.

Ahsan went on to contrast that collaboration with his interactions in the ethics seminar.

> Because there's such a huge variety . . . between senior and junior and middle-level people, and different orientations . . . we didn't find that comfort zone as a cohort.

Like Peter and Sarah, Ahsan thought that seminar participants divided into two groups. And he found that he developed a rapport with the like-minded younger people on his side of the intellectual divide.

> Q: Which of the people were the ones that you had a good comfort zone with?
>
> A: I had . . . the comfort zone . . . with people . . . who were . . . more left-leaning on one hand, people who were also interested in critique of modernism and postmodernism. . . . I think age group . . . [mattered]. I couldn't relate to the more . . . advanced-aged faculty where they had their minds made up. I'm forty-six, and there were people in their fifties, late fifties, sixties.

Ahsan thought the lack of trust was the major reason why the seminar was so conflicted. The organization behavior literature agrees that trust is a key ingredient in creating effective teams. Trust, as well as respect, has been validated in empirical work measuring the constituent factors that promote successful collaboration.[6] Patrick Lencioni argues that "vulnerability-based trust" is the foundational building block of "cohesive and functional" teams.[7] Such trust exists when team members "comfortably and quickly acknowledge . . . their mistakes, weaknesses, failures, and needs for help . . . [and] . . . readily recognize the strengths of others, even when those strengths exceed their own."[8]

Vulnerability-based trust was in short supply in the ethics seminar. I shall have more to say about the role of the group leader in developing such trust in Chapter 7.

Does Ethics "Belong" to Philosophy?

Without taking away from Peter's extreme irritation that Nabila could not carefully define some of the concepts she was using, some of what irked Peter was that she (and others in the seminar) were using the term *ethics* without acknowledging that it "belonged" to philosophy and without understanding its philosophical meaning.

One of the people in the seminar who was most disturbed by Peter's desire to define ethics narrowly, in accord with the philosophical definition, was George, an assistant professor of law. George was interested in interdisciplinarity in part because he thought that his own discipline, law, "might be the most confined or constrained discipline of the ones represented" at the seminar, and he thought that the law was insufficiently inclusive of ethics. George wanted to be sure that the definition of ethics encompassed the ways in which the law is interpreted.

> Lawyers are called upon to give their opinions about all manner of things in our public world, and so to just know what the law requires doesn't help you [to make ethical decisions]. . . . You have to think about what sort of person you are and what sort of goals and aims you have in terms of applying and using that tool.

George bristled at the narrowness of philosophy's definition of ethics. And he didn't like the idea that philosophers seemed to think that they "owned" the topic of ethics. Thinking that law tended to shut out ethics, he didn't then want philosophy to shut out the ethical issues that were of concern to him.

> If we want to . . . have an . . . interdisciplinary discussion about ethics, are we bound to ethics as it is described by the field that it comes from? . . . If ethics falls under the discipline of philosophy, does philosophy own it in such a way

that [if we talk about issues of concern to nonphilosophers] we then are no longer talking about ethics but . . . about something else?

One of the things George wanted to be sure was included in ethics' province was the book by Michael Warner that the seminar read at Nancy's suggestion: *The Trouble with Normal: Sex, Politics, and the Ethics of the Queer Life.* The book argues that the concept of "normal" chokes off desirable societal innovation and creativity. George liked the book because it connected to the work he does on property rights, which are assumed to be inalienable and "normal," but which he increasingly regards as problematic. The book showed him how he could "de-privilege" property rights in the same way that Warner de-privileged home and family, two other concepts that are reified as "normal" in American thinking.

George was troubled by Peter's metaethics, which searches for universals, and by Peter's view that the Warner book, while interesting, was outside the purview of metaethics because gay behavior is exhibited by only a subgroup of the population. Like Warner, George was interested in a subgroup of the population. He was concerned with those who don't own property and sought to devise a social and political metaethics regarding their situation—a situation he thought was precarious not only for them, but potentially also for the larger society.

Boundary Work

Susan Cozzens and Thomas Gieryn use the concept of "boundary work" to illustrate how a discipline (call it X) sets up barriers around the work it does and attempts to keep scholars from other disciplines out by defining work within those boundaries as "belonging" to X.[9] They argue that scholars belonging to discipline X often expend considerable energy policing the territory their discipline has staked out and sanctioning those who speak without that discipline's authority on topics within that domain.[10]

A famous example of boundary work in philosophy took place in 1992 when Jacques Derrida received an honorary degree from Cambridge University and a group of philosophers from all over the world wrote a letter of objection to the *Times*, arguing that Derrida was not a "real" philosopher. Joe Moran quotes Derrida's description of the philosophers' letter.

M. Derrida describes himself as a philosopher, and his writings do indeed bear some of the marks of writing in that discipline. Their influence, however, has been to a striking degree almost entirely in fields outside of philosophy—in departments of film studies, for example, or of French and English literature. . . . We submit that if the works of a physicist (say) were similarly taken to be of merit primarily by those working in other disciplines, this would in itself be sufficient grounds for casting doubt upon the idea that the physicist in question was a suitable candidate for an honorary degree.[11]

The comparison of philosophy with physics is interesting. It suggests that one motivation for the boundary work may have been to maintain the "scientific" status of philosophy.

Boundary work is also common in cultural anthropology and economics. Cultural anthropologists seek to keep others from using their concepts, suggesting, for example, that the concept of culture "belongs" to anthropology and that when others use it, "they get it wrong." In economics, patrolling the border is about what constitutes "real" economics. For example, some mainstream economists refuse to recognize Marxist economics or feminist economics as "economics."[12] At other times, economists will disdainfully say, "That's not 'real' economics; it's sociology."

Michèle Lamont thinks that the "intense disciplinary boundary work" by cultural anthropologists stems from an "atmosphere of crisis [that] seems to have led cultural anthropologists to perceive their discipline's boundaries as fragile and in need of defense against the encroachment of scholars from other fields."[13] Boundary work in economics occurs in a different context. Unlike cultural anthropologists, economists do not adopt the position that only economists can use economic theories and methods. In fact, most mainstream economists are delighted that economics has been so successful in exporting itself to other disciplines, particularly political science and sociology. But in an environment of so much exporting, economists want to be sure that both exporters and importers are quite clear about the "scientific" attributes of the product in question.[14] Hence the recurrent admonition about what is and what is not economics.

Personal Affect

Because of her experience the year before, when anger led to a major blowup in Adams's science studies seminar (see Chapter 3), Nancy began the ethics seminar talking about the emotional challenges of interdisciplinary dialogue.

> I tried actually to just say flat out that I felt that thinking interdisciplinarily, engaging with ideas that were outside . . . our own training, is about as scary a thing as we do. It's almost as scary as the blank page.

Sociologist Andrew Abbott also thinks that academics find it scary to venture out of their discipline.

> Every academic knows the experience of reading something from outside his or her discipline and knows the unsettling feeling it induces. Disciplines in fact provide a core element of the identity of most intellectuals in modern America.[15]

But as Nabila noted above, Peter was not sympathetic to Nancy's idea that the seminar discuss this fear of losing one's identity by engaging in interdisciplinary work. Peter thought there was nothing to be fearful about, that if participants could all agree on the definition of terms, the seminar would proceed smoothly.

Ahsan agreed with Nancy that matters of affect were critical, although he put the issue somewhat differently. He thought that what was important was the affect with which participants put forward their ideas, that ideas put forward tentatively encouraged discussions while ideas put out definitively discouraged them. He thought that what distinguished tentativeness from definitiveness was not discipline but rather geographic origin, with those from countries that had been colonized tending to be less definitive and more tentative in their style of argument.

> Some people were just so single-minded . . . that their ideas [are] just the only ideas that are available, and so it just didn't make for any kind of collaboration and mutual learning. And it actually turned . . . sometimes it turned into a huge battlefield. . . . I think in collaboration . . . there must be a tentativeness to your assumptions and your presentations, in order to solicit the critique.

Ahsan also thought adherents of postmodernism were likely to be more tentative in their thinking.

> I think that there were different epistemological projects going on. . . . Someone like Peter was very positivist and empirical, and others were postmodern, [where] the critique of the South and other is almost foremost, there are no grand narratives . . . no straight answers to things . . . a tentativeness to things.

And in his view, the difference in status between junior and senior faculty further exacerbated affective problems.

> I think there was also an asymmetry problem in [the seminar], asymmetry of people who were at a particular stage in their career and others at another stage of their career. And I think that asymmetry created . . . tension.

Nabila certainly felt that her arguments with Peter had an affective as well as an intellectual component.

> I have to also say I do think that there is some personal animosity in our relationship . . . and I'm not sure that it's all about interdisciplinarity.

But when I asked whether some of that animosity had to do with gender and age, she gave only a tentative assent.

> Yeah. Yeah. I mean, who knows what it is?

Nabila's inability to pinpoint the cause of her discomfort stems from the difficulty of disentangling multiple factors that are highly correlated. Scholars trained in postmodern, poststructural, and postcolonial theory are mostly young relative to others in the academy; they are also more likely than their more senior colleagues to be women, people of color, and scholars from areas of the world that were formerly colonies of European countries. They don't know which of these characteristics—their training, their age, their gender, or their national origin—underlie the challenge they feel as they seek to claim their place at the scholarly table.

However, the work of Barbara Herrnstein Smith, a senior scholar with a sophisticated understanding of epistemological debates, suggests that Nabila's age and gender probably did play a role in Peter's difficulty in understanding what she had to say. Not only do habits of mind act as barriers to new ideas, but when those new ideas are put forth by people we consider to have lower status, the ideas have two strikes against them.

> Theoretical accounts that are more or less incompatible with what we already take for granted as obvious, self-evident or unquestionable are likely to appear inadequate, incredible, or incoherent to us, and also, depending on our sense of the intellectual authority and sometimes other social characteristics of the people who offer them—for example, their . . . age, gender or class—as ignorant, silly, outlandish, wildly radical, or fraudulent.[16]

Yankelovich suggests that one of the requisites for successful dialogue is that participants regard themselves as equal to one another.[17] With rare exceptions, junior and senior faculty do not regard themselves as equals. Given the necessity of ironing out disciplinary power differences in interdisciplinary seminars, it probably would have been helpful if the additional power differential between junior and senior faculty had not been present.

I asked Ahsan whether he saw the battle as drawn particularly between Nabila and Peter.

> Yeah . . . Peter just had this whole thing . . . all worked out. And Nabila was much more tentative. . . . Nabila actually went silent at some point, she just gave up.

When Nabila responded to my question about what the seminar had been like for her, she confirmed that Ahsan was on the mark in using the word *silent* and sensing that she had given up.[18] The seminar had been a silencing experience for her, and what she had given up on was interdisciplinarity.

> I think that the seminar has in some ways made me more attached to my own disciplinary bias. . . . It has sharpened my sense of my own attachment to a form of literary reading. . . . Every discipline has . . . various methodologies of interpretation, and I suppose I began to value and refine my own sense of what mine is in this seminar. . . . I don't think this has been the most successful experience with interdisciplinarity.

I asked Nabila what she might do differently if she were granted a "do-over," an opportunity to participate in the same seminar again.

> I felt by the end of it that I was being bossed around a bit . . . and not really treated with much respect. . . . I suppose I maybe would have in some ways demanded a little more respect from day one, rather than trying to be sort of nice to everyone, if you know what I mean.

Ari shared Nabila's perception that she was not treated with respect. In fact, he thought that the lack of respect in the seminar was a broader problem, that not only did senior people not respect junior people like Nabila, but that junior people did not respect senior faculty either. Sarah also felt that courteousness was sometimes lacking. "There were moments when people got personal with each other," she said.

Disciplinary Affect

While Nancy agreed that there were issues of civility and lack of respect in the seminar, she thought that some of them were the result of different habits of mind across academic disciplines, and that, for example, while the style of critique normative among analytic philosophers seems unduly sharp to those from other disciplines, those same philosophers often think the style of thinking in other disciplines is not rigorous enough.[19]

> We had some problems with civility, but there are different worlds in academia; analytic philosophers can be very sharp with each other; they have certain ways of understanding reason. In fact, they [think they] own rationality and the rest of us [have] this sloppy, unthinking way.[20]

Contrasting the affect of the analytical philosopher with that of the historian in the seminar, Nancy introduced the notion of disciplinary affect.

> He [the analytical philosopher] doesn't come at things with a sense of openness, which the historian in the group is actually remarkable for having. . . . I think there's such a thing as disciplinary affect, and I think we get displays of it all over the place. And so, the historian has an affect of openness, of being willing to hear what you're saying.

When I interviewed Ari, the historian Nancy was referring to, I too found him to be particularly open and positive. And he seemed to have that same view of himself. He told me he thought that the seminar was conflict-ridden and that he was sure that in the course of my interviews I would find that he was the happiest person in the seminar. He referred to himself as a sponge, soaking up scholarly tidbits wherever he found them. He said he was delighted by the opportunity to be tutored in Derrida by the younger generation in the seminar, because he could never have read Derrida on his own, and that postcolonial theory (PCT) had given him important tools that he could use in his own work on nineteenth-century ethnic conflict, because although he and postcolonial theorists use different vocabularies, they deal with similar issues related to hybridity. In particular, he felt that PCT had given him tools to understand how minority communities appropriate from hegemonic communities and what different communities can legitimately demand from one another in the way of cultural openness. He also said that deepening his understanding of some of the main theoretical perspectives of the late twentieth century helped him to feel cultured, a feeling he enjoys. Ari was an intellectual bridge. Peter saw him as a solid thinker who was entirely intelligible, and the postcolonialists saw him as open to their ideas. I wondered if the seminar would have been less conflicted if a historian like Ari had been its leader.

Disciplinary affect may be a habit of mind, but we should not fall into the trap of assuming that all members of a discipline behave in the same way. For example, when I asked George whether Peter's postdoc, also an analytic philosopher, viewed matters that came up in the seminar in the same way that Peter did, his answer made it clear that there is a difference between *seeing* things the same way and *behaving* the same way.

> I think that she does [view them in the same way], but she's not as confron-
> tational about it. . . . Whereas Peter would just say, no, this isn't ethics . . . [his
> postdoc's] approach is more, can you tell me how this is about ethics? I un-
> derstand ethics to be X. Is the way . . . you are talking about [whatever you are
> talking about] . . . a good way to look it?[21]

Although disciplines have habits of mind, there is nonetheless room for individual difference in affect. In the preface to the second edition of *Academic Tribes and Territories*, Tony Becher and Paul Trowler are quite firm on this point: "[Burton] Clark overstates the thesis of the first edition of this book when he characterizes it as arguing that bodies of knowledge 'determine the behavior of individuals'. . . . Such determinism is certainly very far from our current position."[22]

In summary, although central tendencies of affect may exist in many disciplines, there is also considerable variation around these central tendencies. Discipline is not destiny. Moreover, as Geoffrey Hodgson argues, habits of mind are mutable. And one of the dynamics that leads them to change is interaction with institutions.[23] In other words, it is precisely exposure to new ideas in an interdisciplinary conversation that may promote change in habits of mind, including any affect that might be associated with a particular discipline.

Power and Status

Some of what happened in the ethics seminar involved the clash of disciplinary cultures and habits of mind. For example, it is likely that Peter was trained in what Robert Merton has called one of the four basic norms of scientific behavior, "organized skepticism."[24] Careful not to make the error of believing something is true when it is false (what statisticians call a Type 1 error), he is much less concerned about making a Type 2 error, believing something is false when it in fact is true. Having been carefully socialized to sniff out possible Type 1 errors in his own discipline, he was probably even more vigilant in a interdisciplinary seminar, where he didn't know the discipline being presented and could not fall back on his prior knowledge. Much of his sharp questioning was no doubt to ensure against being hoodwinked.

Nabila, too, was behaving according to her disciplinary culture, which included the habits of mind connected to postmodernist thinking: Ask whether truth is constructed or discovered. Ask questions about which knowledge is valid and who has a place at the scholarly table. Question gender, race, and ethnic roles.

But something else was going on as well. Not only did the seminars provide a weekly occasion for reenacting the culture wars, or, as Sarah put it, getting to the fundamentals way too often, they also provided a fertile ground for negotiating power and status.[25]

Pierre Bourdieu's work suggests that we view the conversations as a power struggle as much as a venue for increasing intellectual understanding. His argument is that symbolic capital (prestige) is as important as economic capital (material wealth) and cultural capital (knowledge and skills) in conferring power, and that in power struggles, the trading off of the three kinds of capital often takes place. This notion provides an informative lens through which to view the battles just described.

> A field is always the site of struggles in which individuals seek to maintain or alter the distribution of the forms of capital specific to it. The individuals who participate in these struggles will have differing aims—some will seek to preserve the status quo, others to change it—and differing chances of winning or losing, depending on where they are located in the structured space of positions.[26]

Seminar participants indeed varied in the extent to which they wished to change the status quo (in the society, the university, and the seminar), and they varied in the amount of symbolic capital (prestige) they brought to the seminar. Some were tenured professors with long-standing international reputations, and some were young assistant professors who were laboring to build standing. Some were women or minorities (or both) with few friends in high places, and others were white men with many powerful connections.

They also varied in their economic capital: some came from rich disciplines and had large grants; others came from poor disciplines and ran their research on a shoestring. In general, as might be expected, those with a great deal of symbolic and economic capital had less interest in changing the status quo than did their colleagues with less such power.

Bourdieu's description of a power struggle also accords well with the situation in the seminars with respect to engagement. As he suggests, even those with small amounts of relevant capital (and therefore little power) were absorbed in the proceedings. They all had bought in to the academic notion that intellectual dialogue and battle—explaining their disciplinary perspective, trying to understand some other perspective, arguing against another perspective, or gaining prestige—were important.

> All individuals, whatever their aims and chances of success, will share in common certain fundamental presuppositions. All participants must believe in the game they are playing, and in the value of what is at stake in the struggles they are waging. The very existence and persistence of the game or field presupposes a total and unconditional "investment," a practical and unquestioning belief in the game and its stakes. Hence the conduct of struggle within a field, whether a conflict over the distribution of wealth or over the value of a work of art, always presupposes a fundamental accord or complicity on the part of those who participate in the struggle.[27]

Helen Schwartzman's views on the purpose of meetings also contribute to our understanding of what was going on at the ethics seminars. Schwartzman argues that the idea that meetings are places where people discuss issues and make decisions is woefully inadequate for understanding what really takes place. She views meetings primarily as occasions when people come together to confirm or rearrange their relationships, occasions when they figure out how much power and status they really have and how much they may be able to gain in the course of the proceedings. People are talking about the subject of the meeting, but at the same time they have another agenda.[28]

The ethics seminars were as much about interpreting and validating status as they were about discussing ethics. Because people came from different departments and disciplines and for the most part did not know one another, their first order of business was to establish the status hierarchy. While it is certainly the case that one purpose for Peter's sharp questioning of Nabila was to understand what she was saying, it is also likely that a second purpose was to establish his primacy in the seminar's pecking order. Peter had high status to begin with because he came from philosophy, a high-status discipline, and because he was a senior white man. But his standing within philosophy did not automatically transfer to the seminar because people didn't know him or his work and several people in the seminar were interested in questioning status that was derived from age, race, gender, and discipline. Nor did his status as a faculty member at a high-prestige institution matter much since all the seminar participants had the same institutional status. Peter had to establish his reputation in the ethics seminar in a way that he did not need to do at seminars in his own department or seminars in his own interdisciplinary field. And everyone else did too, including the seminar leader.

I noted earlier that Nancy began the first seminar by talking about the difficulties of interdisciplinary dialogue. This was her area of expertise. She knew much more about interdisciplinarity than about ethics. By choosing to begin with a topic on which she was expert, she sought to establish her status. But Peter challenged her effort to establish her expertise in this domain by saying that the idea that they would have trouble talking with one another was ridiculous. In addition to thwarting an attempt to bring matters of affect to the fore, a strategy that might have worked to enhance the seminar's functioning, Peter's comments took away potential status and power from the seminar leader.

Nabila, Ahsan, and George also had difficulties establishing their status positions, particularly vis-à-vis Peter. Peter was a senior white man, born in the United States; they were junior and either female or men of color. Peter came from analytic philosophy, a discipline with very high status. And James, one of the people Peter counted as on his team, came from medicine, another high-status discipline. Although George came from law, a high-status discipline, the other junior people, including Nancy, were humanists from disciplines with less status.

Bourdieu's concept of habitus, "the set of dispositions that incline agents to act and react in certain ways," is also useful in understanding what happened at the ethics seminar.[29] Even though Bourdieu talks about dispositions as having been acquired in childhood, we can easily argue that for purposes of interdisciplinary discussions, the dispositions that matter are those acquired in the course of doctoral training and academic experience. Habitus, Bourdieu argues, gives people a point of reference, a feel for what is going on, and a sense of how to behave. Because each of the disciplines provided a different habitus for its members, when seminar participants came together, they often misunderstood the habitus of others.

Conclusion

Seminars with multiple cross-currents of difference have tremendous potential for creativity. Indeed, it is often specifically diversity of background and opinion that contributes to creativity. As Randall Collins puts it:

> Creativity is the friction of the attention space at the moment when the structural blocks are grinding against one another the hardest.[30]

But great differences in disciplinary culture and habits of mind also have a high potential for dysfunction. To harness the creative potential of so much difference requires expert leadership. Had Nancy been expert in both ethics and managing participants' jockeying for status and power, the seminar's positive potential might have been achieved.

The management literature on successful teams distinguishes between two types of conflict—A-type (affective) conflict and C-type (cognitive) conflict—and argues that while cognitive conflict fuels creative thinking, affective conflict takes group members away from the task at hand.[31] However, if we take seriously Schwartzman's view that meetings are by definition occasions when people jockey for status and power, we come to realize that the dichotomy between these two types of conflict is not helpful; seminars are inevitably going to have both.

Interdisciplinary meetings that are ostensibly about scholarly topics are filled with affective issues, including disciplinary identity and uneasiness about presenting work to those outside one's "comfort zone." If such seminars are to be successful, they need leaders who recognize that affective conflict is intrinsic to interdisciplinary dialogue. The kind of creative cognitive conflict that proponents of interdisciplinarity are looking for will emerge only if a strong leader can contain and productively channel inevitable affective conflict.

Analysis of the Adams ethics seminar also suggests that productive cognitive conflict might have been more likely if the deans had taken interpersonal relationships into account when they chose participants for the seminar. Ahsan suggested that one way the deans might have done this was to have interviewed all potential participants and figured out "whose personalities would gel."

It also would have been helpful if the deans had given some attention to disciplinary interactions. Just because a faculty member in discipline A is interested in discipline B doesn't mean that he or she will be interested or successful in conversing on issues involving discipline C. Put another way, if we put lots of people interested in interdisciplinarity together, they will not necessarily have a productive dialogue. Anticipating which people in which disciplines might have the knowledge, desire, and interpersonal skills to talk to one another on topics that matter is a supremely challenging task.

It is particularly disheartening that it was a seminar on ethics that had so much difficulty bridging disciplinary cultures. As our societal problems get ever more complex, figuring out how we are going to live ethically is paramount. It would have been reassuring to know that diverse academics could wrestle productively with ethical concerns.

5   Two Cultures Revisited

IN 1959, IN HIS REDE LECTURE AT CAMBRIDGE UNIVERSITY, C. P. Snow said he observed "an unbridgeable division between literary intellectuals and natural scientists."[1] In the half-century since Snow's address, science has become increasingly complex, and it may be that those who specialize in the humanities know even less about science today than they did at the time Snow discerned two cultures. And social scientists, a group left out entirely in Snow's analysis, are generally in the same situation as humanists.

This gap in knowledge about science on the part of humanists and social scientists is increasingly problematic, for not only has science become ever more central to unraveling problems that beset us—slowing climate change, finding alternative sources of energy, improving the health and mobility of an aging population, and discovering cures for fearsome diseases—but solutions to these problems require collaboration with those from the humanities and social sciences.

From a classroom perspective, improving interdisciplinary understanding is also important. When scientists have a working knowledge of the humanities and social sciences, they are better able to find links between those subjects and science, thereby making science more accessible to nonscience majors in their classes. The reverse is also true: some knowledge of science is helpful to faculty seeking to help their students who are science majors to make connections to humanities or social science subjects.

This chapter looks at three seminars, the science seminar at Adams and the consilience and representation seminars at Jefferson. The purpose of the science studies seminar was to look at connections between science, culture, and society, and both Jefferson seminars put particular emphasis on opening dialogue between scientists and nonscientists, the consilience seminar by examining connections among scholarly fields, and the representation seminar by comparing the ways in which the different scholarly fields represent "reality."

The Science Studies Seminar at Adams

Information on the composition of the science studies seminar is in Chapter 3,[2] which analyzes a dispute between a professor of economics and a postdoc in religious studies. Here we focus on two additional disputes in that same seminar.

The first was between Fred, a professor of biology, and two professors not in the interview sample, one in literature and one in philosophy/computer science, and concerns a definition of the combatants in the science wars and their lines of battle. The second disagreement was between the literature professor and the philosophy/computer science professor as seen through the eyes of other seminar members and is about the relationship of science studies to science. We have already observed that the Adams seminar on ethics fought the postmodern wars. Unfortunately, the Adams seminar on science studies fought the science wars.

Who Are the Combatants in the Science Wars and What Are They Fighting About?

The dispute involving Fred was in large part a disagreement about exactly who the combatants in the science wars actually are. Unlike the postmodern wars, where the two sides of the quarrels are fairly clear, exactly who is fighting whom in the science wars remains somewhat muddy. Some think the battles are between scientists and those who study science. Others think that scientists are not combatants at all, but rather those who philosophers and others are fighting *about*.

The second quarrel in the seminar was equally important, and even more opaque. As the comments from Fred, Nancy (the seminar leader), and Larry (the anthropologist/historian) demonstrate, it involved an effort to define the issues in contention between a philosopher and a humanist.

Trevor Pinch locates the dawn of the science wars in a 1939 encounter between mathematician Alan Turing and philosopher Ludwig Wittgenstein.[3] Relying on biographies of both men, Pinch recounts that the two stars in their fields were both at Cambridge University giving independent lectures with the same title, "Foundations of Mathematics," and Turing decided to attend one of Wittgenstein's lectures. According to Wittgenstein's biographer Ray Monk, Wittgenstein said the following in his talk:

> I shall try again and again to show that what is called a mathematical discovery had much better be called a mathematical invention.[4]

In other words, Wittgenstein thought that truth is invented (or constructed) by science rather than discovered. Turing said he understood what Wittgenstein was saying but disagreed with him. Then Wittgenstein countered that Turing didn't *really* disagree with him, but that Turing was afraid to agree for fear that Wittgenstein's idea would diminish mathematics. Wittgenstein thought this was a baseless fear; in his view giving up the idea that truth is out there to be discovered would not be harmful to either the prominence or the power of mathematics.

Although the science wars have become inordinately complex, the dispute between Wittgenstein and Turing remains at their heart. The field of science studies, which emerged in the 1960s and 1970s, took up Wittgenstein's argument, contending that not only is truth invented (or constructed) by science rather than discovered, but that science as a whole is merely another culture and that the scientific method is neither a special nor necessarily the best path to truth.[5]

Those engaged in science studies don't wish to undermine science, but they don't wish to privilege it either. As historian/anthropologist Larry put it:

> There's a debunking edge to science studies; that . . . science is not really scientific, that its own self-proclaimed special status is really sleight of hand.

Nancy described the battle in the science studies seminar as follows:

> The most challenging issue of the seminar stemmed . . . from its topic—science, culture, and society—which encompasses what has come to be known as the "science wars," . . . the split between those who "do" science and those trained to "theorize" it.

But Fred did not see the argument this way. Fred's research was on biomechanics. He had been interested in the intersections of biology and engineering from the very beginning of his career and regularly combined them in both his writing and teaching. In addition, he often team-taught interdisciplinary courses with nonscientists. Rather than seeing himself as a combatant in the science wars, he saw himself as one whose work was being fought *about*. But he said he didn't comprehend this until after the seminar was over:

> I didn't understand the context of that seminar . . . until . . . about a year ago. I attended a meeting of a humanities and technology society . . . a small conference of . . . a lovely bunch of people, who mostly . . . teach . . . English and engineering, . . . and I understood that all the squabbling that went on in the science seminar was fundamentally not a squabble that involved scientists. It was between philosophers of science and sociologists of science.

Fred's comments are reminiscent of a quote from scientist Stephen Jay Gould, who also argued that scientists are not combatants in the science wars but rather their subject. In an article in *Science Magazine* in 2000, Gould said: "A science war can only exist in the minds of critics not engaged in the enterprise supposedly under analysis."[6]

Jay Labinger has noted that although there are many complicated ins and outs concerning the science wars, the one fact most everyone agrees on is that there are not many scientists engaged in the science wars. He cites Paul Gross's estimate that fewer than a dozen are actively involved on his side and suggests that "if we include all practicing scientists who have participated from *any* perspective the numbers might grow by a few fold, but not much more."[7]

Fred said that he had read Paul Gross and Norman Levitt's book *Higher Superstition* about the science wars several years before and "had had a hard time imagining what they got so mad about." But as a result of being in the seminar, he understood.

> My experience of science criticism had only come from the sort of know-nothing right, as opposed to this rather funnier, stranger world, which is generally thought to be on the left, denying that science can make progress, denying that we're actually doing what we say we're doing, and certainly not doing it for the reasons we say we're doing it.

He thought that those who theorize about science completely misunderstand his motivation for doing science, namely, that he is curious about the answers to certain questions. And he could not understand why theorists were focused on matters of power.

> What I was exposed to was a . . . major industry misrepresenting why scientists do science. . . . It was certainly not me they're talking about. . . . It's not my field they're talking about, in terms of anything I could recognize as being familiar. . . . And the scientists, well, we're the guinea pigs they're studying.
>
> Q: So you're not at war?
>
> A: I'm what they're fighting over, not one of the participants. . . . They're talking about power and all of this kind of thing, and I'm thinking about questions I'm curious about.

Fred was particularly puzzled about why a social scientist would say that an introduction to a science paper that traced the intellectual ancestry of an idea would be seen as an effort to assert power.

> You get somebody who will write a book criticizing a scientific paper and going through the introduction of papers saying, you know, all those citations that you make in the introduction are an assertion of power. . . . You want to wrap your stuff in the aura of the continuity with important ancestors and that kind of thing. Oh, my God, I mean, I write an introduction to a paper. Certain things it's got to do to set the stage so that people know where you're coming from . . . the reviewers will reject the paper if I don't put it into the proper context. It never bothered them about that.

I asked Fred whether the search for power could be an unconscious motivation, but he thought that desire for power, if not entirely absent from science, was in any case trivial. He thought that some of the emphasis on power in science has come about because nonscientists have come to think that all of science is like molecular biology and that scientists are generally like James Watson and Francis Crick, who proposed the double-helix structure of the DNA molecule. He believed that molecular biology is particularly competitive because "it's fashionable," it's "overcrowded" (the people/problem ratio is high), and "there's money in it." As for Watson and Crick, he thought they were a special case owing to their "peculiar" personalities. He said he's never seen issues of power arise in his more than forty years in science and gave an example of his own noncompetitiveness and the relative absence of issues of power in his field.

I just went to a meeting where I gave a talk where the entire talk was giving away problems. I said I'm sixty-three years old. I want to know how these things come out, and I'm certainly not going to have a chance to chase them down. Anybody wants me, they have . . . the assurance that I'll do anything I can in terms of advice, whatever.[8]

It may be that the explanation for Fred's discomfort with the philosophers and sociologists who study the field of science was just as Wittgenstein thought: scientists are opposed to analysis of science because they believe that it per se undermines their discipline. Pinch provides an interesting analogy on this: If a woman who has been robbed meets a criminologist who has a wider perspective on crime and explains to the victim the likely sociological roots of the robber's action, the victim may feel angry, believing that the criminologist's analysis has diminished her experience of suffering. Knowing that he was a guinea pig for philosophers and sociologists of science bothered Fred.

But it may be also be that one of the reasons for Fred's bafflement at the notion that scientists wield power is that Fred's definition of power is different from that of his seminar colleagues. Steeped in postmodernism, many of them were likely using the concept of power in written work in the sense that Michel Foucault uses it, to ask whom the discourse serves.[9]

In her essay on autonomy and power in science, Susan Cozzens distinguishes two different types of power: power as dominance and power as mastery. She also differentiates among three different facets of the power of scientists: influence, competitive edge, and autonomy.[10] She sees having power through having a competitive edge as related to dominance; but she views power that manifests in autonomy as related to mastery. Had Fred made this kind of distinction among types of power, he might have agreed that he had autonomy, which stemmed from the mastery he had of his field. But Fred thought about power solely in terms of dominance, and he did not see that he had power over others.

Susan Cozzens and Thomas Gieryn write about power in science in terms of what they call opportunity structures and the need for scientists to obtain funding (what they call sponsors). Their work suggests that Fred may not be alone in failing to recognize the role of power in science. They observe that "for individual scientists . . . control through opportunity structures may be invisible."[11]

No matter which of the many possible definitions of power Fred's colleagues had in mind, the conversations did not adequately translate them. Fred never came to understand what his sociologist and philosopher colleagues meant when they used the term.

Nevertheless, Fred said the seminar had been important for him.

I found the seminar somewhat unsatisfactory, as you probably understand, but it wasn't totally unsatisfactory; it was an important experience in my life.

Q: So if you had it to do over again, would you do it?

A: I think I probably would. And I hadn't thought about it that way, but, yeah. It exposed me to all kinds of things I wouldn't be otherwise exposed to. . . . I understand a lot more now . . . not about science, but about the sort of funny academic . . . attitudes towards science.

The Relationship Between Science and Science Studies

Fred was never really engaged in the seminar's dialogue. He was baffled and annoyed but not really a part of the debates about science studies. Here is his view of the debate between the philosopher and the humanist.

There were squabbles between [them]. . . . And they would lock horns, and I would be sitting there wondering what exactly are they locking horns about, because these things obviously made a great deal of difference to them and they seemed rather remote to anything in my experience or that really seemed to matter to me as a practicing experimental scientist.

Anthropologist/historian Larry, had a similar view:

It was a question of the relationship between science and something that science is supposed to be about—call it nature or call it the world, call it empirical reality, or whatever you like. What you exactly call it was in dispute, and also it was a good question of whether there was something there or whether it was purely a construction or a fabrication of socially arranged practices and discourses.

Nancy, too, reported a great deal of talking back and forth.

The philosopher and humanist talked a lot to each other. One believed she possesses the truth. The other doesn't know what truth is, and so there were good discussions.

In an edited volume with the intriguing title *Einstein Meets Magritte*, Barbara Herrnstein Smith says that the two groups debating the relationship between science and science studies are traditional philosophers of science on the one side and, on the other side, a heterogeneous group of heterodox scholars, including "historians and sociologists of science, epistemological theorists in related fields, and a number of philosophers as well."[12]

About this heterodox group, Smith says this:

> The terms, concepts and distinctions of traditional epistemology and philosophy of science are no longer either workable or, for the most part, necessary in conducting their professional and intellectual lives. For that reason, they find it usually difficult and sometimes . . . impossible to answer theoretical arguments framed in the traditional terms or appealing to traditional distinctions and oppositions.[13]

At the same time, she observes, traditional philosophers of science

> are likely to find the critiques and alternatives elaborated by their heterodox colleagues absurd, arbitrary, and nihilistic . . . reckless abandonments of what is most desirable and indispensable.[14]

She holds out little hope of reconciliation.

While it did not engender the same hostility as the ethics seminar, neither did the science studies seminar promote mutual understanding. The scientist and most of the other members of the seminar were bewildered by the battles between the philosopher and the humanist.[15] Nor did the humanist and the philosopher seem to come any closer to a meeting of minds as the seminar progressed. As Smith suggests in her essay, there is indeed a high likelihood of a failure of convergence between parties to this debate.

Seeking Resolution—David Mermin's Rules

David Mermin, a science studies warrior on the conservative side of the debate, has recently been involved in conversations with members of both sides of the dispute in efforts to use face-to-face conversation to reduce their differences. In an article he wrote about those efforts, he says he has reached several conclusions, which he summarizes as rules. These rules are very much in the spirit of disciplinary cultures and habits of mind. Had members of the science studies seminar instituted Mermin's two rules, they, too, might have made more progress in understanding one another and Fred might have learned more than merely that nonscientists often have a funny attitude toward science.

The two rules are as follows:

Do not expect people from remote disciplines to speak clearly in or understand the nuances of your own disciplinary language.

Do not assume that it is as easy as it may appear for you to penetrate the disciplinary language of others.[16]

In other words, to communicate across disciplines, particularly about controversial matters, it is imperative to constantly keep in mind an awareness of the difficulty of doing so.

The Jefferson Seminars on Consilience and Representation

The Jefferson seminars were much more successful in bridging the science/ nonscience disciplines than was the Adams science studies seminar. Although, as noted in Chapter 3, the mathematician, studio artist, and dramatist had difficulty with the dominant literary habits of mind in the representation seminar, participants in both the consilience and representation seminars found the dialogue between scientists and nonscientists productive.

Background

The funding proposal for both the consilience and the representation seminars was written by Jefferson's dean of arts and sciences, Joyce, a literary scholar, and the provost, Ed, a chemist, and they were jointly in charge of choosing participants for the consilience seminar. They participated in both seminars, and Joyce was the leader of the consilience seminar.

Both saw the purpose of the seminars as an exploration of syntheses among fields. As Joyce put it, in their work as dean and provost, they had come to see that "the impulse in most recent scholarship has been centrifugal"; they wished to "open . . . a conversation among the disciplines . . . and look for commonalities [among them]." And they were particularly interested in using the seminars as a venue for incubating new interdisciplinary courses. They therefore termed the first seminar a consilience seminar, designed specifically to examine the ways in which disciplines intersected.

Because they were jointly in charge of choosing the participants, because

Joyce led the consilience seminar, both choosing the early readings and leading the first set of discussions, and because they both participated in both seminars, the seminars were more closely aligned with their initial visions than were those at the other universities.

As noted in Chapter 1, the Jefferson seminars had more disciplinary diversity than did those at Washington and Adams. Of the fourteen tenured faculty in the consilience seminar, three were in the sciences (biochemistry, chemistry, and physics), four in the social sciences (economics, political science, and sociology), five in the humanities (English, linguistics, literature, philosophy, and religious studies), and two in the arts (musicology and music composition). Ten were professors, three were associate professors, and one was a professor emeritus; 30 percent were women (see Appendix Table A-1).

Four of the participants were administrators: the provost, the dean of arts and sciences, the former dean of arts and sciences, and an associate provost. In addition to the faculty, there were eight postdoctoral fellows—four humanists, two musicians, one physicist, and one sociologist.

All but one of the sessions took place in a comfortable seminar room. One session was held in the laboratories of two of the scientists in the group, the chemist, and the biochemist.

The note taker at Jefferson was a young man who was serving both as an executive assistant to the provost and as a fellow in one of the university's interdisciplinary programs. Although he led one session on his own academic work, he did not generally participate in the discussions, and as a result, he took even more extensive notes than Neil did at Washington. He worked with Joyce to put those notes into an attractive binder with a group picture of participants on its cover, and they gave it as a gift to seminar attendees.

Key Players

I interviewed eight faculty from the consilience seminar: three scientists and five from the humanities, as well as Leon, director of Corporate and Foundation Relations, who was an observer. The scientists were Ed, the provost and a professor of chemistry; Victor, a professor of biochemistry; and Amita, a professor of physics. The humanities faculty were Joel, an associate professor of music; Joyce, former dean of arts and sciences and a professor of literature; Louise, the dean of arts and sciences and a professor of music; Mary, a professor of religious studies; and Sam, a professor of humanities (see Appendix Table A-2).

Ed said he joined the seminars to get to know some of his colleagues and what they were thinking about professionally. He thought the interactions were quite likely to have an impact on his teaching, and that was one of the attractions of the seminar for him.

Biochechemist Victor had a long-standing interest in the humanities and arts and joined the seminar to learn more about them. Victor also thought the seminar would give him an opportunity to educate nonscientists about science, and he enthusiastically embraced that role.

Unlike Victor, Amita had had little exposure to nonscience fields, and her interest in joining the seminar stemmed from her awareness of how narrow her professional life had been.

> I went through all my undergraduate schooling in India, [where] you get thrown into the sciences right when you're eighteen years old. . . . I always felt that I had missed out on an opportunity to have the more liberal kind of education that people have here. So one enticement was to be able to . . . see what people outside the sciences did as part of their research.

Amita was also interested in explaining science to nonscientists, thereby helping to break down barriers between the two groups.

> Often when I talked to people outside the sciences, there was very little understanding . . . of what the day-to-day life is of a scientist. There seemed to be not a clear notion of what [scientists] do.

Composer Joel had interests that intersected with several disciplines.

> I had [already] collaborated with a poet . . . in putting together a book about the relationship between poetry and music. And it interested me to see what kind of other connections I might be able to make between music and poetry, which I already knew, and sciences, humanities, which I didn't know so well.

Literary scholar Joyce had been the dean of arts and sciences for a number of years and had become interested in interdisciplinarity while she held that position. In the summer before the consilience seminar, she stepped down as dean and was thus able to lead the seminar.

Musicologist Louise became the dean of arts and sciences when Joyce stepped down and was a participant in both the consilience and representation seminars, although her administrative duties kept her from attending as regularly as she would have preferred.

Mary, a professor of religious studies, had a long history of working collaboratively in women's studies and was excited to join the seminar.

As noted in Chapter 3, Sam, a professor of humanities, had had many years of experience with interdisciplinarity, including several years leading a multiuniversity interdisciplinary seminar.

Ed, Joyce, Louise, and Sam, as well as Leon (the director of Corporate and Foundation Relations), also participated in the representation seminar. Three additional faculty in the interview sample for the representation seminar—Barry, a professor of mathematics; Evelyn, an associate professor of fine arts; and Jane, an artist-in-residence in drama—were introduced in the second part of Chapter 3.

Readings Designed to Bridge Snow's "Two Cultures"

While issues stemming from the Wittgenstein-Turing dispute were at the center of the science wars that emerged in the science studies seminar, the science issues that surfaced in the two Jefferson seminars link to the questions raised by Snow and E. O. Wilson, whose book *Consilience: The Unity of Knowledge* was the first reading for both the consilience and representation seminars. Drawing on an 1840 definition from William Whewell, Wilson defines consilience as a "'jumping together' of knowledge . . . across disciplines to create a common groundwork of explanation."[17]

Wilson begins with the notion of the Ionian Enchantment, a term that physicist and historian of science Gerald Holton uses to mean a belief in the unity of the sciences, and extends that notion to a belief in consilience, the unity of *all* knowledge. Perhaps not surprisingly, for he is after all a scientist, Wilson wishes to base the unification of all knowledge, including the social sciences and humanities, on a foundation of science. His book is an effort to show how this might be accomplished.

Participants also read Jared Diamond's book *Guns, Germs, and Steel*, which also examines interactions between science and nonscience, in this case with respect to economic growth. And quite early on in the consilience seminar, Joyce assigned three plays that integrate science and nonscience: *Arcadia, Copenhagen,* and *The Tempest.* Although Sam was quite hostile to Wilson's notion that all knowledge could be unified under the science rubric, Sam used almost all of the same readings Joyce had used the year before, including Wilson's book *Consilience.*

At the beginning of the spring semester of the consilience seminar, Joyce came back to the question of the unity and disunity of knowledge and led a session based on *The Two Cultures,* by C. P. Snow, and two books taking off from Snow's examination of the differences between the sciences and the humanities: *Two Cultures? The Significance of C. P. Snow,* by F. R. Leavis, and *Beyond Culture,* by Lionel Trilling. For the remainder of the semester, faculty and postdocs presented their own work, either singly or in groups. For the penultimate session, Joyce asked participants to talk about their own intellectual autobiographies, which they had shared in advance with one another; during the last session, also led by Joyce, faculty commented on one another's proposals for new courses.

Humanists and Artists

Humanists and artists in the seminars were positively affected by their interactions with scientists and the science they learned during the year. In both years the scientists in the seminar opened their labs to participants and gave them a taste of what it's like to do experiments, and they found these visits particularly satisfying. (Interestingly, although the seminar agreed enthusiastically to do lab visits, they did not agree to do a studio visit for artist Evelyn.)

According to religious studies scholar Mary, she was the initial proponent of lab visits. She said found them exciting and said the experience gave her the confidence to ask questions of the scientists.[18]

> We went to Ed's lab . . . and then we went to Victor's lab . . . and I was fascinated. . . . Since then, I feel that I can ask questions better, I just jump in. . . . I think, with the natural sciences, there is the feeling on the part of the general public and on the part of people, [including] many people teaching in the natural sciences, that this is so complicated that nobody can understand it, and there's no way to explain it, and you have to have a lot of background or you're not going to understand it. Well, I don't have the background; I'm not going to have the time to get the background. I'm doing other things, but I still would love to know what's going on. And so now, I just ask. And . . . if I don't understand, I just keep asking, and I'm just going to keep asking.

Mary said one of the most important understandings she got from the seminar was that humanists are not alone in presenting evidence in a way that accords with their perspective, that scientists do this as well. Before the seminar, she had assumed that scientists were "objective" when they presented evidence. Usually, it is sociologists or philosophers of science who make the point that science is less objective than scientists like to believe. But in this case, it was Ed, a practicing chemist, who helped Mary to come to this key insight of science studies.

> In the humanities, we usually stress that . . . there is no objective truth, that there is no interpretation of the . . . text . . . that is without perspective and that . . . perspective shapes the way you present the material. [But] Ed gave an example . . . of an academic paper in the natural sciences [where] . . . the kind of example that you select, the words that you select . . . the table you use, the colors that you use in the table [also depend on perspective and affect how the evidence is presented].

Studio artist Evelyn also got a great deal out of the lab visits.

> I loved going to Ed's lab. . . . I loved [how] . . . he let us work, he let us make things. My God, that was just so satisfying, and then . . . we got to watch the results.

Evelyn said that because of the seminar and her exposure to science she was more open to her brother's proposal to link art and science.

> My brother is a neurobiologist, and he was invited to Jefferson to talk to the neurobiologists. He makes images, really beautiful images of neurons. . . . And people are always telling him he's an artist. And he said he wanted to talk to the artists at Jefferson about how scientists make images. He thinks there's a lot of similarity between the way scientists and artists work. Now, I might have said a couple years ago, "I don't think so" . . . but because of the seminar [I was open to the idea].[19]

Dramatist Jane was surprised by the connections she made in her own mind among the fields of drama, chemistry, and economics.

> I went in expecting one thing and found the economist was more able to speak with me and the chemist was more able to speak with me than people from the English department.

I asked Jane what she thought it was about chemistry or economics that she felt connected to.

> The willingness to explore and search. They have to think creatively, based upon

certain knowns and certain speculations, and then they have to devise an exploration route, and then they have to assess the results. So they're much more comfortable living in the imaginative and in the unknown.

Then I asked her what it was about English that made her feel unconnected.

They felt that they had to know and demonstrate [everything] . . . and be right all the time. They were not comfortable with living in the unknown at all.

Composer Joel said the seminar enabled him to engage with the neuroscientists and clarify his views on the extent to which appreciation of music is "hard-wired" or cultural. He had thought about this before, but in the interactions with scientists in the seminar he was forced to think more deeply and come up with arguments and examples to make his case.

Sounds have no value in and of themselves; it's just whatever value culture gives to a combination of sounds that make it into something. . . . So, if . . . [appreciation of music is hard-wired], then there should [be a lot more things about music that are held in common across cultures]. But . . . there aren't.

As part of the consilience seminar, Wilson came to present his ideas and answer questions. The reactions to both his book and his visit were decidedly mixed. Composer Joel was negative.

Strangely enough, I was most under whelmed when E. O. Wilson actually came and talked.

But dramatist Jane, true to her habit of trying on ideas rather than critiquing them, enjoyed both his book and visit.

Other people were responding to him on a political level, and I was responding to his story. And I was looking for what was valuable in the story. . . . I appreciated going on that journey. It was fun, and I learned things on the way, and the political implications . . . were not even secondary . . . whereas, they were primary for, I would say, the majority of the seminar.

The politics Jane was referring to were not the politics of left versus right or progressive versus conservative, but rather the politics of knowledge production. In that sense, the debates about Wilson are quite similar to those in the science wars. Both concern the degree to which science should be privileged in the structure of knowledge. Scholars in science studies wish to show that, as historian Larry in the science studies seminar put it, science's "own self-proclaimed special status is really sleight of hand." Critics of Wilson wish to show that the efforts of consilience to make science preeminent are seriously misplaced.

One of Wilson's critics is Sam, who said that the seminar was extremely useful to him in crystallizing his objections to Wilson's ideas, which he calls scientism.

> What I got out of the seminar [was] a better ability to formulate my objection to scientism . . . which is not an objection to science but to the hubris of science when it tries to explain everything.

Sam was absolutely opposed to the possibility of a unity of knowledge based on science. He thought that Wilson could conceive of such a unity only because he completely misunderstood the humanities.

> I think Wilson's notion . . . that the problem with the humanities is . . . [that] it's insufficiently positivistic and insufficiently scientific . . . [is] wrong. I think he's tone deaf; he doesn't really know what's online with humanities.

Sam said the high level of interchange in the first year's seminar enabled him to carefully martial his objections to Wilson.

> Those people who tried to defend Wilson were smart and made arguments that were challenging to me. And, in fact, then I wrote an article, an essay that came out of the experience of the seminar.

It is certainly not the case that all scientists agree with Wilson's notions of consilience. Scientist Stephen Jay Gould was also opposed to it. Although, like Wilson, Gould believed cooperation between the sciences and humanities is a desirable goal, he disagreed with Wilson's view that science should be preeminent in the coming together of disciplines. Gould's alternative to consilience was *e pluribus unum,* from many, one, with equal status assigned to science and the humanities. In his words:

> I too seek a consilience, a "jumping together" of science and the humanities into far greater and more fruitful contact and coherence—but a *consilience of equal regard* that respects the inherent differences, [and] acknowledges the comparable but distinct worthiness . . . [of all fields].[20]

Scientists

While the humanists and artists were enjoying learning about science, the scientists in the Jefferson seminars were excited by what they learned from their nonscience colleagues. Chemist Ed found a potential collaboration between chemistry and sociology.

> At one point last year, there was a sociologist who was studying communities . . . where there were Native Americans and . . . Scandinavian immigrants, and she was looking at . . . how these groups distributed themselves geographically. . . . And it occurred to me . . . I study pattern formation in chemical systems, and some of the ideas that one uses to describe how patterns form in chemically reacting systems could be used to try to predict [and] understand the groupings that would form when you have different populations distributed geographically.
>
> Q: So, the mathematics of the two are similar?
>
> A: Yeah. Or at least in one way of looking at them.

Biologist Victor was surprised by the degree to which he saw scholars and researchers in the nonscience disciplines trying to become more like natural scientists.

> One of the threads that ran through the whole seminar . . . was that for those disciplines that were not what I would call hard sciences . . . there was a constant effort to make what they do more grounded in a scientific vocabulary or scientific methods, scientific reasoning processes.

The reason for his surprise was that both he and the other scientists saw science as so different from the other disciplines and never suspected that the other disciplines would wish to be more like science.

> There was an attempt [by the scientists in the group] to explain to the other disciplines how very different the life we live, the questions we think about, the way we go about investigating them really is to anything that they do.

Jane saw connections between art and chemistry because they both are involved in exploration of the unknown. Victor saw connections between scientists and artists because they are both motivated by a need for self-expression.

> I think I do science for exactly the same reason that an artist paints, as a means of self-expression. I could no more imagine not doing science than an artist

could imagine not painting. Well, you paint because you have a need, not necessarily to sell paintings, right, but to put down on a canvas the way you see the world. . . . I do science because the questions I ask . . . are . . . an intrinsic part of me, and I find beauty and truth and meaning in the answers. Actually, I find beauty and truth and meaning in the inquiry process itself. . . . I think there is an artistic flavor to what we do.

Victor felt that the most important outcomes of the seminar were that the nonscientists got a sense of how scientists work and that the scientists figured out how to better provide nonscientists with an understanding of what scientists do.

When we did our little skit about a day in the life of a physicist . . . I could see from the looks in their eyes that several people suddenly understood aspects of the life of a scientist and the way a scientist worked and thought that they hadn't really understood before. . . . I think it's enormously important to communicate what we do to people who aren't scientists—not just the implications of what we do, but everything about what we do, from the way we think to how we go about answering questions, to how we go about figuring out that we haven't answered a question, or that our answers are wrong.

Physicist Amita, also was pleased that the seminar provided her an opportunity to understand better how to communicate science to nonscientists.

I really enjoyed . . . talking to [nonscientists] and being able to . . . get across a flavor of the way we [scientists] approach research problems. . . . I think it made me much more aware of the kinds of barriers that we as scientists put up, which need to be broken down to be able to communicate to the nonscientist community about what we do.

I asked Amita what kind of barriers she thought were important to break down. She mentioned two—jargon and approach to problems.

We get so embroiled in our own jargon. . . . We have . . . our own language, and we don't realize that that really puts up barriers. . . . And if I don't make the effort to explain what I'm doing, keeping in mind that the way we think . . . is not universal . . . then there can be lots of misunderstandings.

One of the insights Amita highlighted was that she and the other scientists didn't realize that the nonscientists were unaware of scientists' search for beauty in their work.

So one of the first things . . . the . . . scientists in the group . . . realized is that there is quite a bit of misconception about how we approach things. For example, . . . when one of us first mentioned that we really look for beauty in what we do, like even if I'm doing something mathematical, we look for an elegant solution because that's very pleasing, that seemed to be a complete surprise to a lot of them.

A second insight for Amita, which I found fascinating, was that some of the young humanists in the group did not want scientific understanding to take the "mystery" out of the universe for them.

The other thing I realized was we . . . have different objectives. Scientists are always trying to demystify things. I always want answers. . . . Mysteries are enticing, but mysteries are there to be solved. But . . . part of the allure of some of the humanities is to keep the mystery there and not analyze it to the point of completely taking away the mystery. And that, to me, was a big surprise. I hadn't realized that there was a difference in basic perspective.

Conclusion

Attempts to bridge the two cultures are clearly challenging. Not only are the language and concepts of science difficult for nonscientists, but the culture of science and the habits of mind of both scientists and nonscientists make communication across the science/nonscience divide laborious. Nonetheless, this chapter shows that under the right conditions, even though faculty remain aware that the two cultures continue to exist, scientists and nonscientists can learn from one another. The Jefferson seminars represent a major accomplishment in this regard. Had C. P. Snow been a fly on the wall, he would have been pleased.

Joyce, the leader of the consilience seminar, said that from the beginning she and Ed thought that the purpose of the interdisciplinary seminars at Jefferson was to examine commonalities across faculty's fields. It was this unambiguous commitment to explore syntheses that allowed conversations to begin to bridge the science/nonscience divide. As a literary scholar and as a chemist, respectively, Joyce and Ed, the two scholars who wrote the proposal and chose participants for the seminars, were themselves bridging science and the humanities. All of the other seminar proposals were put together by humanists only.

Moreover, Joyce chose readings for the first few weeks of the seminar that were specifically designed to examine science/nonscience connections, readings such as E. O. Wilson's *Consilience*, Shakespeare's *The Tempest*, Tom Stoppard's *Arcadia*, and Jared Diamond's *Guns, Germs, and Steel*. And in leading the seminar conversations, Joyce went to some lengths to get participants to explicitly examine the connections between science and nonscience in these readings.

In choosing seminar participants, Joyce and Ed selected scientists who were dedicated to helping nonscientists learn about science. Several of the Jefferson scientists mentioned that the opportunity to teach their colleagues about science was one of the reasons they sought to join the seminar.

A final factor that undoubtedly contributed to the seminar's success was the willingness of the humanists who led the seminars to accept the suggestion from literary scholar Mary in the consilience seminar that they do visits to laboratories in order to learn first-hand about science, a suggestion they did not take with respect to studio art. For many in the seminars, the laboratory visits were the best part of the year's experience.

The contrast between the Jefferson seminars and the science studies seminar is dramatic. The bridges built over the science/nonscience gulf in the science studies seminar were weak, and participants' appreciation of one another's perspectives was lacking. Moreover, most seminar members had only a vague comprehension of the debates between the philosopher and the humanist.

Differences in leadership go a long way toward explaining the different outcomes in the Jefferson conversations as compared to the science studies exchanges, and in Chapter 8 we shall return to the matter of leadership. But first, in the next chapter, we turn to the social science seminars and the question of how interdisciplinary conversations fare when the participants are all from the same broad field.

6 Interdisciplinary Dialogue Within a Broad Field: The Case of the Social Sciences

IT WOULD BE EASY TO ASSUME THAT SUCCESSFUL INTERDISCI-
plinary conversations are more easily accomplished among scholars
and researchers from a single broad area of knowledge than across more disparate fields. However, the two social science seminars at Washington suggest
that this is not necessarily the case. Indeed, they confirm what Muzafer Sherif
and Carolyn Sherif noted in 1969:

> Interdisciplinary ventures [in the social sciences] have not always, or even typi-
> cally ... produced rounded pictures of a problem area. Many have fallen far
> short of providing the advantages potentially inherent in mutual borrowing
> across the lines of disciplines for the benefit of all.[1]

The Seminars at Washington

The president of Washington, a humanist, had a deep-seated belief that creativity, and hence advances in knowledge, could be stimulated by interdisciplinary exchange. With assistance from his staff, he wrote the proposal to
fund interdisciplinary seminars at Washington, and from the beginning he
and the provost, also from the humanities, planned to attend them, saying
they represented an unprecedented opportunity to broaden their own intellectual horizons.

The Social Science Seminar

The president chose Robert, an eminent faculty member in political science, to lead the first year's seminar, and it was Robert who proposed that it be focused on the social sciences, a suggestion the president and the provost readily accepted. The social sciences at Washington had been weaker than the sciences and humanities for some time, and the president and provost had some decisions to make about how to remedy the situation. They thought that extended conversations with social scientists, led by Robert, could inform their thinking.

Robert had considerable leeway, in consultation with the provost, in choosing participants. His first "pick" was Neil, a cultural anthropologist whom he knew well and admired and who also was concerned about the treatment of the social sciences at Washington. Neil would serve as a participant-observer so that a record of the discussions would be available. Adept at the participant-observer role from his fieldwork experiences, Neil took extensive notes on the seminars, which he posted on a Web site, and also prepared summaries of the proceedings at the end of each semester.

In all, the social sciences seminar was made up of eighteen tenured faculty (including the president, the provost, and two professors emeriti). Nine were from disciplines that are considered the core social sciences (sociology, political science, psychology, anthropology, and economics), but of those, several had their primary appointments outside disciplinary departments. Four were from disciplines that are close to the social sciences (two each from law and history). One was a scientist. About 30 percent were women. There were also five postdoctoral fellows in the seminar (see Appendix Table A-1).[2]

Key Players

The five participants I interviewed were Robert, a professor of political science; Neil, a professor of anthropology; Evan, a professor of sociology; Karen, a professor of law; and Nick, a professor of limnology (the scientific study of fresh waters, especially lakes and ponds) (see Appendix Table A-2).

Robert hoped that the seminar would make clear to the president and the provost that one could not judge the strength of the social sciences at an institution by the degree to which they agree with one another. He anticipated that as the president and provost read the materials for the seminar and listened to the discussions they would come to better understand that the diversity of the social sciences was in fact their strength and would be persuaded to provide increased funding both for social science departments and for efforts to enhance social science interdisciplinarity.

Neil had been a proponent of interdisciplinarity during his entire career and had been a director of a series of interdisciplinary institutes at Washington. But his primary reason for joining the seminar was less his interest in interdisciplinarity and more his concern about the social sciences at Washington. Evan and Nick also said that they joined the seminar primarily because they were interested in improving the social sciences at Washington.

Like Neil, law professor Karen had a long history of working across disciplines. She had been an early participant in the movement to incorporate social science research into law and was heading up a major multiuniversity, multiyear interdisciplinary seminar. She had come to Washington only recently and thought the seminar on the social sciences would provide an ideal entry to more interdisciplinarity in her work on campus. But unlike the other interviewees, she thought that attempting to educate the president and the provost would dilute the intellectual quality of the seminar and was not in favor of making that a seminar goal.

Bridging the Disciplines and Educating the President and the Provost

Just as C. P. Snow's *Two Cultures* and E. O. Wilson's *Consilience* were the foundational texts for the Jefferson seminars, their counterpart for the social science seminar was *Open the Social Sciences*, a report by the Gulbenkian Commission chaired by sociologist Immanuel Wallerstein. A highly abstract tract that begins with a history of the social sciences since the eighteenth century, the book concludes that the sharp distinctions that have grown up among social science disciplines interfere with their ability to solve real-world problems, which inevitably traverse disciplinary lines:

> The major issues facing a complex society cannot be solved by decomposing them into small parts that seem easy to manage analytically, but rather by attempting to treat these problems . . . in their complexity and interrelations.[3]

One purpose of the social sciences seminar was to have faculty explore creative ways of doing exactly what the Gulbenkian Commission suggested: treat social science problems in all their complexity and interrelations. This meant fostering discussion across the disciplines.

Neil described the seminar format:

> Robert set out some ground rules, and if you knew Robert, you'd know that people were likely to follow the ground rules. He has a very persuasive way. Nobody was allowed to ... require their own work to be read. No presentations were allowed to be longer than thirty minutes, and he was quite rigorous about maintaining that. The assigned readings were ... to be short, two to three articles maximum. . . . The emphasis was obviously the discussion and debate.

Nonetheless, Neil said, the discussions were slow in getting started.

> People were nervous with each other; [it's] very interesting to see how nervous senior faculty are in each other's presence when they are not used to talking together.

Others have observed similar interactions in interdisciplinary seminars. Discussing the Sloan seminars at the School of Engineering at the University of Illinois, Hugh Petrie notes that the seminar was slow getting started: participants "remarked over and over that they seem to spend almost all semester simply learning what each other is like and getting their biases and interests on the table, before they feel they can really get to work."[4] And commenting on the Luce seminars at Emory University, Susan Frost and Paul Jean note: "Despite the high marks for lowering the clashing of egos and ideologies, we found some potential evidence . . . that interdisciplinary dialogue often produces high levels of anxiety and defensiveness."[5]

Like Nancy, the leader of the ethics seminar, Neil found that in the social science seminar, participants were fearful of losing their disciplinary identity.

> To the extent that we pushed the issues of interdisciplinarity hard ... people who were willing to play along up to a certain point started to get very nervous ... the sense of, gosh, if we don't have disciplinary identity, then maybe we'll evaporate into outer space. Fearful reaction, confused, too; some combination of fear and confusion.

Neil reported that disciplinary stereotypes were prominent.

> As people became more frank with one another ... there were lots and lots of stereotypes. Everybody was irritated by the stereotype about their discipline. And that became a subject of conversation which I think was very productive in the long run: how bad our images are of one another.

Neil was surprised that these stereotypes persisted despite the fact that Washington had numerous interdisciplinary centers, institutes, and programs.

> What interests me . . . is that in spite of all of that, there was no space for discussion of disciplines. . . . And so the discussion [at the seminar] was much less advanced than you would expect in a place where there is so much interdisciplinary activity.

He thought that the seminar might have made more progress in bridging disciplines if there had been more continuity of discussion from seminar to seminar. I asked him how he thought that might have been achieved.

> It would have taken a very different model. . . . [Robert] mostly let people talk. . . . I think if you wanted to get progress . . . you would have had to set up a structure that was designed to produce progress on [particular] concepts.

Law professor Karen also thought the seminar lacked structure, and like Neil, she thought its absence was a direct result of the seminar's basic design, having people talk about their work without giving all of them the same set of questions to answer in the course of presenting. "There was no thread that ran through [the seminar]," she said. Karen had suggested a different seminar format, but her suggestion hadn't been accepted.

> What I had suggested we do was to organize [the seminar] around . . . methodological substance across disciplines. . . . I said that if we looked at how the various disciplines thought about evidence, that that might be really good. What constitutes proof? . . . I just thought if we did that, then there would be something that we could kind of grapple with every week that would give it some structure.

The same power politics we observed in the ethics seminar and discussed in terms of Pierre Bourdieu's and Helen Schwartzman's work was evident in the social science seminar. Karen thought that as the politics played out, the seminar became primarily about jockeying for power.

> There were so many different levels of tension and competition going on. It wasn't really about working together; it was really about establishing your own position.

In the research for their 1969 book about interdisciplinarity in the social sciences, Sherif and Sherif also observed power scrambles. "Interdisciplinary ventures become arenas for jockeying for position, symbols and instruments of power."[6]

Karen thought that one of the reasons for the prominence of power politics was the presence of the president and the provost, which she thought skewed the seminar's proceedings.

> I thought that it was actually . . . not a good idea to have them [the president and the provost] there . . . because some people were . . . pitching their own agenda in the context of the meetings. . . . So what . . . was getting hammered out . . . [was] . . . just how much support . . . the social sciences . . . merited.

I asked Karen if she could remember any exciting intellectual moments from the seminar.

> I actually don't. I was really . . . disappointed. . . . I enjoyed meeting individuals and got a lot in that way. But the group sessions themselves, I did not get very much from them. . . . There weren't highs or lows. . . . It was just kind of bland.

Sociologist Evan had a different objection to the provost and the president attending the seminar.

> I would say their attendance wasn't stellar. They would have gotten a C in my class. They came when they could. And that, I think, was discouraging to people. It was to me.

But scientist Nick was very positive about the president and the provost being there.

> I was incredibly impressed that they actually had done all the readings. . . . I don't know how they found the time. I barely found the time. . . . And they would come in, they had not only done the readings, they were prepared; they had questions to ask and insightful comments to make, and they liked some things they read, and they definitely didn't like other things.

Brian, a psychologist in the inequality seminar, which the president and the provost also attended in the second year of the grant, was even more positive about their presence.

> The provost, the vice-provost . . . and the president, were all terrific. . . . These folks . . . seriously should have honorary social science degrees. . . . I am so impressed because I cannot do it in their fields. They're humanists, and if you gave

me some literary criticism or something, I could not hold my own; whereas, you put these regression equations up on the overhead projector, and they're talking about, well, what's the B coefficient for this interaction?

The Split Between Quantitative Research and Action Research

The main split in the social science seminar was between those who did positive social science and those who did action research. Action research seeks to erase distinctions between researchers and subjects and to enlist subjects as active partners. Proponents of action research believe that experts and subjects each have only part of the knowledge needed to solve a problem and that it is only when the two groups partner as equals that problems have a chance of being solved. Action researchers also think that to solve a problem, researchers must give it sustained attention, that there are no quick solutions to the kinds of problems action researchers work on.[7]

Evan explained the components of action research:

[Action research is] critical of . . . positivist social science and really deeply committed to . . . reciprocal learning between those affected by a problem and those studying it. . . . [It is] very place-oriented. . . . To really understand and make a difference in a place, you've got to spend real time. So this notion of being the professional expert consultant all over the planet, being called from one great meeting to another, being a guru in flight, that's . . . anathema. . . . I prefer going in, digging in to a place until you can understand it, and then with folks finding a pathway to a better outcome.[8]

Not being an action researcher himself, Robert was unusually sympathetic to it.

It's a whole different form of social science. And I regard it as utterly respectable and legitimate on its own terms, when you think about both the ideology and methodology of it. . . . Now, the typical Ivy League–oriented . . . social scientists and the core faculty of Washington would regard this as wacko: this is no place [for such research]; social science is not about that. . . . I think that's wrong. I think . . . it would be institutionally irresponsible not to think through those issues [that action researchers tackle].

Evan and Neil agreed that action research was not given proper recognition at Washington. Evan talked about the difficulties action researchers have in establishing themselves as credible academics. His concerns are echoed in a 2006 article in the *Chronicle of Higher Education* on action research, by Nancy Cantor and Steven Lavine, cochairs of a national organization to help develop policies that will allow colleges and universities to evaluate and give credit toward tenure for public scholarship and community engagement in the arts and humanities.

> While . . . community engagement is flourishing, the graduate students and faculty who are fueling the trend are not. . . . Scholars who want to collaborate with diverse groups off their campuses are still pressured to defer community-based research and civic collaborations until they receive tenure.[9]

Other Methodological Tensions

Reflections from Nick, the only scientist in the social science seminar, provide a quite interesting perspective on methodological tensions in the social sciences in general and in the seminar in particular. He said he found those methodological tensions quite similar to those in the natural sciences.

> I learned a lot about how social scientists think, how the arguments that we have in the natural sciences are the same arguments that they have about how knowledge *should* be gained, how it *can* be gained, what are going to be the most productive approaches.

Nick noted that the usual assumption made by social scientists (and others) about science being done according to the scientific method, starting with a hypothesis and then testing it, is not in fact the way much of science is done.

> There is this . . . abstract view of the natural sciences, that there is *a* way that the natural sciences do science. Well, there is no [one] way that the natural sciences . . . [do science]. . . . When it came my turn to . . . lead a seminar session, I had everybody read these debates that go on in the natural sciences about . . . the right way to do science.

I asked Nick if science has the equivalent of qualitative methods—anything similar to the interview I was doing with him?

> Nothing quite so qualitative, but there's a lot of storytelling that goes on. . . . In a sense, what you're doing is what we would call natural history, where an ecol-

ogist goes out into the field and just makes observations about what organisms are there, what interactions he or she sees out there, what the conditions were like at the time.... How do you decide which organisms to put into your cage together [for an experiment] if you never go out in the field and look at them interacting and see what the dynamic is?

He noted that, like social scientists, scientists have a difficult time getting qualitative research funded. And he thought Darwin, one of the great qualitative researchers, would have trouble getting a voyage on the *Beagle* funded today.

Darwin ... was a great naturalist storyteller.... But you still couldn't write a grant proposal to the National Science Foundation saying, "I want to go out and look at how these organisms are interacting in nature just by using my two eyes." You'd never get it funded.

Nick said his accounts of methodological debates in the natural sciences got the social scientists arguing "vehemently" about their own methodological disputes. Prior to his presentation, he felt that participants had been more or less "dancing around" their methodological disputes, not wanting to directly confront one another; but under the guise of arguing about science, they were able to argue forcefully about social science.

When I asked Nick his opinion of the most exciting moment in the seminar, he talked about seeing parallels between his work and the work of a social historian in the group.

When a member of the seminar talked about the way she does her work, from a historical perspective, I could identify a lot with that. A lot of what I do is taking sediment cores in lakes and reading the history out, layer by layer.

Nick felt that the quantitative social scientists in the seminar did not respect the work of their more qualitative colleagues and that the more qualitative researchers could feel the disrespect. (This is the same problem that appeared in the story I related at the beginning of the book about doctoral students working on my own interdisciplinary project.) He said he could identify with the feelings of the more qualitative researchers because he had experienced similar feelings of disrespect from the more quantitative researchers in molecular biology.

The President, the Provost, and Institutional Support

For Robert, it was exceedingly important that the president and the provost see the splits in the social sciences, and he deemed the seminar a success because he thought they gained some fundamental insights into the incredible variety of approaches taken by social scientists.

> You know, they got it. They didn't get it [before the seminar] when the social sciences initial task force reported . . . because that task force had been appointed, and it represented [only] one branch of the social sciences. [When] there was a public hearing [on its findings] . . . the other half of the social sciences rebelled in public. And one could see [from] the body language and the eye contact between the provost and president that they didn't understand what the hell was going on because they didn't understand that part of the social sciences is really part of the hard sciences, part of the social sciences is really part of the humanities, and in other parts we straddle [the two].

He also felt the seminar would result in more institutional support for the social sciences.

> [The president and the provost] were religious in attending the meetings. They participated actively, and in the end, the university has made—is, I assume, this year on the verge of making—a fairly sustained, modest commitment to reinvigorating the social sciences.

Robert's view of the president and provost's attendance was quite opposite to Evan's. Robert termed their attendance "religious," while Evan gave it a C. Such are the pitfalls of eyewitness accounts.

But Robert and Evan disagreed on more than attendance. While Robert thought the president and provost were on the verge of a "fairly sustained, modest commitment," Evan thought they still didn't understand the importance of action research.

> Neil and another seminar member and I spent a lot of time preparing . . . the engaged scholarship/action research material. . . . I wouldn't say it got much of a hearing. [The direction in which the administration decided to go] was very unlike the direction that Neil and I and a few others in the seminar were suggesting would be most appropriate.

Evan was also highly critical of the underlying assumptions of the president and provost about how to strengthen the social sciences.

Their approach basically was . . . there's mediocrity among the social sciences, and the way we're going to solve it is the way we did it in sociology, which was to hire four senior people with very long lists of refereed journal articles and overnight move our . . . NRC [National Research Council] rankings from not ranked to the top fifteen. That's viewed as a great success . . . the resurrection of the sociology department. It doesn't appear to be a very nurturing intellectual environment for students at any level, nor are faculty apparently very happy being there, but they've "solved," quote, unquote, their problem with excellence in sociology. . . . There were many of us who just thought that was absurd.

Q: What would you have liked to have seen?

An interdisciplinary center for applied research that would have seed money for teams of scholars that cut across disciplines to look at the most critical issues facing . . . this region.

Like Evan, Neil was far less satisfied than Robert was with the outcome of the seminar.

My curiosity was about whether the institution could change or not and whether it would have the will to change. I think the answer is no.

The Inequality Seminar

The inequality seminar provides yet another test of how scholars from a single broad field of knowledge might bridge disciplinary culture and habits of mind, but this time the topic on which they came together, inequality, was even more focused than in the first social science seminar. Still, the qualitative/quantitative gap entailed habits of mind that were hard to overcome.

For the second year of the seminar, the provost and the president at Washington wanted to continue emphasizing the social sciences, but they wanted the readings and discussions to be less theoretical and methodological and more subject-focused. In terms of leadership, they again wanted a respected scholar with a strong personality who would signal to the faculty that the seminars were an "important intellectual venture." They chose an economist, Sheila, and were excited about her suggestion that the seminar focus on the topic of inequality. In terms of seminar purpose, although the president and the provost continued to attend, the seminar was focused on the topic of inequality and *not* on the social sciences at Washington.

Consulting with the provost, Sheila assembled eighteen tenured faculty, including the president, the provost, a vice-provost, and a professor emeritus. All three administrators were from the humanities, and the emeritus professor was a scientist. Thirteen participants were from the core social sciences: five economists, four sociologists, two psychologists, and two anthropologists. One professor was from law. As in the first Washington seminar, many of the social scientists had their primary appointment outside of disciplinary departments. One-third of the participants were women. There were also three postdoctoral fellows (see Appendix Table A-1).[10]

As in the social sciences seminar, Neil served as participant-observer and prepared a comprehensive report at the end of each semester. He continued to post weekly notes on a seminar Web site but said that, in contrast to the first year there were very few postings by seminar members.

At the first session, Sheila had participants introduce themselves and then jointly plan the remainder of the first semester. After that, at each subsequent session, a faculty member made a presentation based on his or her own articles, which they asked colleagues to read in advance. There were no time limits placed on the presentations, as there had been in the social science seminar, and no formal discussants assigned as there had been in the Adams seminars.

In the second semester, although several of the participants made interdisciplinary intellectual connections they thought were important, some were dissatisfied with the seminar process and felt that the sessions seemed to run out of steam. Sheila tried a few times to tie the presentations to the central theme. Early in the second semester, she and Neil led a session called "Cross-Cutting Themes," and midway into the second semester she led a roundtable in which participants made short presentations, prepared in advance, on how they viewed inequality—its causes, problems, and possible solutions. But some participants still thought the second semester lacked sufficient focus.

Key Players

I interviewed seven faculty in the inequality seminar: Donna, a professor of sociology; Brian, a professor of psychology; Karl, a professor of political science; Neil, a professor of anthropology; and Matt, Omar, and Sheila, all professors of economics (see Appendix Table A-2).

Donna had initial reservations about joining the seminar. Although she worked regularly on campus with scholars in women's studies outside of sociology and had participated in numerous interdisciplinary collaborations, she said that when Sheila first approached her, she realized she would be one of only two nonquantitative social scientists in the seminar. (She did not consider the law professor a nonquantitative social scientist.) She thought the discussions would be largely positivist and not of particular interest and said she would have preferred to join an interdisciplinary seminar with a broader reach. Ultimately she did participate in the inequality seminar because the seminar leader was "so persuasive."

Psychologist Brian also had long experience in interdisciplinary work and was the editor of an interdisciplinary journal. He said he joined the seminar despite its topic, which was not close to his own work. He saw himself as much more interested in interdisciplinarity than are many of his fellow psychologists.

> Some of my colleagues . . . just don't see the need to do interdisciplinary stuff; they're quite happily buzzing along doing the research they're doing and talking to the same audiences they've been talking to, and that's fine. For others of us, I think we have been persuaded or excited by what we perceive to be very significant contributions to be gained by it for our field.

Unlike Donna and Brian, political scientist Karl joined the inequality seminar precisely because of his deep interest in the topic, although the opportunity to teach fewer courses for a year was also a draw.

Economist Matt also joined the inequality seminar because of his interest in the topic, but in addition he appreciated the opportunity to interact with the president and the provost and with faculty who did related work in other parts of the university.

Omar, a development economist, joined the seminar in part because of its topic and in part because of his broad interests.

> I am interested with a . . . firm foot in economics, in exploring interdisciplinary interactions. . . . Partly, I think, it's . . . my academic background. I was an undergraduate at Cambridge . . . England, so there's a certain European perspective, which is different from a mainstream [narrow] U.S. graduate school economics perspective.

The Quantitative/Qualitative Split and Questions About the Seminar's Effectiveness

Most of the seminar members were quantitative researchers, and although they came from a variety of social science disciplines, their quantitative methodology and adherence to economic thinking made them rather similar. There were only three qualitative researchers in the group: Neil, an anthropologist and action researcher; Donna, a qualitative sociologist; and a law professor.

Donna felt like a fish out of water.

> So I gave a talk . . . and I was quite nervous . . . because I felt it was orthogonal to the way people were thinking about measurements of inequality.

She also felt that the questions participants were asking about inequality were not the questions she was interested in.

> [They had] big datasets or small ones. How many [ways can] you break down . . . different panel data and cross-sectional data? . . . I can talk that game, you know . . . but I've chosen to put my . . . efforts into other kinds of questions. So, I didn't feel that the kinds of questions that most concerned me were the kinds of questions that animated the discussion.

But Donna's major difficulty came when she presented. She felt the quantitative researchers in the group were not willing to engage with her and learn from her type of work. She found the experience ego-deflating and wound up shutting down in the same way that Nabila had done in the ethics seminar.

> So, when I gave my talk . . . I was trying to say, okay, we're really here to learn from each other; I'll put mine on the table. . . . It wasn't trashed by any means, but people didn't really get it and weren't excited by that kind of conversation. So I ended up being much more quiet after a few efforts at forays into sort of pushing discussion or questioning what people meant.

I asked Donna if she had it all to do over again whether she would choose to participate. She said she would not.

> And not because I didn't want to be part of a group of people discussing interdisciplinary work. . . . I would have liked to be recognized, and I really mind that I wasn't.

Donna thought the seminar had too much presentation and not enough conversation, not enough productive engagement or playing with ideas. She was quite specific about the big ideas she wished the seminar had discussed.

> I was disappointed that we didn't take on substantive questions. What do you think about inequality? What does it mean? Why is it important to imagine it as

a driving issue? . . . How does it articulate itself differently across gender, class, race, ethnic lines? That was not part of this seminar at all. In fact, . . . it ended up being how did you measure this?

Donna also felt that participants didn't engage enough in the rough and tumble of heated discussion and that when people interrupted the presenter, the presenter seemed primarily interested in finishing the presentation, not engaging in conversation.

> People were a little polite in the seminar. . . . But polite . . . means that you couldn't really say "You've got to be kidding," or "How do you make that assumption?" or "What happens if you made this assumption? How would it play out?" . . . And I think, for me, it didn't push the boundaries. . . . It turned into people giving presentations . . . but I wanted it to be a conversation. . . . Here are smart people; they all seem to be nice people. Let's play.

Neil was also disappointed in the seminar. He thought that the absence of researchers for whom race and ethnicity were central was a major problem.[11] He also felt that too much of the discussion was from an economic and political perspective and too little effort was given to interweaving economic and cultural analyses. In his report on the seminars, he said:

> Stereotypes, life course expectations, career structures and their enshrinement in law, race/ethnic ideologies, ideas about class, cultural explanations of failure and success are all essential parts of an analysis of inequality. It is not that these were ignored. Rather, it is that we did not find a way to bring the two broad streams of our analyses of inequality together in any way other than by juxtaposition.

Neil thought that the seminar did not achieve any integration of perspectives because there was not enough attention paid to the ways in which seminar participants thought about the problem of inequality. His report continued:

> We did not inquire systematically into the deeply held different starting points of different schools of analysis. Some of us adhere mainly to rationality paradigms. . . . Others focus on the psychological and emotional elements that underlie behavior and cognitive structuring of the world. Still others build our analyses out of cultural and historical materials and are dubious about rationality frameworks. And a few of us see issues like inequality as products of large-

scale processes of exploitation and suppression. Though these different framings of the issues of inequality never came into open conflict, they also did not produce a larger integration.

Paradoxically, the absence of conflict in the seminar, while welcome to most of the participants, may indeed have made the seminar less cognitively interesting. A modicum of cognitive conflict produces tension and lively questioning. Without it, there is not much creativity. I think Neil is right that without conflict there was little motivation to seek an integration of perspectives. In David Sill's words, "Creative tension is the driving force for integrative thought, providing the motivation to integrate."[12]

In his interview, Neil took off his reporter hat and spoke from the perspective of an action researcher.

> I just couldn't relate to an abstract discussion of a concrete social issue. . . . Getting clear on what a group of hothouse academics think about inequality, at the very same time the country is ripping itself apart in terms of structures of inequality?

Like Donna, Neil felt that the discussions were lackluster:

> There wasn't any real fire in the discussion; where the first year, there had been. People got either upset or got excited or enthusiastic, and so on, but this was a very genteel discussion of a very nongenteel subject.

Neil felt the people who did most of the talking were economists, plus one political scientist with an economics perspective.

> It became a subgroup dialogue with other people mostly watching.

I asked him whether he recalled any particularly difficult moments in the seminar.

> No. The stakes were never high enough. . . . Some people got on each other's nerves, but only in the sense of gobbling the air time too much or not listening and then repeating back just exactly the opposite of what somebody had said— those sorts of fracases. But there wasn't any kind of real [engagement].

Like Karen, the law professor in the social science seminar, Neil thought that having the president and the provost at the seminar may have contributed to an absence of liveliness.

Having the president and provost there ... probably put something of a damper on rabble-rousing. I don't think this group would have rabble-roused very much, but the setting probably did influence it some.

It was not only the qualitative researchers who expressed reservations about the seminar. Quantitative political scientist Karl said he had a sense that in the second semester the seminar was searching for its own raison d'etre.

Two-thirds into it, there wasn't ... a plan for the last third ... and I think it proved difficult for the group.

I asked Karl if there had been any attempt to derive overarching themes in the presentations or whether there were any threads that tied things together. He thought that Neil had made an effort to do that, but that it hadn't taken hold.

I'm not exactly sure how it went, but that was in some sense Neil's role in all of this ... and he wrote copious notes and circulated notes. And I think that at least on one occasion he did attempt to kind of draw a picture for us of what we were talking about by doing a kind of meta-analysis.... [But] I think that by that time ... everybody was ... tired.... It ... didn't end on a bang.... It ... ended on a whimper.

Karl thought that perhaps for the second semester the larger group should have split into smaller clusters that reflected the particular interests of sub-group members. Despite the fact that all participants were social scientists, he felt they had run out of issues they could talk about productively across their fields. At that juncture, he was more interested in making progress on the issues of interest to him than in fostering interdisciplinary dialogue.

Omar, a development economist and also a quantitative researcher, felt the seminar was less challenging than it might have been because the group was inbred. (Interestingly, he didn't even note that Donna or Neil were seminar participants, perhaps because after a time they had stopped speaking up.) But ironically he thought that the inbred nature of the group was precisely what led to the seminar's success!

The way that Sheila selected people, sure, they were from different disciplines, but broadly speaking, they were all quantitative in their orientation.... So, there wasn't a serious challenge to that. Nobody stood up and said, this is rubbish, all this quantitative stuff.... You think you're getting something, but you're getting nothing, really.

Q: So the methodological issues that surfaced were in a narrow range?

A: Exactly. And that accounts partly for the success of the thing, you know. You didn't have great big stand-up battles. . . . So, for example, . . . nobody was putting forward a Marxist perspective on these things.

Clearly Omar's criteria for success were different from Neil's and Donna's.

The Social Sciences in Context

An interesting study by Rik Pieters and Hans Baumgartner concludes that there is not much communication among social scientists. In an article titled "Who Talks to Whom?" they examined the cross-citation patterns for the three-year period 1995–1997 among the five most influential economics journals and ten other journals: the five most influential journals in anthropology, political science, psychology, and sociology, and the five most influential in accounting, finance, management, marketing, and management information systems/operations research. While the study is limited in its scope because it excludes books and conference proceedings, it nonetheless provides a useful window on interdisciplinary communication. Two of the study's main conclusions are that there is very little interdisciplinary citation among the social sciences and that although political science and sociology seem to be learning a great deal from economics, economics does not appear to be learning much from them.[13]

A National Science Foundation study of 1997 citation patterns in social science journals also shows economics to be particularly insular, with slightly more than 80 percent of citations being to material within economics. This compares with sociology, anthropology and archaeology, and geography, which had only about half of its citations to material within the discipline.[14] In psychology, about two-thirds of citations were within the discipline.[15]

The stability of some of these patterns over time is interesting. A study of cross-citation patterns in the social sciences in the leading journal in each discipline between 1936 and 1975 also found that economists had about an 80 percent within-discipline citation rate (78.8 percent), as compared to about a 50 percent rate for anthropologists. Sociologists had a somewhat higher within-discipline rate in the 1936–1975 period as compared to 1997, about 60 percent versus about 50 percent.[16]

In Chapter 3, in connection with the dispute between the economist and the postdoc in religious studies, I cited Axel Leijonhufvud's 1973 satire on the customs of the Econ tribe. In that article, Leijonhufvud observed that when economists talk to other social scientists, their status is decreased. Talking about the Econ tribe, he noted the following:

> Their young are brought up to feel contempt for the softer living in the warmer lands of the neighbours, such as the Polscis and Sociogs. Despite a common genetical heritage, relations with these tribes are strained—the distrust that the average Econ feels for these neighbours being heartily reciprocated by the latter—and social intercourse with them is inhibited by numerous taboos.[17]

In the years since 1973, relations between economists and other social scientists have changed; economists' efforts to mathematize and bring rational choice theory to the other social sciences have been successful, and some political scientists and sociologists clearly admire economic analysis. But Pieters and Baumgartner's work suggests that it is still the case that while political science and sociology borrow from economics, economics maintains a taboo against borrowing from them. However, economists' views about borrowing from psychology have changed. As we shall see in the next chapter, several economists in the inequality seminar thought the ideas of one of the psychologists were interesting, and certainly nationally, behavioral economics, which involves explicit borrowing from psychology, is becoming not only acceptable but even fashionable among economists.

In an article aptly titled "Separate Tables," Gabriel Almond noted that political science was an extraordinarily diverse discipline with scholars divided into four groups—soft/left, hard/left, soft/right, and hard/right. Although Almond's categories are a bit pat, they do show the incredible variety in methodology and worldview among political scientists, and indeed among social scientists in general.

Almond characterized those in the soft/left group as those who do "thickly descriptive" clinical studies and argue that "objectivity is inappropriate," that scholarly analysis and political action should be joined, and that social science should be used to bring about a better world.[18] He painted the hard/right on the opposite pole with respect to both method and ideology; it uses quantitative analysis, including mathematical modeling, sophisticated statistical techniques and sometimes experimental designs, and believes that the market, rather than political intervention, should be relied on to make economic decisions.

While none of the participants in the two social science seminars at Washington fell neatly into Almond's categories, the vast majority were of the "hard," that is quantitative, persuasion. The participants on the soft side were Neil and Evan, who called themselves action researchers, Donna and a law professor, who called themselves qualitative researchers, as well as political scientist Robert and law professor Karen, who were theorists.

The splits in the social science seminars were the same that exist in the social sciences internationally, with disagreement on the following fundamental questions:

How should social scientists build theories?

Should they sit back and theorize and then translate their theories into verbal propositions? Or should they translate their theories into mathematical models? Is the gain in precision worth the loss of reality in translating theories into mathematical models?

Or should they not engage in armchair theorizing at all, but instead go out and observe, building theories only *after* real information from real people has been collected? If they have no theories to begin with, how will they decide *what* to observe?

How should social scientists test theories?

Should verbal evidence be gathered, or should social scientists use statistical techniques? Should social scientists do experiments?

Who should go out and observe?

Should it be expert social scientists or people who live the phenomenon being researched? Should there be a sharp distinction between researchers and research subjects, or should social scientists seek to blur such distinctions?

What kinds of problems should social scientists study?

Should social scientists engage in research if it has no benefit for those being studied? How can researchers ensure that those who are studied benefit from research?

While the ecumenical answer to many of these questions may be "Let a thousand flowers bloom," or "The methodology should depend on the particular question being asked," or "Two methods are often better than one," few social scientists who have been socialized by their doctoral programs and become acculturated to their discipline and subfield in the early years of their faculty appointments have that degree of openness to research methodology.[19]

Anthropologists are wed to field observations without having a theory in advance, and they rarely use mathematics except to count. Economists are distrustful of asking people about the motivations for their behavior (they think most people lie to researchers) and prefer to use "hard" quantitative demographic and economic data and infer motives from sophisticated statistical analysis. Experimental psychologists think truth is best obtained by observing in carefully designed laboratory experiments.

Conclusion

We began this chapter asking whether interdisciplinarity is easier to foster within the social sciences than across wider disciplinary groups. The answer is clearly, no. Diversity of perspective and methodology within the social sciences is perhaps as great as diversity across the larger fields of humanities, social sciences, and natural sciences. History and anthropology are close to being humanist fields. Parts of psychology are basically natural sciences. Economics aspires to be as close to physics as possible, and much of sociology and political science aspire to be close to economics.

In the social sciences seminar, there seemed to be three problems that inhibited intellectual discussions. First, there was difficulty in getting the seminar started, partly because the reading that Robert began with, *Open the Social Sciences*, was dense and difficult to understand, and partly because faculty came to the seminar with stereotypes about their colleagues, and some feared losing their disciplinary identity by deep interdisciplinary engagement. This generalized anxiety may have been partly responsible for the jockeying for power and status that took place, although, as we noted in the chapter on the ethics seminar, power politics goes along with the territory for meetings in general and for interdisciplinary conversations in particular, since many of the established status distinctions within disciplines are disrupted when faculty come together from different fields. None of these issues—stereotyping, disciplinary identity and anxiety about its possible loss, and jockeying for power and status—were ever discussed directly in the seminar; perhaps if they had been, the conversations would have proceeded more easily. Although it may be that with the president and the provost in attendance, faculty would have been reluctant to have a frank discussion of these matters.

There was also a second problem having to do with continuity of the conversations. As Karen pointed out, there was no set of questions that all pre-senters were asked to address, and so the underlying intellectual purpose of the seminar was not clear. This was made even more difficult by the fact that the seminar had two purposes, one intellectual and one political, having to do with educating the president and the provost so that they would provide enhanced financial support for the social sciences.

A third problem in the social sciences seminar concerned the long-standing split between the qualitative action researchers and the more positivist scholars. As was the case in the ethics seminar, where respect for opposing perspectives was in short supply, Nick observed that mutual respect was lacking between quantitative and qualitative researchers in the social sciences seminar. Also, worthy of note is Nick's observation that it was only his willingness to talk about the quantitative/qualitative debates in science that brought the same debate in the social sciences into open discussion. Robert's sense that it "would be interesting" to have a scientist in a seminar on the social sciences turned out to be quite right.

The presence of the president and the provost affected both seminars. In the social sciences seminar, their presence may have impeded frank explo-ration and muddied the waters concerning the purposes of the intellectual discussions. In the inequality seminar, it may be that some of the blandness a few people experienced came from a sense of needing to be on good behavior in order to impress powerful administrators. Perhaps the disorder necessary to achieve creative conflict was simply not forthcoming.

But the blandness in the second seminar also came from too little diver-sity of perspective. The quantitative researchers in economics, sociology, and political science, despite their different disciplines, were of a similar mind, and the few qualitative researchers ceased being vocal as the seminar pro-gressed. Most of the diversity in perspective came from the psychologists, and it was the interactions between the psychologists and the others that seemed to produce most of the seminar's intellectual excitement, as we shall see in the next chapter.

Like participants in the social sciences seminar, those in the inequal-ity seminar saw a rift between qualitative and quantitative researchers, and Donna, like Nabila in the ethics seminar, felt a lack of respect for her work. Also, the inequality seminar, like the social sciences seminar, did not have a clear thread running through it that participants could follow. Some felt the goal of the seminar was unclear and that the various sessions did not fit together.

Although, as we shall see in Chapter 8, many faculty in both Washington seminars obtained valuable intellectual insights, because of differences in habits of mind and seminar organization and leadership, the conversations did not achieve their full potential for creative interdisciplinary interaction.

III WHAT HAVE WE LEARNED?

7   Leadership: The Key to Success

EFFECTIVE LEADERSHIP IS THE SINGLE MOST IMPORTANT ingredient for creating successful interdisciplinary conversations, whether they take place in a faculty seminar or in the course of a teaching or research project. But providing such leadership is a daunting task.[1] In situations where there are independent, experienced faculty members from multiple disciplines whose disciplinary cultures and styles of conversation are poles apart, leaders must walk a fine line, providing both structure and ample space to explore intellectual differences. In addition, to permit intellectual discovery to move forward, an effective leader must be skilled at creating trust and resolving interpersonal conflicts.[2]

Hans-Georg Gadamer is a proponent of providing virtually no leadership for conversations. For him it is important that conversations be permitted to go wherever participants lead them. One might say he advocates not simply laissez-faire, but anarchy.

> It is said that we "conduct" a conversation, but the more genuine a conversation is, the less its conduct lies within the will of either partner. Thus, a genuine conversation is never the one that we wanted to conduct.... The partners conversing are far less the leaders of it than the led. No one knows in advance what will "come out" of a conversation.[3]

An alternative style of leadership is proposed by Marilyn Amey and Dennis Brown, based on their study of faculty in an interdisciplinary project at

Michigan State University. They argue that a successful leader of an interdisciplinary group must emphasize "facilitating member growth across discipline orientation."[4] He or she must be a leader of learning, "a boundary agent, midwife and steward."[5]

Nancy's leadership style in the Adams seminars was close to the one Gadamer proposes. Sheila's style in the inequality seminar was also somewhat laissez-faire, although far less so than Nancy's; she seemed less a facilitator of interdisciplinary learning and more a discussion leader of issues on inequality. On the other hand, Robert, Joyce, and Sam, who led the seminars in social sciences, consilience, and representation, respectively, were more directive in their leadership and seemed to see themselves precisely as leaders of interdisciplinary learning.

While a sample size of six is far too small to test the hypothesis that a leadership style that emphasizes interdisciplinary learning is more likely to produce such learning, it is fair to say that the risky laissez-faire strategy that Nancy chose did not pay off in terms of creating productive conversation and that the strategies that Joyce and to a lesser extent Robert and Sam employed were more successful in creating productive interdisciplinary dialogue. Keeping their goals for the conversations firmly in mind, carefully selecting an initial set of readings and presentations, and transparently weaving connections among sessions, Joyce and Sam produced exciting and fruitful dialogues. And in the social science seminar, although several participants were unclear about the purpose of the seminar, Robert's leadership led to the president and provost deciding to provide increased funding for the social sciences, particularly for interdisciplinary initiatives in the social sciences.[6]

This chapter looks at how five elements of good leadership played out (or didn't): clearly communicating the seminar's purpose; paying attention to group dynamics (including in the initial choice of participants); having sufficient authority to lead; creating productive conflict; and bridging disciplinary cultures.[7] Faculty and administrators who wish to initiate their own interdisciplinary conversations or projects and government agencies or private foundations that wish to fund them have much to learn from this discussion.

Clearly Communicating the Purpose
of the Conversation

Citing his studies of highly successful groups, organizations theorist Warren Bennis argues that to be an effective group leader one must continually convey to participants the substance and significance of the group's purpose. In his words, successful group leaders "remind people of what's important and why their work makes a difference."[8] This leadership characteristic is central because it is precisely a clear understanding of the group's mission that motivates its members to continue their participation at the highest levels of interest and effort.[9]

Although at Jefferson all the seminar participants I interviewed were clear about the purpose of their seminar, those at Washington and Adams often were not, and some had difficulty envisioning how each session connected to some overall objective.

In the social science seminar at Washington, law professor Karen said the objective of the seminar was never made clear to her, and she remained confused about the seeming lack of connection among sessions.

> What we did was to just have people . . . pick a few readings from their own discipline to show something. I don't know what we were supposed to show, and I didn't think it worked, because there was no continuity. There was no thread that ran through it. . . . [The seminar] had a lot of potential, but it never realized its potential.

In the inequality seminar, especially in the latter part of the second semester, political scientist Karl felt that he did not have a clear idea of the seminar's goal.

> Q: How did you think the seminar leader did in leading the seminar?
>
> A: I think it was fine. . . . It was obviously very competent, and there were no sort of obvious glitches. [But] . . . two-thirds into it, there wasn't . . . a plan for the last third.

In that same seminar, economist Matt thought the seminar leader needed to, in his phrase, "shape" the seminar and tie the various sessions more tightly to the overall theme.

> I think it could have been shaped a bit more. . . . There was something to be said for doing some show-and-tell, where we would present our work, but I guess

the way I would have shaped it was, maybe with hindsight, would be trying to do more of the identifying the theme area or an issue where we would have multiple presentations. . . . I would have done that more, sooner, and more of it because I thought that was the most valuable part of it.

The question of how democratic a leader of an interdisciplinary project should be is a matter of personal taste. Some leaders favor making solo decisions, while others choose a more collaborative process. Still, no matter the style, successful leadership requires making the purpose of the endeavor clear and structuring each session so that everyone understands how it relates to the project's overall purpose.[10] Without that kind of unambiguous structuring, participants get lost and lose interest. If leaders favor a democratic approach, they can lead a discussion on how to structure sessions. But that discussion should be held long before participants feel at sea. And in the end, if there is no agreement, the path taken must be decided upon by the leader.

In the science studies seminar, economist Jack was also critical of the way in which the purpose of the seminar was conveyed. He said he simply couldn't figure out what he or the others were supposed to be doing. He had joined because of his interest in science studies, but when he got there, he found most participants were not interested in that subject. He thought the seminar leader, Nancy, was lost at the beginning, and he was unable to sort out what he saw as conflicting messages as to purpose from the dean, the vice-provost, and the foundation that funded the seminars.[11] Although others saw his leaving the seminar as a response to an insult from one of the other participants, he said that that incident was merely the last straw. For him, the seminar had simply never gotten off the ground.

Martin, a psychologist in the science studies seminar, agreed that the seminar goal was not clear and thought a clear goal would have helped participants to know at the end whether or not the goal had been achieved. But the reason why a seminar should have a clear goal is not merely so that its output can be evaluated. Having a goal that everyone understands and buys into has an enormous effect on the seminar's process. Larry, the anthropologist/historian in the science studies seminar, makes this point using the metaphor of building a bridge:

If we were trying to build a bridge and we had these fights . . . that would . . . give some way [to ask the question] . . . "Is this useful for what we're trying to build?" You couldn't ask if [something] . . . was useful for where we were trying to go, because where we were trying to go was in so many different directions. . . . No one could . . . say, "Come on, let's get back to the topic. Let's try to figure out how we can build this bridge."

The dean and the vice provost, who wrote the grant proposal for Adams, were interested in using the seminars to pave the way for two new programs, one in science studies and one in ethics. Laying out a detailed interdisciplinary intellectual agenda for these programs could have been a goal for the groups, but since that goal had not been communicated well to Nancy, neither group worked toward that purpose.

The stated goal in each of the universities' grant proposals was to have the seminars be springboards to the creation of interdisciplinary courses and research projects. That could have been a goal that would have focused participants' attention. But that goal was extremely loosely linked to the seminar proceedings and did not function as a unifying theme in any of the conversations.

Leaders could have devised benchmarks toward which participants were working throughout the year. Whether such benchmarks might have mitigated some of the squabbling is not clear, but creating benchmarks was antithetical to Nancy's leadership style, which saw conversations the way Gadamer did, where lack of direction is inextricably bound up with excitement and understanding.

Paying Attention to Group Dynamics

Before an interdisciplinary project or seminar ever convenes its first session, its success or failure may have already been decided by which faculty have been chosen to participate. The mix of personalities, disciplines, and interdisciplinary interests will play a large role in determining whether the seminar has productive conflict, blows up, or is largely flat. If participants are intolerant of alternative points of view, behave rudely, or monopolize the conversation, the seminar is unlikely to build the trust required for collaboration. At the same time, if participants are too similar to one another in terms of background or approach, there will be insufficient grinding of creative gears.

Julie Thompson Klein lists several characteristics associated with faculty who are successful at interdisciplinary work: reliability, flexibility, patience, resilience, sensitivity to others, risk-taking, a thick skin, and a preference for diversity and new social roles.[12] Had those who chose seminar participants kept Klein's list of attributes in mind, particularly flexibility, patience, and sensitivity to others, much of the squabbling that took place in the Adams seminar might have been avoided.

One of the reasons why the consilience seminar at Jefferson was particularly satisfying to participants was that Joyce made her faculty selections with potential interpersonal interactions in mind. Because of her experience as dean, she was familiar with the personalities and intellectual agendas of each of those she chose. She said she sought people who would contribute to the conversation but not monopolize it.

Moreover, Joyce paid attention to interpersonal dynamics throughout the year, whenever they arose, and acted quickly to neutralize anger and smooth hurt feelings. In many ways, her leadership included the skills of a family therapist.[13]

> I would get little e-mails from people saying, "So-and-so insulted me last time, and I'm feeling like maybe I don't want to come back next time." And so I would talk to that person, and then I would talk to the other person. . . . For me, the group dynamic was always, in this particular enterprise, most important. I am not wishy-washy, and I don't fear controversy, as you know, but in this particular situation, I really wanted all channels to be staying open.

Sam, the leader of the representation seminar at Jefferson, did not have a say in the selection of its participants and felt that this put both his leadership and the seminar participants at a disadvantage. An emeritus professor with almost fifty years in academia, Sam had served as an interdisciplinary seminar leader on numerous occasions and had a clear philosophy about choosing participants. He was not particularly pleased with the mix of faculty that had been chosen for him.

> There were several instances in which I thought that other choices should have been made, not because the people were not good, but because I think they did not have the right kind of personality for a faculty seminar.

Sam said he thought it was ironic that in their role as teachers faculty members instruct their students to behave in ways that foster productive classroom conversations, but that when they become seminar participants, they often overlook what they preach.

> It's interesting, when faculty get together, they forget their own behavior as teachers and they act like smart-ass students.

Karen, a participant in the social sciences seminar, was another veteran interdisciplinary seminar leader. She said that sometimes she did invite "prickly people" to her seminars because she thought their intellectual contribution would outweigh their negative personality traits, but that when she did this she was on the alert for when she might need to run some interference.

It would have been useful if Nancy had run some interference in the two seminars she led at Adams. When James, the physician in the ethics seminar, responded to my question about the most difficult moments in the seminar, he said they occurred when "people were angry and cross-talking," and he faulted Nancy for "not playing a role in defusing anger."

Ahsan, a participant from religious studies in that same ethics seminar, commented that not only did Nancy fail to defuse anger, but she sometimes promoted it, with unfortunate results.

> Sometimes the coordinator, Nancy, tried to act as a . . . provocateur, and I think sometimes she intentionally tried to antagonize Peter because she just took some pleasure out of that and because Peter could so easily be antagonized. And I think, sometimes . . . her interventions were not entirely productive.

Ahsan thought Nancy should have worked harder outside the seminar to mediate disagreements and that she also should have encouraged people to meet one-on-one outside of the seminar without her. He thought that not only would that have reduced anger and misunderstanding, but that gaining greater understanding of others' positions would have productively affected the conversations within the seminar.

> There was money for lunches and dinners et cetera, which we really never exploited. . . . I think the coordinator should have every two weeks, say, said, "Which two of you guys want to go for lunch, and can I be the fly on the wall? Or if you guys don't want me there, just go and have the conversation." . . . That would have created more intensity . . . Or, if you really want to make a breakthrough with Peter and Nabila . . . go and take them out to lunch and converse.

Having Sufficient Authority to Lead

The seminar leaders at Washington and Jefferson were prestigious senior faculty who selected themes, organized the first session, and demonstrated early on that they had command of the seminar's subject matter. This was not true for Nancy, who had four strikes against her from the outset. She had no say in choosing participants, no say in choosing the themes, no expertise in the seminars' subject matter, and no faculty status. And she was asked to lead some extremely prominent scholars.

Particularly for the ethics seminar, which was the second that Nancy led, she had a good sense of the challenges she faced.

> I tried to learn from last year's seminar, to think more about what my role was. Because my role is peculiar, being neither an expert in science studies nor ethics. I mean, I knew a little bit at least about debates in science; in ethics, I knew nothing . . . and nevertheless, trying to think about what should my role here be? I'm not going to be an intellectual leader, for any number of reasons, so how do I run this show? How do I get people to get the most out of the . . . project?

Surprisingly, political scientist Sarah did not think that Nancy's lack of faculty status was a problem, or at least not the main problem. And historian Ari said that while having a senior faculty member in charge might have avoided some of the problems and tensions in the first place, what happened was that faculty in the seminar wound up filling the leadership gap when necessary.

Psychologist Martin said he felt great admiration for Nancy and the challenge she faced.

> What a woman. She had a lot of big shots who've been doing this for a long time. . . . And I think it would have been very hard for anyone. If they'd let [two prominent members of the seminar] or [Jack] . . . run this, they may have been able, by age, to say, "Come on, let's cut it out, let's get back to it. . . . This is going off too far. It's too personal." But Nancy, there's no way she could do that. . . . I mean, I think she did a good job, but I think I wouldn't want the job of moderating that group.

Reading between the lines, it may be that what Martin was really saying was that given the seniority and high status of many of the participants in the science studies seminar, the job of seminar leader should have been given to someone with similar prestige and experience. I agree.

Creating Productive Conflict

Three aspects of creating productive conflict were mentioned by participants. The first concerned choosing the right mix of participants; the second was creation of more in-depth or "uncomfortable" discussions; and the third involved keeping discussions on point.

Choosing the right mix of participants in order to produce productive tension was an issue only in the inequality seminar. Several participants thought the seminar did not live up to its potential because there was insufficient divergence of perspective (too many economists). They attributed that problem to the leader's selection strategy, although others pointed out that Sheila was somewhat constrained in her choices because there was a multidisciplinary humanities seminar going on in the same year, which took some of the participants that she might have wished to tap for the inequality seminar.

The desire for more in-depth discussions came up in the social science seminar. Evan, the action researcher, thought that perhaps more meaningful discussions would have emerged if Robert had been less directive and major decisions about seminar direction had come from participants. He also thought that the sheer number of topics that surfaced crowded out the ability to focus deeply on some subset of them.

In the inequality seminar, economist Matt thought that the leader could have played more of a role in keeping the conversation on point. When I asked him if he felt there had been any difficult moments in the seminar, he responded as follows:

> [A seminar participant] was kind of rambling on, and she got . . . academically esoteric, and I could see the president was . . . losing it at one point. And he said, . . . "Well, let's get to the point. What the hell are you really doing?" It wasn't "what the hell"; he said it politer than that, but it was like "What is really going on here?" . . . Sheila exercises her old soft hand there; that's her style. . . . She could have cut her off, but she didn't. She just let her ramble on.

Psychologist Brian had a different view. He felt that, if anything, Sheila intervened too frequently, but he thought that on balance her leadership style worked well.

> She stepped on people's toes probably every week because she was so excited and so interested in everything. She has one of these promiscuous tastes for knowledge. I don't care what you talk about, Sheila is interested in it. [But] . . . I think the downside is in your role as leader. If you're that interested, you're in the thick of it all the time, and other people are trying to sort of elbow their way in to get their two cents in. So Sheila would sometimes . . . exercise her prerogative as being the leader to talk the most, and I think if it was annoying to people,

it was mildly annoying, and the upside was that you had this very excited, committed person, very smart person. . . . Having said that, I also think that if she talked a little bit less, it would have been even better.

As already noted, in the Adams seminars Nancy's leadership style was exceedingly laissez-faire. She viewed the sessions much more as conversations than seminars and referred to herself not as a leader, but a convener.

Despite the major altercation between the economist and the postdoc from religious studies, Fred, the scientist in the science studies seminar, was supportive of Nancy's leadership.

I think she did about as well as she could do, given the disparate personalities. The old trite expression "herding cats," you know, she was herding cats. . . . I don't have a sense of how one would do it. . . . I would have done worse. I could argue that she should have taken a stronger hand, but I think that would have only made trouble. Which stronger hand? We sort of self-organized, and we didn't know what we were doing or how to proceed.

Most of the points raised by Jefferson seminar participants about productive discussions concerned the leaders' difficulties keeping the conversations on point. This was particularly true for participants in the representation seminar.

Only Evelyn, the studio artist, said she wished the conversations in the representation seminar had been more in-depth or uncomfortable. I asked her if there had been difficult moments in the seminar, times when she felt uncomfortable or things didn't seem quite right. She said there hadn't been enough of such moments.

That was the problem; everything stayed a little bit too breezy. There weren't any arguments. I don't think we invested enough of ourselves in the seminar, so we weren't challenged. . . . I think . . . among the humanists . . . there might have been tensions, but . . . I don't know. I never felt uncomfortable.

Bio-chemist Victor thought that keeping the conversation on point was Joyce's biggest challenge in the consilience seminar.

It was so easy to go off on tangents because you have bright people whose minds make connections and leaps, and there was a lot of that. . . . It meant that sometimes one left the seminar feeling like you'd never really gotten anywhere. You'd learned a lot of fascinating facts but . . . nothing had ever come to any kind of resolution. I think it was very difficult, not just for Joyce, but for all of us to keep bringing the focus back to any given day's discussion. Sometimes it happened; sometimes it didn't.

But most of the other seminar participants gave Joyce very high marks for leadership. Mary, a humanist, saw her as a facilitator.

> She did a wonderful job . . . because she was both well prepared, as far as having information, material to share, and such, but she did not dominate the discussion. She genuinely facilitated the discussion.

To physicist Amita, she was a mediator.

> I think Joyce did very well . . . a fine . . . job of mediating the whole thing. It was very well done.

The words Mary and Amita used to describe Joyce, *facilitating* and *mediating,* are worth our attention. They are precisely the behaviors that walk the fine line between being too laissez-faire and too dominating in trying to create just the right amount of productive conflict.

Leon, the head of Jefferson's foundations and corporate relations office, who attended both years' seminars, had kudos for both Joyce and Sam, but he pointed out that their approaches to moving the conversation along were quite different, with Joyce leading in a rather open-ended way and Sam being more directive.

> They each approached the seminar in a different way. . . . Joyce . . . was simply interested in developing a conversation and stimulating people to talk. And in rare moments when people weren't immediately jumping in—and often you had four or five people who wanted to jump in at the same time—Joyce would . . . ask questions that would help move the conversation along. . . . Sam was . . . trying to explore a question that he had, and it was a very good question, that he thought might be a unifying factor in the conversations.

Louise, the musicologist and former dean of arts and sciences, who had likewise participated in both Jefferson seminars, also contrasted the two leadership styles.

> Joyce had a very nice touch in the first seminar. . . . I think Sam wasn't . . . as attuned to group dynamics, and so sometimes he was a little too authoritarian and too prickly. So there was some discomfort at his leadership.

Joyce herself observed the difference between the ways that she and Sam led the conversations.

> Sam is very interested in bodies of knowledge and understanding intellectually what the issues are and what the different key points of difference are. . . . My goal wasn't just to expose differences among disciplines but also to lead people into a new kind of discourse and a different way of thinking and let them sort of play around with it.

Louise noted that one of Sam's problems was an inability (or unwillingness) to control some English professors who tended to monopolize the conversation.

> There were too many English professors who would fight with one another, or disagree with one another, sort of show off, and two of them were long-winded and [since] . . . he had also been in English . . . he had trouble . . . controlling his former colleagues.[14]

Joyce offered advice on the monopolization matter:

> I would say that if somebody is monopolizing a conversation, the seminar leader has to be ballsy enough to speak to that person and say, "Look, you are a major star and it's mesmerizing to listen to you, but . . . you can't monopolize the conversation." And I think that, actually, for these people, we'd be doing them a huge favor.

Assisting Participants to Bridge Disciplinary Cultures

Patrick Lencioni argues that trust among participants is a foundational requirement for success in all types of groups. He calls the kind of trust needed for group success "vulnerability-based trust," a situation in which each member of a group readily admits his or her own limitations and with good grace acknowledges the strengths of others.[15] As we saw in Chapter 4, on the ethics seminar, which did not have a baseline of trust among its members, trust is particularly critical to the success of an interdisciplinary conversation.

In Lencioni's view, the only way for a leader to create a milieu of trust is to model it: "The only way to initiate it is for the leader to go first."[16] One of the reasons why Joyce's leadership style was successful was that she did model vulnerability, readily admitting her lack of expertise outside of the humanities, especially in the sciences, and equally willing to extol the capabilities of others in their own fields. Her actions led others to do the same, thereby quickly establishing trust in the group.

It is difficult for prestigious academics to admit intellectual shortcomings and encourage others to follow suit. Faculty who head interdisciplinary groups at research universities generally have received manifold accolades for decades; they are scholars accustomed to intellectual adulation. But as is always the case, paradoxically, exhibiting vulnerability makes one stronger. And this is particularly so for leaders of interdisciplinary conversations who need to persuade other equally distinguished colleagues to open their minds.

Organizations expert Warren Bennis also believes that the ability to create trust is an essential characteristic of an effective group leader. But his definition of trust is different from Lencioni's. Bennis thinks that what is important is for the leader to create trust *in the group itself* and also in its leadership. He argues that it is the presence of this dual trust that allows the group to "accept dissent and ride through the turbulence of the group process."[17] In the ethics seminar, Nancy's inability to create trust in either the group or her leadership was one reason why the group was unable to profit from its turbulence.

Just as therapists need to be aware of their own psychodynamics before they can help patients, so too before leaders of interdisciplinary seminars or projects can assist participants to bridge disciplinary cultures, they need to be aware of their own biases, disciplinary as well as political, and seek to neutralize them. One of the problems with the ethics seminar was that Nancy was a player rather than a referee in the battles that erupted. She clearly identified with the younger, more politically radical scholars. Sarah said this was obvious in the seminar and thought it took away from Nancy's effectiveness as a leader.

But seeking to neutralize one's own biases is not merely about not taking sides; it is about becoming aware of one's disciplinary habits of mind and seeking to broaden them. As we saw in Chapter 3, although Sam was not seen as "partisan" in the same way that Sarah saw Nancy as favoring one group in the seminar at the expense of another, he was not aware of his disciplinary biases. He came to the seminar as an English professor, with disciplinary habits of mind garnered through his training and many years of experience. And, interestingly, despite his many years of leading interdisciplinary seminars, he did not seem to have a conscious awareness of the culture-bound behaviors that his training and experience had imposed on his seminar leadership.

In each of the seminars, the leaders brought to the table their own disciplinary style of organization and direction. Guided by their own disciplinary cultures, they instituted rules with regard to level of civility, degree of democratic decision making, style of presentations, style of discussion of texts, and style of moderating in an unconscious fashion and without group discussion. Not surprisingly, participants whose disciplinary culture was closest to that of the seminar leader tended to report that they felt most comfortable in the seminar, while participants whose disciplinary cultures were different from that of the seminar leader often reported that they were uncomfortable and that their discomfort often interfered with learning.

It is as impossible for leaders of interdisciplinary seminars and projects to jettison their cultural baggage as it is for the secretary general of the United Nations to dispose of his.[18] But in the same way that we expect leaders of international organizations to be sensitive to the fact that people across the world have different ideas and customs, we should expect leaders of interdisciplinary conversations to recognize that academics have divergent disciplinary habits of mind. Moreover, they need to get seminar members to become aware of these habits of mind as well so that the group can work collectively to communicate across cultural barriers.

Once leaders become aware of their own disciplinary biases, they can work with participants to help them become ethnographers of their own disciplines. Leaders can specifically introduce material on disciplinary cultures and habits of mind. Similarly, they can explicitly initiate a discussion on creating a climate of trust among participants and creating group norms.

Conclusion

Although some of the seminar leaders did well in creating trust, resolving interpersonal conflicts, conveying purpose, and fostering understanding across disciplines, they could have done more. Nobody thought about training seminar leaders. The assumption seemed to be that academics know how to lead seminars. But these were interdisciplinary seminars, and most of the leaders could have used help in understanding their own disciplinary biases as well as helping seminar participants to understand one another's prejudices and preconceptions. They also could have used some help in learning to defuse anger and keep people from monopolizing the conversation.

One aspect of leadership training should concentrate on helping leaders to become crystal clear about the goals of the conversations they are about to lead and should give them an opportunity to discuss means of achieving those goals. As we will see in the next chapter, although there were numerous positive benefits that faculty obtained from the seminars, the conversations failed to achieve the goal set out in the grant proposals: creation of interdisciplinary courses and research ideas. Part of the reason for this is that the seminar leaders did not tie achievement of that goal to the seminar discussions.

8 Outcomes of the Conversations

A S NOTED IN CHAPTER 1, I LOOK AT SIX OUTCOMES OF THE
seminar conversations: acquisition of new knowledge; the transe
lation of that new knowledge into interdisciplinary courses and research; new
relationships with colleagues from other fields; enhanced intellectual self-esteem; intellectual enjoyment and excitement; and seminar tone. I also examine the absence of seminar follow-up by administrators.

Despite the difficult dialogues and conflicts reported in earlier chapters,
when I asked faculty what they had taken away from their experiences, many
had positive stories to tell. In a few instances they had already incorporated
their new knowledge into their courses or research, and one person had already designed a new course that he would teach alone. However, none had
made firm commitments to team-teach new courses with other seminar
members; nor were there ongoing discussions about new collaborative research.

Thus, although faculty gained a great deal from their conversations, few
of these gains translated into interdisciplinary courses or research, and none
translated into team-teaching or collaborative research. To have created team-
taught courses and collaborative research projects, seminar leaders would
have had to link the seminar conversations more tightly to this goal. And administrators would have had to design follow-up activities to the seminars
and remove bureaucratic barriers to team-teaching.

Effects on Research, Scholarship, and Art

Several participants said that the conversations had implications for their research. I begin with the scientists, and then move to the social scientists, humanists, and artists, respectively.

Biochemist Victor thought the representation seminar had quite a large effect on the kind of research he does.

> I spent the first twenty-five years of my life doing absolutely nothing that had the slightest practical significance whatsoever, and I was damn proud of that. . . . Then . . . that suddenly started not to be enough for me, and now, about a third of what I do is directly looking at neurodegenerative diseases. . . . I think wanting to do that was to some extent catalyzed by that seminar. . . . I might have gotten there anyway, but I suspect I sure got there faster because of the seminar. And maybe I would have never gotten there at all.

Environmental scientist Nick found the social science seminar useful in his continuing efforts to understand and collaborate with social scientists on research projects, collaboration that is now regularly mandated by various funding agencies.

> It's very common in ecological sciences now for the National Science Foundation to mandate that there be a social science component to what we do. . . . When this first came out, there were some really awkward interactions. Even . . . everybody going in with good will, people are just speaking completely different languages. . . . I think this seminar probably made that easier for me.

In the inequality seminar, psychologist Brian thought his research was directly impacted by the economists in the group.

> In my field, we tend to rely heavily on what we call cognitive predictors, so if you want to know what the best predictor of lifetime earnings is, or life satisfaction . . . an IQ score is not a great predictor, but it's better than anything else that we have looked at. . . . And one of the things that the economists in the seminar said was that psychologists have missed it on this, that far better predictors are social skills: showing up on time, getting along with your colleagues, et cetera. . . . So here I come from a profession who's never heard that message. . . . I can tell you as a result of that kind of thinking, I have a doctoral student . . . who is doing research . . . now to really see if the economists are right.

Also in the inequality seminar, political scientist Karl found the group discussions helpful with his research; the ways in which the psychologists and sociologists in the seminar thought about inequality led him to a less abstract view of the subject, which in turn motivated his current book project.

> The biggest impact the seminar . . . had . . . is that I'm actually . . . right now . . . trying to stake out a new book project, and [it] is going to be much more sensitive to issues . . . from the psychologists who were obviously interested in reference groups. . . . It's also related . . . to [a sociologist in the seminar's] work—which I didn't know about before I started this [seminar].

Economist Matt, in the inequality seminar, saw the seminar as helpful not in his research per se but in how he explains it to others.

> There was a . . . really interesting session where Karl, Sheila, and I were discussing/debating various approaches toward assessing the role of economic and social policy on inequality. . . . Sheila and Karl, in different ways, had used econometric methods, and I was arguing that [we] . . . needed to look at things more . . . institutionally. . . . It forced me to sit down and prepare for the discussion and think through my thoughts. . . . Trying to explain them to others at the seminar who didn't know anything about these debates . . . was . . . most rewarding to me.

Like Matt, composer Joel in the consilience seminar felt he gained a better understanding of what he does by having to explain his work to colleagues outside of his field.

> In preparing my presentation, which is a whole hour long, not the sort of thing I usually do for people who are not musicians, I came to a lot of . . . large-scale realizations about what it is I do, where I fit, where what I do fits, and maybe a more specific definition of what's the difference between an audience and a market.

Historian/anthropologist Larry, in the seminar on science studies, also mentioned that the seminar experience helped him situate his own work, and Liz thought that hearing multiple views about the definition of ethics was helpful in understanding how her work fit in to the broader landscape of ethics scholarship.

Joyce, the leader of the consilience seminar, said that the reading the seminar did on chaos theory deeply affected the way in which she was writing about Dostoevsky in her new book.

There are moments when . . . Dostoevsky writes about the ways in which he thinks things are connected, and he describes the great ocean of being in the world. And it's actually uncannily close at certain moments to what is being described in James Glick's book on chaos: how very small changes in a system at one end of it can produce such hugely different results. And that deepens my take on Dostoevsky.

While chaos theory affected Joyce's work, Joyce herself affected the creative process for studio artist Evelyn. Evelyn felt her relationship with Joyce created an openness that led her to learn more about illustration of texts, and that in turn led her to create paintings in a different way. In her studio, Evelyn showed me some of her more recent paintings based on her new technique, and I could see for myself how different they were from earlier paintings she showed me.

Evelyn said that her original motivation for joining the representation seminar was to decrease the sense of isolation she felt at the university. In her interactions with Joyce she felt her isolation somewhat lessened. She felt a conversation she had with Joyce outside of the seminar was transformative. The links she explained were complex, especially for a listener not familiar with the way in which painters go about their work.

I then did this research into illustration, which I never thought I was interested in . . . and . . . realized, looking at my paintings, that I was developing a theme that reminded me of the fairy tale "Cinderella," but in a totally different way than we normally think of "Cinderella," which is a rags-to-riches story. I was identifying with the stepmother, being in a house with daughters . . . and I realized I had . . . something going on that reminded me of . . . the house of Cinderella. So I've been painting domestic interiors, but suddenly I'm bringing this narrative to the painting.

Evelyn said she had only begun to benefit from her interactions with Joyce. She wanted more.

I need to talk to Joyce again. I need to get her back and help me deal with the narratives in the painting. . . . I would love for her to make a studio visit and read the paintings with me . . . and maybe suggest things to me that I haven't noticed.

However, I didn't get the sense that there would necessarily be any further interaction. Once faculty resumed their usual routines, it seemed hard to nurture relationships that had begun in the seminar.

Effects on Teaching and Advising

The seminars influenced faculty teaching, but for the most part the effects were subtle. In one case, a potential effect was entirely unrealized. And while several faculty planned team-taught courses, none were sanguine about the possibility of teaching them, partly because they lacked the time to teach new courses and partly because of administrative barriers.

Of course, many of the intellectual insights described in this chapter are likely to find their way into classrooms. For example, Karl's new understanding about how people think about inequality, Joyce's new ways of looking at Dostoyevsky, and Matt's new ability to explain institutional economics to noneconomists will undoubtedly be reflected in each of their courses. Anthropologist/historian Larry said a new course he taught on the enlightenment had already been influenced by his experience in the science studies seminar.

The only person who said unequivocally that he didn't think the seminar would influence his teaching was economist Omar in the inequality seminar. He explained that he teaches only economics graduate courses and that, in his view, they have to be "hard line," purely disciplinary.

Several faculty thought that the seminar would affect their teaching, but they couldn't say precisely how. Fred, the biologist who worked on biomechanics, put it this way:

> I'm aware of certain things that I wasn't aware of before; how this actually impacts, I'm not too sure. There are things rattling around in my head that would not have been rattling around . . . otherwise.[1]

Like Fred, Liz in the ethics seminar, thought that she could not yet predict all the effects the seminar might have on her teaching.

> I was thinking about [how the seminar might affect my teaching]. I think it's going to probably be more long-term . . . rather than immediate . . . because, honestly, I think it takes a really . . . long time to be able to distill some of the conversations we had among faculty into material that's accessible and useful for undergraduates. . . . It takes some time to . . . do the act of translation back

into terms that make sense for them. . . . If I rushed it, it's too . . . difficult and it seems irrelevant.

Chemist Ed at Jefferson also talked about subtle effects on his teaching, particularly in the way he presents material.

> I think that when I'm teaching, I'm more apt to find some example or some analogy that comes from the humanities or the social sciences or the arts. . . . I started off this year . . . teaching freshman chemistry by saying that although the textbooks tend not to look at it this way . . . we're going to be talking about some of the great creative ideas that people have developed over the ages, and that coming up with the atomic theory is just like writing a Beethoven symphony or a Shakespeare play. And I might not have said that.

Physicist Amita said that being exposed to other disciplines in the representation seminar had affected her teaching because it led to an awareness that the nonscientists among her students might be thinking about the world in a different way than she does.

> I don't want to fall into this rut of saying that scientists think in one way, nonscientists think in other ways, but I think different people have different ways of thinking—and I think I got a much better flavor of that through this seminar. So, when I'm teaching, I think I do keep constantly reminding myself . . . that the way I'm thinking about the problem is not necessarily the way the students are thinking about it.

Joel, the composer at Jefferson, thought that by leading him to clarify his views on the role of culture in music composition and appreciation, the seminar helped him to reframe the way he explains music and music theory to students.

> Students coming in to take courses in theory and music . . . have less and less preparation in classical music. . . . It's just not as much in schools anymore. And they always have questions [about] why do we need to know this and what is this all about, anyway. . . . And now, I tend to answer in . . . a cultural context, rather than simply just say, well, this is the way they did it so that's why you're learning it.

Ironically, despite his feeling that the effects of the seminar would be mostly long-term, Fred was the only faculty member who, at the time of interview had already created a new course which he attributed to his experience in the seminar. The course was about how tools, weapons, and structures were built in the past, and Fred's coteacher was an anthropologist who had not been in the seminar. They taught the course through an already-existing entity for team-taught undergraduate courses where both faculty members had appointments.

Victor, the biologist at Jefferson, seemed likely to teach a multidisciplinary course in the near future. But like Fred, Victor intended to choose a coteacher who had not been in the seminar.

> [The seminar] made me bound and determined to put together a course, which I've not completed but which I intend to do, about the view of science and scientists by nonscientists in the twentieth and twenty-first centuries. I've been thinking about how to do that, and it occurred to me that one way to trace that is through the treatment of science and scientists in the contemporary film.

The courses being contemplated by other interviewees seemed less likely to be taught in the near term. For example, as a result of his experience in the inequality seminar, psychologist Brian developed a great respect for the seminar leader, economist Sheila, and said he would like to co-teach or create a joint research project with her.

> I mean, probably someday, when I get time to think my way through it, I'm going to go back to one of the readings that [Sheila] assigned that she and a colleague of hers did that I found really provocative and interesting. And I've talked to her about it, and there's probably either a course we can co-teach, a seminar, or . . . collaborative research between us. We're both interested. . . . I could easily see Sheila and I doing a doctoral seminar . . . that would force my students to learn some econometric approaches and some economics theory and open her students to some of the psychological constructs in the literature.

While Brian didn't think it would be easy for him and Sheila to both get full credit for teaching a joint course, he thought they could eventually get their respective deans to cooperate in cross-listing a course. His comments portray the bureaucratic impediments they would need to overcome.

> The institution often supports [team-teaching]. They often pay lip service to it; they don't stand in your way, but you've got to make it happen. So, if I want it to happen with Sheila . . . I've got to someday say, "Let's have lunch. Let's talk about this. Can your dean and my dean get together? Can they agree that we can cross-list a course so that it satisfies requirements in your college and in my

college and satisfies the teaching requirement for you and the teaching requirement for me?" And probably, probably we could get the higher-ups to sign off
on it.

Composer Joel also said he would like to co-teach a course in the future, one
on music and philosophy, but noted the barriers to doing so.

One of these days, I'd like to put together . . . a philosophy of music course.
That would be fun because he [philosopher in the seminar] knows the philosophy, I know the music, and he's also very interested in classical music. . . . While
he's chairman, I don't think he's really got the time to do something like that,
but once he's no longer chairman, and if they don't make me chairman, I'd like
to do philosophy of music with him.

Also at Jefferson, chemist Ed and dramatist Jane had proposed a team-
taught course that was on hold. Here is Ed's description of the course:

I actually put together with a member of our theater arts department a proposal
for a course . . . "Science as Drama." . . . This was . . . an exercise at the end of the
second-year seminar . . . and we were going to pick eight or ten plays that had a
scientific theme . . . Brecht's *Galileo, Proof* . . . and work through them with the
students. . . . She was going to look at them from the dramatic point of view,
and I was going to provide a little scientific background for each one. We were
going to do *Copenhagen,* and we were hoping we would get a . . . seminar . . . a
mix of science students and nonscience students. But that would involve us
both finding the right year to do this.

I asked Ed what he thought the right year would be and again got a good sense
of the bureaucratic impediments to team-teaching.

Well, one where the [chemistry] department needs a general education course
and could spare me from doing what I'm now doing, which is teaching two
hundred freshmen.

In my interview with Jane, Ed's would-be teaching partner, she also mentioned the course, and she too noted that time constraints made joint teaching difficult.

Ed and I had proposed a course on theater and science, because there are so
many plays now that are like *Proof* and *Arcadia.* . . . One that . . . I would be interested in doing is about the atomic bomb, where the actual physics and the

history could be taught of what was going on during that time. . . . There's a number of plays, like, *In the Matter of J. Robert Oppenheimer:* this new play called *Raindance* is about Los Alamos; *The Seven Streams of the River Odo*, which covers Japan at the time that the bomb was dropped and follows it for several generations; *Copenhagen.*

I asked Jane the same question I asked Ed: whether in fact they would teach the course.

I don't know, because I have a lot of courses that I have to teach every semester. . . . I will say that this interview has made me rethink . . . that course and . . . maybe I should really get in touch with Ed immediately and see if that's something that he has the time for.

I had the sense that if someone from the Jefferson administration had debriefed seminar participants, they might have been able to encourage Ed and Jane to team-teach. Both seemed eager to do the class. A nudge and some flexibility in teaching schedules might well have resulted in an extremely interesting interdisciplinary seminar.

Another instance where administrative debriefing might have had salutary effects concerned Jefferson mathematician Barry. Most of my interviewees in the representation seminar commented that when Barry gave a session on his own work they found it incomprehensible. Some were angry that his pedagogy was so poor. Interestingly, Barry himself, as a result of watching his colleagues' presentations, became aware that his teaching could be improved.

Some of the presentations were really amazing, really engaging. [I was] really, really impressed with . . . my colleagues' ability to convey their ideas in ways that got the rest of us involved. . . . Whether I can translate their . . . teaching skills to what I do in mathematics, I don't know. I can't say that I've actively tried to.

In talking with Barry, I felt that this new awareness of what teaching *could* be like was important to him. However, since no one (except me) ever debriefed seminar participants, no one ever offered to help him improve his teaching. The teachable moment was lost.

Getting to Know Colleagues

Participants from all three universities said that getting to know colleagues from other parts of campus was an important outcome of the seminars. They stated that as a result of dialogues with these new colleagues they now felt that they belonged to something bigger than their own field or department, that they belonged to a common institution, a university of which they felt proud.

Here are comments from Evan, who participated in the social sciences seminar.

> I met some marvelous colleagues whose work I was unfamiliar with, and that was really quite exciting. I mean the folks in limnology—they really engaged in the social science discussions, and they were very, very sharp and compelling. It was great fun to meet the . . . scholars in the law school who were doing law in society. I think there were a lot of overlaps between what we do . . . and some of the things they're concerned with.

In the inequality seminar, economist Omar thought that getting to know colleagues was the most important effect of the seminar and that those connections in turn influenced his research.

> What was very important, I think . . . were the personal connections that were established in this seminar. . . . For example, I got to know [a member of the seminar] . . . who is a professor of law. . . . So we had exchanges of our papers and discussions over lunch . . . and that was the basis for further work.

Omar thought the relatively small size of the seminar was important for creating new collegial relationships.

> I've . . . thought a little bit about what it is about the . . . seminar that's good. . . . And, ultimately, I think it's creating this base of connections. . . . I mean, we have fifteen people in the room every week. . . . It's like being back at grad school. Each of them have to make a presentation; they have to come to meetings on time, and so on. And it had . . . the grad school reading group type feel to it. And sure . . . it's fairly resource-intensive. Obviously it would be more cost-effective to have thirty people in the group . . . but . . . you wouldn't make the same connections. It wouldn't be the same thing if you had thirty people.

Omar thought it was hard to predict when or which of the contacts he made would turn out to be important for him.

> And you . . . can't tell where it's going to pop up; . . . so it's dormant, lying there, and suddenly something comes up in psychology or whatever it is, and I call up Brian . . . and say, "Hey, what do you think about this?" . . . I don't know if I would have done that quite so easily had it not been for this seminar.

Even Karen from Washington and Peter and Jack from Adams, all of whom were on the whole quite disappointed in their seminars, mentioned meeting new colleagues and wanting to maintain ongoing dialogues with them as positive experiences.

Evan, from the social sciences seminar, has sought to maintain his new collegial relationships and thinks they have somewhat changed his intellectual life.

> We've tried to, since then, maintain some of these connections [with faculty in the law school] by inviting them over for colloquy, urging our students to look at some of their courses; so I think it changed my advising a bit, and it changed a little bit who we've invited in to contribute to debate in our fields. I think that was very positive.

However, Neil, the reporter for both Washington seminars, was pessimistic about the staying power of the new relationships. Although he said that some new colleagues he met in the seminar were helpful to him when he wanted to broker a joint appointment between his department and the law school, he felt it was unlikely that any of the new relationships would last.

> I think it was like leaving summer camp; get back into the traces and. . . . There should be some residue there, but I'm not at all sure what it is.

Matt, in the inequality seminar, also said he hadn't maintained contact with colleagues he met in the seminar.

> Typical style—we all go back to our own little office, and I interact with people at my [department] . . . but most of the people [from the seminar] . . . I don't ever see, so it hasn't led to a sustained interaction.

Affective Effects

In earlier chapters, we saw evidence of the negative effects the seminar had on several seminar participants' sense of self. But four seminar members also mentioned positive effects on their self-confidence. Interestingly, three of these were at Jefferson.

The leader of the consilience seminar, Joyce, was pleased to learn of her ability to ask sensible and useful questions of a computer scientist and comprehend the answers. Louise, a musicologist in the representation seminar, was delighted to find she could keep up with the highly technical presentation by mathematician Barry, and in that same seminar, studio artist Evelyn said that watching one of the literary scholars had a positive effect on the confidence with which she paints.

> I really enjoyed . . . the way [the literary scholar's] mind would work and free associate, the kind of ease with which she would move from idea to idea. I was very inspired by that, and that is something that I think has . . . given me confidence to be more open to things that . . . come through my mind while I'm painting.

Finally, Larry, the historian/anthropologist in the science studies seminar, found the seminar experience to be an overall ego boost.

> I had a sense coming out of the seminar that my own interdisciplinary stuff was respectable . . . beyond the reaches of the disciplines that I'm usually working in, that it would still hold up quite well . . . for a psychologist or for a philosopher, or whatever, that they would be able to read my stuff and say, yes, this is a reasonable position, even if they disagreed with it.

Intellectual "Play" and Enjoyment

The kind of play and enjoyment that faculty experienced in the seminars was not of the ordinary kind, not akin to attending a comedy show, laughing with friends, or playing with one's children or grandchildren. In his book on play, Stephen Nachmanovitch comes closer to describing the kind of play and enjoyment that faculty got from the group conversations.

> There is an old Sanskrit word, *lila*, which means play. Richer than our word, it means divine play, the play of creation, destruction, and re-creation, the folding and unfolding of the cosmos.[2]

And in his book *Truth and Method*, Hans-Georg Gadamer further contributes to an understanding of the kind of serious play in which faculty engaged:

It can be said that for the player play is not serious; that is why he plays. . . . [But] play itself contains its own, even sacred seriousness. . . . Seriousness is not merely something that calls us away from play; rather, seriousness in playing is necessary to make the play wholly play.[3]

Victor, a biologist in the consilience seminar, was one of the most enthusiastic about his play experience. For him, it epitomized what university life should be about.

I had a great time in that seminar; it was the most fun I've had in a sitting position in a long time. It reminded me of why I'm glad I'm at a university.

Victor likened watching great minds play together to watching an all-star sports team on the field.

I was blown away by how smart some of my colleagues are. . . . And in many cases, it was just such a pleasure to sit there and watch their minds work.

Composer Joel, also in the consilience seminar, enjoyed coming to understand some philosophy.

Oh, yes, when the philosophers started talking, everything they said was just really exciting, because philosophy was always kind of unclear to me, and they spoke about it . . . very plainly, in ways that made sense to me.

Joel particularly liked arguing with one of the philosophers about music.

And . . . [one of the philosophers] . . . knew very much what the nineteenth-century Germans wrote about music, and he had sort of presumed that this applied to all music, all these things about the strong man and what notes do and so forth. And it was fun . . . trying to contradict him and to show that that was only a very narrow, Western way of looking at music.

Jane, the dramatist in the representation seminar, was greatly pleased that her fellow participants were willing to engage in serious play with her.

I asked my colleagues, when it was my turn for the presentation, to come wearing tennis shoes and sweat pants. I was so gratified when they did and that they played with me for the day.

In the inequality seminar, Omar also said he had fun. And, in his case, as an economist, the fact that having fun was also an efficient way to learn made the experience doubly satisfying.

Well, it was enormous fun; it really was enormous fun ... an easy exposure to things that I would not normally have experienced. So when Brian ... for example, made a presentation on his work, on ... the psychological bases of inequality, ... this ... was a very efficient way for me to immerse myself in the thing, rather than Brian ... sending me four papers ... and saying, well, you read through it.

In that same inequality seminar, Donna, a sociologist who was generally critical of the seminar, nonetheless particularly enjoyed watching and listening to one of the humanists.

[He] is always so interesting to watch. . . . He likes to play with ideas. . . . I like the way his mind works, and he picks up this stuff and plays with it in interesting sorts of ways.

In the science studies seminar, historian/anthropologist Larry also found pleasure.

The high point was the readings. . . . I thought the papers that we read ... were really excellent. . . . It was just very much fun keeping up with the readings.

Also in the science studies seminar, psychologist Martin used the word *fun* to describe his experience.

I think [what I liked most] was watching the styles of argumentation, watching what constituted evidence and what constituted a convincing argument for people.

Intellectual Insights

We have already examined some the intellectual insights faculty had in our discussion of the conversations' effects on teaching and research. However, faculty also had intellectual insights of a broader nature, insights that might or might not make their way directly into their teaching and research.

Political scientist Karl and economist Omar were both stimulated by presentations from the psychologists. Karl put it this way:

I had never taken any psychology courses. . . . The ... almost laboratory nature of their work ... the way of ... manipulating your subjects in certain ways to get certain kinds of effects. . . . I had not fully understood ... that there is a social science that can take that form.

Economist Omar said:

> So this was my first . . . exposure to social psychology. . . . Brian and another
> psychologist . . . did a joint presentation . . . about test scores and how . . . some
> people think they've done better than they have done in the test, and other
> people think they have done worse than they have done. . . . I recall that as a
> very interesting thing, and how that then related to their other characteristics.

Omar was interested in relating his new psychological knowledge to behavioral economics.

> I'd been thinking a lot about the new behavioral economics and particularly
> its implications for development economics . . . and, of course, behavioral eco-
> nomics essentially uses the insights of psychology.

Economist Matt was excited by anthropological approaches to inequality.

> There was a very interesting presentation by a woman who was . . . in anthro-
> pology, about . . . declining industrial communities and what inequality meant
> in those kinds of communities. . . . I don't take the time to read what anthro-
> pologists write about inequality. . . . I didn't agree with a fair amount of what
> she was concluding . . . but I thought what she was observing and the method
> was really interesting.

Insights About Interdisciplinarity

One type of intellectual insight that several participants mentioned was developing a more nuanced understanding of interdisciplinarity and the conditions under which it flourishes. Interestingly, all of these insights came from
participants in the science studies and ethics seminars, the two seminars that
probably had the most difficulty with interdisciplinary dialogue.

In the ethics seminar, humanist Liz discovered what has been called the
difference between instrumental and radical interdisciplinarity. Researchers
who are instrumental in their interdisciplinarity use another discipline at a
certain stage in a project because they realize they need its tools. Those who
are radical in their interdisciplinarity are quite different in that they turn to
multiple disciplines at the very beginning of their work, at the conceptual
stage.

> I think that for some of the people . . . interdisciplinarity was more strategic

in that one did interdisciplinary work . . . when one came across a question that your particular field didn't have the answer to but the guys next door's did. . . . For me . . . interdisciplinarity is happening before you even decide what questions you're going to be asking.

Liz observed that she thought radical interdisciplinarity was more common in younger people.

I think [my kind of interdisciplinarity] is more common in . . . junior faculty, in people . . . who've been doing interdisciplinary work from course work into their dissertations, rather than having, say . . . worked for ten years within a certain discipline. . . . I think that it's really part of a generational formation.

Liz's insights about interdisciplinary conversations also concerned the difficulties when some participants work in Western countries (the center) and others work in non-Western countries (the periphery).

[The seminar] reinforced . . . familiar themes for someone working in any non-Western [country] . . . the global south . . . the periphery. It made me once again realize the privilege of . . . writing in English and publishing in English or French or German, in terms of what is considered theoretical or philosophical and what is not.

And she wryly observed that it seemed as though theoretical propositions can only come from outside of the global south.

Anything that doesn't come from the center can be dismissed as a case study, as too specific to be theoretical. So, therefore, if you work on . . . Latin America, you're supposed to take theory from Paris or Berlin, or such places.

In the ethics seminar, Nabila had some insights about interdisciplinary work. Mostly what she learned was that she liked her own discipline, English. But like Liz, she felt that cohort was important and that if the person outside her field was from her own generation, she was able to relate to him or her intellectually.

I feel as if I've only said negative things about the seminar . . . but . . . I do think that in some ways, part of what's interesting about a seminar like this one is that you realize who you want to engage with more . . . who really can be useful to your work, even if they are from the outside, who will sort of sharpen your awareness, and also who you will not want to engage with.

When I asked her which particular members of the seminar she might like to meet with to sharpen ideas, the people she named were either in her own or closely related disciplines or in her own age cohort, people she called allies.

> Those people seem like allies because we've gone through university within the same fifteen years and because there has been a general movement in intellectual thought that everyone, or most people, are exposed to.

Sarah, a political scientist in the ethics seminar, felt that although the seminar was "awful" she learned a lot about how (and how not) to engage in interdisciplinary dialogue, knowledge she was using in another interdisciplinary seminar on another topic in which she was then participating.

Sarah also made a most interesting comment about the way that, paradoxically, although interdisciplinarity is much touted in universities today as a way of achieving a broadening of scholarship, in a certain respect it is intellectually narrowing.

> It has struck me that there are ways in which interdisciplinarity actually is intellectually narrowing in the university, that the logic of it is that disciplines are narrow, we're all in boxes with blinders, and that we will be stimulated and expanded by the diversity of ideas we find in interchange with people in other disciplines. . . . But if you do enough of that, what happens is I think you start to get dominant paradigms in groups of disciplines and you've actually narrowed the amount of variety there is in the intellectual menu in universities.

When I asked Sarah for an example, the one she chose first described precisely what had happened in the inequality seminar.

> So, for example, in the social sciences, the rational choice paradigm starting with economics is moving through political science, sociology, a number of other disciplines, and you can have a very interdisciplinary group where people are actually incredibly like-minded.

And her second example described the ethics seminar, in which she had participated.

> Likewise in the humanities, the French philosophers, poststructuralists and postmodernists, have had a huge impact, and you can get people together from a whole set of romance languages, literature, history, whatever, and they're actually all speaking the same language and reading the same books, and there isn't really much variety in intellectual ideas out there at all.

She summarized her point:

> Nobody's actually doing what you think they're supposed to be doing; political scientists are doing economics, cultural anthropologists are doing political science, literature people are doing philosophy, and the names of the disciplines don't actually match what's going on.

Sarah's point echoes Stanley Fish's 1989 argument that interdisciplinarity is really nothing more than a rearrangement of the academic deck chairs: "The interdisciplinary impulse finally does not liberate us from the narrow confines of academic ghettos to something more capacious; it merely redomiciles us in enclosures that do not advertise themselves as such."[4] This observation, often neglected in paeans to interdisciplinarity, is important. If the purpose of interdisciplinarity is to capitalize on cognitive difference, the creation of overarching paradigms to which numerous disciplines adhere may diminish rather than augment opportunities for diverse thinking.

Achievement of Other Goals

As noted earlier, both Washington and Adams sought to achieve goals in addition to those outlined in their proposals for funding. It is useful for our discussion of outcomes to examine the extent to which those goals were achieved.

At Washington, although the leader of the social science seminar put forth a strong secondary goal of developing a new interdisciplinary social science program, the president and the provost did not give the seminar the task of outlining its specifics; rather, they gave that assignment to a special task force whose membership included a few seminar participants but also faculty not in the seminar. At the end of the year, in part because of what they learned in the social science seminar and in part because of the task force's work, the president and the provost did allocate funding for an interdisciplinary social science program for faculty, which by many accounts has been quite successful.

At Adams the dean and the vice-provost wished to use the seminars to develop major programs in science studies and ethics, but as noted earlier, the leader of the seminars said she did not know about that goal and did not use the seminar conversations to promote it. Adams did eventually develop a science studies program for undergraduates, but only one member of the science studies seminar is part of it, and its director is a faculty member who was not in the seminar. It provides little in the way of interdisciplinary course work, and as is generally the case in undergraduate interdisciplinary programs at research universities, each course is taught by a single faculty member from his or her disciplinary perspective.

A similar situation prevails in ethics. A new undergraduate program was developed in that field, but it is headed by someone who was not in the seminar, and only one member of the seminar is on its faculty. Like the program in science studies, the ethics program is largely discipline-based, although the introductory course, while taught by a single social scientist (not a member of the ethics seminar), seems to draw on knowledge from multiple disciplines.

Conclusion

Although faculty changed their teaching and research somewhat as a result of the seminar, and it is likely that in the future more changes in these activities will percolate from the conversations, the goal of getting new collaborative interdisciplinary teaching and research was not achieved. Perhaps if that goal had been more tightly tied to the seminar structure and procedures, the outcome would have been different. But seminar leaders did not do this; they treated the goal as a hope or neglected it entirely. Even in the representation seminar, where Joyce scheduled one session to which faculty were asked to bring and discuss team-taught course proposals, there was no follow-up on the courses faculty designed.

Without a strong expectation on the part of seminar leaders that new courses and research were to come out of the conversations, and without a seminar structure that worked toward achieving these goals, faculty behaved like magpies. They collected numerous shiny bits for their own nests, but never put them into larger structures. The list of individual interdisciplinary insights was extremely interesting. Very smart people got a tremendous amount out of relating their own work to that of their colleagues and to the high-level interdisciplinary readings.

Administrators could have played their parts better. The conversations yielded fragile sprigs of greenery that needed additional watering. But with the end of the seminars, watering ceased. To harvest the potential of the seminar conversations, university administrators needed to arrange follow-up activities and lessen bureaucratic impediments to team-teaching; they needed to continue to water the plants they had seeded.

It is unrealistic to think that new interdisciplinary courses and research projects can be launched after only twenty or so conversations. The work faculty did in these conversations was merely an overture to more serious work. As it turned out, the overtures were not always well led, and more could no doubt have been accomplished in them. But it takes time for people to learn one another's disciplines, build trust, and get to know one another well enough to begin collaborating. Recall that Lucy Shapiro reported that the four faculty who started the interdisciplinary research institute Bio X at Stanford met every Saturday morning for two years before they were ready to begin their collaboration. In their book on interdisciplinarity, Liora Salter and Alison Hearn noted that it takes about two years of submersion for a cultural anthropologist to be able to work effectively in a new culture.[5] What faculty do when working with collaborators from another discipline is learn a new culture. They need more than a year to accomplish this.

Perhaps one reason why there was so little follow-up to the six seminars is that follow-up would have cost money that administrators did not have in their grants. It is telling that when these universities sought additional funds from foundations for interdisciplinary work it was for *new* interdisciplinary seminars, not for follow-up on the initial seminars. Administrators believed that new seminars would be more attractive to foundations than would follow-up for previously funded projects. And they were probably right.

Funding team-teaching (by ensuring that both faculty members receive full credit for teaching a team-taught course) is the major follow-up activity that would have been expensive. Since none of these institutions wished to increase average class size or hire more part-time faculty to teach some of the full-time faculty members' courses, giving full credit to both faculty members for team teaching would have required increasing the size of the full-time faculty. And despite their commitment to more interdisciplinarity, administrators were not prepared to do this.

But administrators could have made changes at the margin, substituting new interdisciplinary courses for some of the single-discipline courses already on the books. In the same way that government agencies with fixed budgets need to make choices between funding single-discipline projects and those involving multiple disciplines, university administrators need to make choices about course offerings. If they do not wish to hire new faculty, some single-discipline courses need to be removed from the course offerings, or taught less frequently, to make room for new interdisciplinary courses.

Moreover, some of the possible follow-up activities would not have been expensive at all and would have involved little in the way of time trade-offs. For example, administrators might have done exit interviews with seminar participants to see where administrative follow-up might pay off (as in the case of helping Barry to improve his mathematics teaching); they could have set up reunions so that seminar members could retain and renew their interdisciplinary contacts. Most likely, administrators simply did not think about these opportunities. As a result, the payoff from the faculty conversations was much smaller than it might have been.

However, absence of follow up should not take away from the success that some of the seminars achieved in creating productive interchange among an extremely cognitively diverse group. And in all of the seminars, faculty took away important interdisciplinary insights for their own teaching and research.

The consilience seminar in particular accomplished a great deal, creating productive dialogue in a friendly and civil atmosphere and helping to reduce gaps in understanding and appreciation between scientists and nonscientists. Joyce's careful structuring of the seminar and her leadership strategies should be carefully studied as means of mitigating the barriers that habits of mind and disciplinary cultures present for successful interdisciplinary conversations.

9 Talking Across Disciplines

IN HIS BOOK ON INTERDISCIPLINARITY, JOE MORAN ARGUES that at first blush interdisciplinarity seems inherently appealing, "a democratic, dynamic and co-operative alternative to the old-fashioned inward-looking and cliquish nature of disciplines."[1] He cites Roberta Frank's colorful elaboration of this idea:

> "Interdisciplinary" has something to please everyone. Its base, *discipline*, is hoary and antiseptic; its prefix, *inter*, is hairy and friendly. Unlike fields with their mud, cows, and corn, the Latinate *discipline* comes encased in stainless steel: it suggests something rigorous, aggressive, hazardous to master; *inter* hints that knowledge is a warm, mutually developing, consultative thing.[2]

But as we have seen from our close reading of the six faculty conversations, interdisciplinarity is not necessarily warm and friendly. In fact, the opposite is generally the case; engaging in interdisciplinary dialogue is tough work and conflicts are recurrent. In order to create conversations that are both enjoyable and intellectually productive, it is necessary to manage them carefully.

This chapter returns to the two central questions of this book: What makes interdisciplinary conversations so difficult? What are the hallmarks of fruitful interdisciplinary conversations? The first section answers the first question, examining three types of barriers to interdisciplinary conversations: those that occur before the conversations even start, those that occur during the conversations, and those that come into play afterward and limit the sustainability of the conversations' outcomes. The second section briefly summarizes the social science explanations for these barriers and reviews ways in which some of the leaders moderated the effects of these barriers to make the conversations more productive. The third section makes additional suggestions for nurturing interdisciplinary conversations. The chapter's conclusion focuses on the centrality of open-mindedness to successful conversations.

Barriers to Interdisciplinary Conversations

Barriers Faculty Bring with Them

The first set of barriers to interdisciplinary conversations are internal, fears that faculty have even though they are unaware of them. A prominent fear for many humanists and some qualitatively oriented social scientists is that they may be unequal to the task of understanding concepts and methods that involve mathematics or science. Lack of sufficient background to understand or appreciate a particular discipline creates not only fear, but also a sense of alienation and isolation. Both Louise and Joyce in the Jefferson seminars were delighted to find that their fears about being unable to understand technical material were unfounded.

Then there are fears associated with presenting one's own discipline-based work to colleagues in other fields. Will the work's basic premises and contributions be understood? What will have to be explained that is normally taken for granted? Will the work garner respect? Will status have to be renegotiated? Neil observed that these kinds of fears were at hand in the first few sessions of the social sciences seminar at Washington.

Faculty (and doctoral students) also bring stereotypes and negative feelings about certain disciplines to interdisciplinary conversations. We saw these in the anecdote about the research meeting of historians and quantitative social science researchers that opened Chapter 1, and in interviews about the social science seminar at Washington, Neil noted his surprise (and consternation) at the disciplinary stereotypes faculty held about one another. Also in the social science seminar, scientist Nick noted the lack of mutual respect between qualitative and quantitative researchers. In the ethics seminar, several participants commented on the lack of respect for postmodern work. And in the inequality and ethics seminars, respectively, Donna, the qualitative sociologist, and Nabila, from English and women's studies, felt a lack of respect from colleagues.

Having an ineffective leader or the wrong mix of participants can also be a problem at the outset. Selections of both leader and participants need to be made with great care. Does the leader have the authority to lead? Is he or she knowledgeable about the subject, highly respected, and able to successfully resolve disputes? Are the participants flexible in outlook? Are they interested in learning from one another? Is there enough disciplinary diversity to achieve productive conflict? Is there so much diversity that there are no themes of common interest? Are the participants interpersonally compatible?

Only Joyce said that she took interpersonal compatibility into account when choosing seminar members. Sam felt that the representation seminar would have been more successful if he had been able to select participants; he said he would have avoided people who he knew had a tendency to monopolize conversation. Nancy, too, had no role in choosing the participants for the seminars she led. Perhaps she too would have reduced the friction in the Adams seminars if she had been able to select participants based on their openness to new ideas and their ability to work with one another, although one of the problems with the Adams seminar was that Nancy did not have the authority to lead or the ability to defuse conflict.

Barriers That Emerge During the Conversations

A second set of barriers emerges during the conversations themselves. No matter how careful the selection procedure, no matter the skills of the leader, there will be jockeying for position as faculty interpret and validate their power and status or attempt to draw boundaries around their disciplinary knowledge, and all participants will bring their disciplinary habits of mind and disciplinary cultures with them.

Diversity of disciplinary cultures and habits of mind are serious obstacles to interdisciplinary conversation.[3] Not only do participants have to learn one another's disciplinary language, they have to learn one another's approaches to knowledge acquisition and truth claims, as well as one another's styles of intellectual interaction.

Disciplinary cultures vary considerably across disciplines, yet faculty trained in a discipline learn only that particular discipline's cultural practices; as a result, when colleagues from different disciplines come together, the cultural gulfs they need to bridge are large, perhaps as large as those in international organizations. In a similar vein, disciplines train people to see quite different realities. And they inculcate habits of mind—habits that are

practiced so frequently in a disciplinary context that they become unconscious. But in interdisciplinary settings, the divergent habits collide.

Members of the representation seminar did not understand why Barry
was silent all year; they never appreciated how foreign their habits of mind
were for him. Nor did he recognize how impossible it was for most of the
others in the group to understand his complex mathematical presentation.
In the ethics seminar, neither the economist nor the postdoc who censured
him understood that they came from entirely different disciplinary cultures
with respect to norms for questioning presenters. And when members of the
representation seminar told Evelyn, the studio artist, that they preferred her
to show slides in a classroom rather than go to her studio to see her paintings,
they were not aware that they were imposing their own habits of mind and
were being disrespectful of hers.

It is critical for participants in interdisciplinary conversations to recognize
that the political jockeying for status that goes on in academic settings is exacerbated in situations where more than one discipline is involved.[4] Pecking
orders that have been established within departments or disciplines over long
periods of time suddenly need to be renegotiated. Numerous questions need
to be settled diplomatically: Whose discipline is primary to the endeavor and
whose is secondary or tertiary? Whose status is highest in a situation where
all the players are used to being kingpins in their fields? How will high status
be rewarded?

Leaders and participants in interdisciplinary conversations should take
for granted that there will be a shaking out of power and status hierarchies
at the beginning and realize that disputes about status and power may come
to the fore again if, for example, decisions need to be made about who becomes first author on a paper or a grant proposal or who presents work at a
conference. But if power issues remain prominent throughout the process of
collaboration, they constitute a serious barrier to interdisciplinarity. In the
ethics seminar, squabbling about power and status as well as efforts to loosen
(or maintain) disciplinary borders continued all year and were impediments
to enjoyment and intellectual growth for many participants.

Barriers That Emerge After the Conversations
Have Been Completed: Absence of Follow-up
I have already noted that administrators at Jefferson who failed to do exit
interviews of faculty who participated in the interdisciplinary conversations

missed an opportunity to improve Barry's mathematics teaching. And at both Jefferson and Washington, administrators missed opportunities to facilitate team-taught courses that faculty were considering. Unless one understands the irrationality of large organizations, it seems strange that administrators would write grant proposals for seminars that would produce creative ideas for new interdisciplinary courses and then put administrative hurdles in the way so that faculty could never teach those courses. But that is in fact what happened.

In one of the meetings of all the seminar leaders and reporters that Atlantic Philanthropies arranged, I asked a question about team-teaching: If two people who are from different departments want to teach a course together, does each get credit for that course? The answer from Washington was, "It depends on their clout." At Jefferson, the answer was, "Even clout doesn't do it . . . but if you had a department chair, a dean and a provost, all of whom were interested in making this happen, you could make it happen." The Adams response was different: "You can do it without any problem and both can get credit." But when I probed a bit, it turned out that while both faculty members who designed a new team-taught course would get full credit the first time they taught it, after that they would have to alternate the credit, each getting full credit only every other year.

A team-taught course is not the equivalent of half a course. Indeed, taking account of the coordination required, the work is the equivalent of more than one regularly taught course. If administrators want more interdisciplinary teaching, they need to figure out how to give full credit to both people who teach a team-taught course.[5]

If university administrators are serious about fostering interdisciplinarity, the ball is in their court. As noted in the Gulbenkian Commission's Report, foundations can give grants to foster creative interdisciplinary projects, but it is university departments and central administrations that play the major role in determining how much interdisciplinarity takes place on a campus.[6]

Although the leaders of the Jefferson seminars had asked faculty to write proposals for interdisciplinary courses and spent one session discussing those proposals, there were no follow-up activities that might have helped faculty to plan those courses. In my interview with dramatist Jane, she said that she feared that the course she and chemist Ed had considered teaching about plays with science themes might turn out to be dilettantish, with not enough deep material on either science or drama. There was no venue in which she could verbalize those fears, let alone work with Ed toward creating a course that was not superficial.

Also, there was no follow-up training for faculty about how to make team-taught interdisciplinary courses integrative. In reviewing the literature about how to create successful integration in such courses, James Davis notes the importance of collaboration in the planning process as well as in the teaching, grading, and evaluation of the course.[7] In follow-up sessions to the seminars, it would have been useful to convey this type of knowledge to participants considering such collaboration. Jefferson lost an opportunity to provide some of its students and faculty with valuable interdisciplinary classroom experiences.

Absence of follow-up not only constituted a significant barrier to realizing the original goals of the seminars (the creation of new interdisciplinary courses and research projects), it also made participants' intellectual insights and new collegial relationships more ephemeral. At Jefferson, both Jane and Evelyn said they wished their seminar had had a reunion, that the whole experience seemed so "one-shot." At Washington, both Neil and Matt said they doubted that the interactions with new colleagues that they had enjoyed during the seminar would be sustained. Neil likened the seminar experience to summer camp, where one rarely keeps up with friends after getting back to the city. Holding a reunion a few times a semester for several years might well have sustained those relationships.

In their book on interdisciplinarity, Liora Salter and Alison Hearn note that it takes about two years of submersion for a cultural anthropologist to be able to work effectively in a new culture.[8] At Stanford, the faculty from medicine, physics, and engineering who set up Bio X, a large interdisciplinary science center, met with one another at least once a week for two years to learn one another's disciplinary cultures, habits of mind, and content before they were able to begin their collaboration.[9]

At Adams, even with follow-up, the seminars would probably not have achieved much in the way of collaboration. Most of the participants seemed glad that the conversations were over. But at both Washington and Jefferson, follow-up might well have led to more permanent and substantial outcomes.

Mitigating Barriers and Making
Conversations More Productive

Three strategies used by seminar leaders served to mitigate the barriers noted above: having a clear vision about what the conversations were to accomplish and structuring the seminars accordingly; explicitly committing to the exploration of synthesis; and creating trust among participants and attending to interpersonal dynamics. Three additional strategies, not used by any of the leaders, could have served to make the conversations even more productive: specifically discussing the concepts of disciplinary cultures and habits of thought; encouraging participants to set group norms and vary their approaches to learning; and seeking formative evaluation early in the course of the conversations.

Having a Clearly Communicated Vision and
Structuring the Seminar Tightly

Having a well-defined and well-communicated thread that weaves through all of the conversations appears to be central to making interdisciplinary conversations productive. One of the reasons for the success of the consilience seminar was that in implementing it Joyce kept her vision of its purpose clearly in mind and communicated it lucidly to participants. Everything about the seminar process was in service of the seminar's purpose—choosing participants, choosing readings, and tying sessions together. Joyce did not have faculty choose readings and make presentations until after a good many sessions that she had structured herself, until the purpose of the seminar and the habit of exploring syntheses were well established.

Sam, the leader of the representation seminar at Jefferson, was also clear about the purpose of the seminar (exploration of how different disciplines represent reality), and he too communicated its purpose unambiguously. He also tightly structured the first few sessions, building largely on what Joyce had done the year before, and in the remaining sessions kept asking participants to explain how their disciplines viewed "reality" and how they represented it.

At Adams, the dean and the vice-provost initially had a clear vision of the purpose of the seminars, but it seemed to get lost when they appointed Nancy as seminar leader. Nancy had no vision of the seminars' purposes, and participants were confused about what they were supposed to accomplish. Probably the best description of the Adams seminars' goal was the one Clifford Geertz propounded, having colleagues from a variety of disciplines give a credible account of themselves to one another. Larry, a participant in the science studies seminar, thought that goal was too diffuse. He suggested that the conversations would have been more productive and less conflict-ridden if the group had had a goal against which they could benchmark their progress.

In the case of Washington, the original vision for the seminars was clear, but the social science seminar was changed as a result of Robert's desire for the president and provost to become educated about the social sciences so that they would provide additional financial support for them. In effect, the social science seminar operated with two visions, and law professor Karen felt they sometimes conflicted.

Karen also thought that Robert had not structured the social science seminar tightly enough. She said she thought that merely having people talk about their work to one another without giving all of them the same set of questions to answer in the course of their presentation meant that there was no common thread that ran through the seminar.

In the inequality seminar, Sheila set the purpose of the conversations (to explore the different disciplinary perspectives and findings about inequality) and successfully communicated it to participants. But there was again relatively little structuring; each participant talked about his or her work, and the connections among the sessions were not clearly drawn. Midway into the year, it was unclear to some participants what the task was for the second semester.

Explicitly Committing to the Exploration of Synthesis

One of the most important reasons for the success of the consilience seminar was Joyce's explicit commitment to the exploration of syntheses among the various disciplines. In particular, she aimed to select participants who wanted to explore syntheses between science and humanities. And she structured the readings and discussions to build, week after week, on the syntheses of the previous sessions.

Another reason for the success of that seminar was that at each session Joyce encouraged participants to think about how various disciplinary approaches could be combined. She particularly wanted scientists and humanists to see the intersections of their fields, but she also wanted artists and social scientists to explore syntheses with other fields.

To promote interdisciplinary collaboration, leaders need to structure discussions so that participants observe and give voice to ideas that connect with those of their colleagues' presentations. In her criticism of the inequality seminar, Donna said she thought there was too much emphasis on finishing presentations and not enough "conversation." This is another way of saying that participants did not have an opportunity to reflect out loud about the presentation of the day and make connections to their own work. It is ironic that several participants in the inequality seminar said the proceedings seemed to run out of ideas for sessions. The "empty" sessions could have been the conversations Donna was seeking, opportunities for participants to consider what they had heard from colleagues and to explore syntheses.

Creating Trust and Attending to Interpersonal Dynamics

One of the most important prerequisites for productive interdisciplinary dialogue is trust. Not only do differences in disciplinary style make it hard to establish trust, so too do differences in age, gender, national origin, and race. The inability to establish trust results in some people being out of other people's "comfort zone." This, in turn, leads to the development of factions that place severe restraints on fruitful conversations.

Joyce began the work of establishing trust by selecting participants who had reasonably good interpersonal skills and who she thought could work together. In addition, whenever there were interpersonal conflicts, she worked to smooth them over. She also established a norm of fairness by preventing people from monopolizing the conversation. And her willingness to pay attention to the feelings of participants who contacted her outside of the seminar created an environment of trust in that dissatisfied colleagues felt they had an ally in the leader.

Robert, Sheila, and Sam all were reasonably successful in creating trust among seminar participants, partly because of their own intellectual stature. But Nancy had difficulty creating an atmosphere of trust. Ahsan was probably correct that Nancy could have improved trust among participants had she taken groups of them to lunch (or coffee) separately and sought to help them iron out their disagreements and disaffections or even encouraged them to meet without her being present.

Additional Strategies to Nurture
Interdisciplinary Conversations

We come now to three additional strategies that are likely to diminish the effects of disciplinary cultures and habits of mind.

Specifically Discuss Disciplinary Cultures and Habits of Mind

Leaders of interdisciplinary conversations need to help participants understand and discuss the concepts of disciplinary cultures and habits of mind. If serious interdisciplinary collaboration is to result from faculty interactions, a primary task for participants is to become ethnographers of their own disciplines, encouraging one another to understand how their disciplines' habits of mind and cultural practices structure their thinking. Reading this book and several of the theoretical frameworks it cites would be a good way to begin.

Robert did deal indirectly with facets of disciplinary cultures by asking participants to read the Gulbenkian Report on the difficulties of getting social scientists to work together. But that report is exceedingly technical and doesn't directly discuss the concepts of disciplinary cultures or habits of mind.

At the beginning of the ethics seminar, Nancy tried to introduce the idea that faculty often fear presenting to colleagues outside their discipline because they are concerned about being misunderstood and that this apprehension becomes a barrier to interdisciplinary dialogue. But the effort to get discussion of that notion failed because Peter countered that if everyone spoke plainly there would be no need to fear being misunderstood. Nancy's efforts might have been more successful had she taken a sociological approach to the difficulties of interdisciplinary communication and introduced the concepts of disciplinary cultures rather than taking a psychological approach, which required faculty to acknowledge fears.

Allow Participants to Set Group Norms
and Vary Approaches to Learning

Once participants in an interdisciplinary conversation understand the concepts of disciplinary cultures and habits of mind and recognize that their own disciplinary norms are not necessarily shared by others, it is easy to introduce the notion that the group needs to devise its own norms.[10] To that end, the group needs to agree on answers to questions such as the following: How formal should presentations be? How much time should be allowed for presentation and how much for discussion? At what point in a presentation may a participant interrupt for clarification or argumentation? How sharply may presenters be questioned? What are the norms for civility? How are conflicts to be resolved?

Understanding habits of mind and disciplinary cultures also leads to awareness that any particular format is only one of many possible ways to organize presentations and conversations. At Jefferson, scientists introduced a bit of variety by having participants do lab visits, and dramatist Jane had her colleagues engage in some acting exercises. But artist Evelyn was unsuccessful in getting her colleagues to leave the classroom and come to her studio for her presentation.

Interdisciplinary discussions need to experiment with techniques for presentations and conversations that are not necessarily familiar to the leader—for example, discussing questions in small subgroups, sending groups of participants out to find answers to questions on their own, asking participants to role-play, having participants question one another one-on-one, or asking participants to write down a few ideas on any given topic and then share them with the group. In any interdisciplinary conversation, it is likely that one or another of these styles will in fact be a common way to interact with colleagues, a familiar habit of mind. The main point is to allow variation so that it is not only the leader's way of engaging in conversation that is used.

A pedagogical technique used in fiction-writing classes is to have the group read a group member's story in advance and then discuss it without any presentation by the author. The author's job is to be an active listener, taking careful notes on what his or her critics have to say. Only at the end of the session may the author speak, and then only to clarify comments that were unclear or raise questions that others did not.

After I learned this technique, I tried it in my doctoral dissertation workshop. The dynamics of the class changed entirely. There was no "defending" by the student whose work was being discussed, and students felt they learned a great deal about how to give and receive constructive feedback. I note this not only because I think it is a good technique, but also to inspire people who lead interdisciplinary conversations to experiment with multiple discussion formats. There is nothing sacred about the formats we learned as graduate students.

Seek Formative Evaluation Early in the Conversations

The use of formative evaluation is a third strategy that would have enhanced interdisciplinary learning in the conversations studied here. None of the leaders asked participants for a written anonymous evaluation early in the year, although several asked informally. However, just as a professor cannot casually ask students "off the record" how a course is going and necessarily get an honest answer, so too some leaders were mistaken when they assumed participants were satisfied just because they said they were in response to an offhand question. Leaders might have been able to make significant changes had they known early on the kinds of dissatisfactions participants had.

Conclusion

In Chapter 3, we met dramatist Jane, a participant in Jefferson's representation seminar. Troubled by the critical stance her colleagues took early in conversations, Jane said she preferred to "try on" ideas before she judged them. I noted that Jane's practice of ascertaining the truth of an idea by first trying it on is akin to what Peter Elbow calls the believing game, in which one follows the dictum "*credo ut intelligam:* I believe in order to understand."[11] The believing game may be contrasted with the doubting game, which ascertains truth by starting with doubt and deems a new idea worthy only if it is able to overcome an initial negative predisposition.

The doubting game is adversarial and seeks to ferret out error. The believing game is cooperative and seeks to unearth truth. In playing the believing game, one runs the risk of believing something that is untrue, but one increases the possibility of learning a surprising new truth. The reverse is the case with the doubting game; one reduces the possibility of believing something false, but increases the possibility of missing something not in accordance with one's initial prejudices that is in fact true (or useful).[12]

Playing the doubting game is one of academe's principal norms. Indeed, doubting new ideas and effectively arguing against them is often equated with being a serious scholar. But in interdisciplinary conversations, where one is seeking new truths in new intellectual territory, it is useful to play the believing game first. We have already discussed the value of having an interdisciplinary group specifically create its own norms. Choosing to play the believing game before the doubting game creates a new metanorm for the conversation.

For you, the reader, the believing game is also likely to be far less familiar than the doubting game. As you read these paragraphs on the advantages of the believing game, you might note the extent to which you yourself can defer relying on your usual habits of thought and disciplinary cultures and peruse with an open mind. It may be that you will have a direct experience of how difficult interdisciplinarity can be.

The believing game requires that participants in an interdisciplinary dialogue listen to one another with empathy.[13] It requires that they suspend their habits of mind and disciplinary cultures and listen so carefully and consistently that they begin to get into one another's heads. The believing game has to be played over a considerable period of time. It takes time for participants in an interdisciplinary conversation to suspend habits of mind and disciplinary cultures so that they can absorb new ideas and frameworks.

It also takes time to play the second stage of the believing game: connecting one's own disciplinary knowledge with ideas and frameworks being learned from other disciplines. It is in this second stage that a leader can play a significant role, specifically structuring sessions to allow participants to synthesize ideas and frameworks.

In the synthesis stage of the believing game, it is useful to think about the rules for improvisational acting. Improv actors, as they call themselves, think about cocreating scenes. Each builds on what their fellow actors have already completed. Each seeks to make their partner look brilliant. Each seeks to "serve the scene," not his or her own ego.[14]

Of course, some degree of doubting and assessing will take place at the synthesis stage of an interdisciplinary conversation. It is impossible to connect one's own disciplinary understandings with *all* the new ideas one has learned. One must make some judgments about which concepts and frameworks will be most interesting to pursue. Nonetheless, it is useful to continue in a brainstorming mode, not discarding new ideas prematurely.

The process of synthesizing ideas from disparate disciplines is unfamiliar and uncomfortable. But it is precisely in that discomfort that the seeds of creativity lie, and if the group can continue to play the believing game—not insisting on certainty, closure, or judgments—participants may ultimately move to new truths and imaginative solutions. It is instructive to imagine how some of the altercations and misunderstandings reported in the prior chapters might have played out differently had participants been committed to playing the believing game, listening with empathy rather than being quick to argue, attempting to build on one another's ideas rather than judge them.

For example, in the ethics conversation, Nabila and Peter spent the seminar talking past one another. Peter did not see any benefit to taking Nabila's postmodern perspectives into account; he put on his doubting hat quickly, saw her ideas as sloppy thinking, and began to question her in a way that made her uncomfortable. And Nabila was no more interested in seeking common ground than was Peter. His ideas were the very ones against which she had been taught to rebel.

Yet they could have learned from one another. Peter was interested in drawing generalizations that would apply as broadly as possible. Nabila was interested in *not* generalizing; to her, ethical issues were about the erasure of difference. Surely both their ideas are germane to the study of ethics. For example, in the ethics of politics, questions about balancing majority and minority rights originate precisely in debates about the need to protect subgroups from erasure while still allowing majority rule. The two perspectives also relate to ethical questions in the social sciences where quantitative researchers like to "throw out" outliers in order to reach more robust statistical generalizations and qualitative researchers believe a great deal can be learned by *not* throwing them out and instead investigating them carefully.

Had the seminar been playing the believing game, the difference in perspectives between Nabila and Peter could have been the start of a rich discussion about ethics in numerous situations, perhaps even a new collaboration. But playing the doubting game from the start foreclosed those possibilities.

One of the major reasons why interdisciplinarity is currently being encouraged is that cognitive diversity *can* enhance creativity and develop new solutions to complex problems.[15] Practicing the believing game before engaging in the more familiar doubting game might go a long way toward realizing the creative potential of interdisciplinary conversations.

Appendix: Details of the Study

USING A SEMISTRUCTURED INTERVIEW FORMAT, I TALKED with forty faculty members, at least six from each seminar, including all of the seminar leaders. The questions I asked are listed in Table A-3 and were approved by the Human Subjects Committee at Stanford. I also interviewed key administrators at each of the institutions. All interviewees who were audiotaped signed consent forms.

Thirty-two of the interviews were recorded and transcribed; in eight cases, I took notes as the respondent spoke to me. Before beginning to write, I read all of the interview transcripts several times to discern their major themes and selected quotes that were helpful in clarifying those themes. In editing quotes, I took out phrases like "kind of" and "sort of" and eliminated repetition. I use ellipsis points to indicate that I have eliminated a word, phrase, or sentence, and square brackets to indicate that I have added a word or phrase for clarity.

In some cases, the interviewees were people suggested by the seminar leaders because they had played a major role in the conversations. In other cases, I interviewed faculty suggested by other seminar participants. Table A-1 provides a summary of the seminars' organization, and Table A-2 provides a list of the interviewees in each seminar.

Most interviews lasted about one hour, but those with seminar leaders and several participants ran longer—between two and four hours. The interviews took place over a three-year period. For some participants, the conversations recounted were freshly in mind; for others, the incidents they recalled had occurred one or two years earlier.

I also read the reports of the note takers for the seminars at Washington and Jefferson, a number of the books and articles assigned in the various seminars, the intellectual biographies prepared by many participants, the three institutions' final reports to Atlantic Philanthropies, several proposals for new courses, the literature on interdisciplinarity, and books and articles that provide a theoretical framework for my findings.

TABLE A.1 Details About the Seminars

	1	2	3	4	5	6
Name	Washington—Social Sciences	Washington—Inequality	Adams—Science Studies	Adams—Ethics	Jefferson—Consilience	Jefferson—Representation
Proposal Writers	President and staff	President and staff	Dean of arts and sciences and a vice-provost	Dean of arts and sciences and a vice-provost	Joyce, professor of literature and dean of arts and sciences; Ed, professor of chemistry and provost	Joyce and Ed
Leader	Robert, professor of political science	Sheila, professor of economics	Nancy, Ph.D. in English (not a faculty member)	Nancy, Ph.D. in English (not a faculty member)	Joyce	Sam, professor of humanities, emeritus
Who chose participants?	Robert, in consultation with provost	Sheila, in consultation with provost	Dean of arts and sciences and a vice-provost	Dean of arts and sciences and a vice-provost	Joyce and Ed	Louise, professor of music and dean of arts and sciences, and Ed
Recorder	Neil, professor of anthropology	Neil, professor of anthropology	None	None	Staff member	Staff member
Faculty	18 tenured, including president and provost	18 tenured, including president, provost, and a vice provost	8 plus Nancy	9 plus Nancy	14 tenured, including provost and dean of arts and sciences	14 tenured, including dean of arts and sciences plus one artist in residence
Faculty fields	3 humanities 2 sciences 9 social sciences 2 law 2 history	3 humanities 1 sciences 13 social sciences: 1 law	2 humanities 2 sciences 2 social sciences 1 anthropology and history 1 philosophy and computer sciences	1 medicine 5 humanities 1 social sciences 1 law 1 history	5 humanities 3 sciences 4 social sciences 2 arts	5 humanities 3 sciences 4 social sciences 3 arts
Percentage women	28	33⅓	33⅓	40	29	53
Postdoctoral fellows	5	3	5	3	8	9
Number of meetings	24	26	19	24	26	25

TABLE A.2 Faculty in Sample

	1	2	3	4	5	6
Name of Seminar	Washington—Social Sciences	Washington—Inequality	Adams—Science Studies	Adams—Ethics	Jefferson—Consilience	Jefferson—Representation
Faculty Participants	Evan—professor of sociology	Brian—professor of psychology	Fred—professor of biology	Ahsan—associate professor of religious studies	Amita—professor of physics	Barry—professor of mathematics
	Karen—professor of law	Donna—professor of sociology	Jack—professor of economics	Ari—associate professor of history	Ed—professor of chemistry and provost	Ed—professor of chemistry
	Neil—professor of anthropology	Karl—professor of political science	Larry—professor of anthropology and history	George—assistant professor of law	Joel—associate professor of music	Evelyn—associate professor of fine arts
	Nick—professor of limnology	Matt—professor of economics	Martin—professor of psychology	James—professor of medicine	Joyce—professor of literature	Jane—artist-in-residence, theater
	Robert—professor of political science	Neil—professor of anthropology	Nancy -Ph.D., English (not a faculty member)	Liz—assistant professor of languages	Leon—director of corporate and foundation relations	Joyce—professor of literature
	President and provost	Omar—professor of economics	William—professor of mathematics	Nabila—assistant professor of English	Louise—professor of music and dean of arts and sciences	Leon—director of corporate and foundation relations
		Sheila—professor of economics		Nancy—Ph.D., English (not a faculty member)	Sam—professor of humanities, emeritus	Louise—professor of music and dean of arts and sciences
		President and provost		Peter—professor of philosophy	Victor—professor of biochemistry	Sam—professor of humanities, emeritus
				Sarah—professor of political science		

TABLE A.3 Questionnaire for Study on Interdisciplinary Seminars

1. What was your interest in being in the interdisciplinary seminar?
2. What do you see as the most important issues that the seminar dealt with?
3. As you look back, what has the seminar meant for you?
4. What were the seminar's most difficult moments? Exciting moments?
5. How did you think the seminar leader did in leading the seminar?
6. Did the seminar have any effects that you are aware of on your teaching? Research? Or just the way you think about the world?
7. If you had it to do over again, would you participate in the seminar? Why or why not?
8. Has your institution built in any way on the interdisciplinary seminar?
9. Are there any other things about the seminar that you would like to talk about?
10. Is there anything I should have asked about the interdisciplinary seminar that I didn't?

Notes

Chapter 1

An earlier version of several of the ideas in this book may be found in Strober (2006).

1. These students were not alone among qualitative researchers who have difficulty with quantitative work. Michèle Lamont, in her study of academics who served on panels to evaluate proposals from multiple disciplines, quoted the following from a cultural anthropologist: "There's certainly a number of anthropologists, including some very influential ones, [who] look askance at people who work with numbers, and tend to be dismissive" (2009: 90).

2. I have spent the vast majority of my forty-plus years in academia at Stanford's School of Education. I have also spent a good deal of time at Stanford's Graduate School of Business. Both of these are ostensibly interdisciplinary places with faculty from a wide variety of the social sciences. But, in fact, few faculty members at either school are interdisciplinary. Many of us, myself included, have a doctorate in a particular social science discipline. But, with only a few exceptions, even those who have a doctorate in education or business do their work in a particular social science discipline—economics, psychology, sociology, anthropology, or political science—and train their doctoral students to work in that same discipline. And when their doctoral students complete their degrees and go on to the academic job market, they are not recruited as scholars of education or business, but as disciples of a particular field—education psychology, the economics of education, finance, marketing, or organization behavior. Wolfram Swoboda mentions this challenge to interdisciplinarity in the field of education: "Even academic areas that by definition would seem to call for an interdisciplinary approach—such as education—have been recast in a disciplinary mold" (1979: 81).

3. Taylor (2009).

4. Jacobs and Frickel (2009); Jacobs (2009).

5. Klein (1990: 195).

6. See Amey and Brown (2004); Caruso and Rhoten (2001); Davis (1995); Frost and Jean (2003); Hollingsworth and Hollingsworth (2000); Scerri (2000); Lamont (2009); Lattuca (2001); and Stokols and Hall et al. (2008). There have also been studies of "big science," such as the Manhattan Project. For a listing of these, see Scerri (2000: 194).

7. National Academy of Sciences (2005: 3).

8. See Stokols and Hall et al. (2008: S78).

9. Of course, it is true, as Jerry Jacobs and Scott Frickel point out (2009: 48), that collaboration among faculty can also be difficult even within a single discipline; the contention here is that collaborating across disciplines adds another layer of difficulties on top of those involved in single-discipline collaboration.

10. See Feller (2002, 2007); Brint (2005); Sá (2008); and Jacobs and Frickel (2009).

11. Giving to Stanford. "The Stanford Challenge." https://thestanfordchallenge. stanford.edu, accessed January 28, 2010.

12. University of Southern California, Office of the Provost. "Strategic Planning." http://www.usc.edu/admin/provost/strategicplan/, accessed January 28, 2010.

13. Purdue University. "2008–2014 Strategic Plan." http://www.purdue.edu/strategic_plan/, accessed January 28, 2010.

14. Gregorian (2004).

15. National Institute of Medicine (2003).

16. The seminars studied here were initial stages in interdisciplinary dialogues. Some such initial conversations are purely faculty-initiated and do not make use of outside funding. Others are initiated by calls for proposals from foundations or government agencies, or by university administrators offering seed money. Many are simultaneously bottom-up and top-down, resulting from long-term conversations among faculty, administrators, and funders. This was the case for the three proposals funded by Atlantic.

17. Geertz (1983: 160–161).

18. In their chapter on interdisciplinary groups and cognitive processes, Angela O'Donnell and Sharon Derry (2005: 59) cite I. D. Steiner's (1972) typology of group tasks. Using that typology, the group product the six groups studied here were asked to produce would be called "additive," the category of product requiring the least amount of coordination and collaboration. O'Donnell and Derry's example of an additive group product is a clean house that is produced by a group of house cleaners, each working independently. But even a clean house is more of a group product than the products desired from the six groups studied here.

19. Interdisciplinary faculty seminars closest to those funded by Atlantic were those funded at Emory University by the Luce Foundation over an eight-year period, from 1989 to 1996. In 2003, Susan Frost and Paul Jean published an article, based on interviews with twenty-five seminar participants, which discussed outcomes but not the interactions that took place during the seminars.

20. This is why researchers who study team science examine the affective side of interdisciplinary collaborations as well as their scientific outcomes. See Stokols and Hall et al. (2008: S78). Whether there are associations between intellectual insights and either enjoyment or seminar tone is unclear. The literature, though sparse, indicates that more enjoyable group processes produce better group outcomes, but the reasons for this relationship are not understood. However, in this study there was no group outcome, and as we shall see, some faculty who found their conversations difficult nonetheless obtained important intellectual insights, while others who said their conversations were reasonably enjoyable reported that the lack of productive conflict limited their learning. See Amey and Brown (2004); Derry and Schunn (2005); Mansilla (2006); Klein (2008); and Stokols and Hall et al. (2008: S81).

Chapter 2

1. As Carol Folt, dean of the Faculty of Arts and Sciences at Dartmouth put it: "Complex problems don't respect disciplinary boundaries" (Knapp, 2006: 1).

2. One way of ascertaining the amount of interdisciplinarity that already exists is to examine citation patterns. However, such patterns depend heavily on the set of disciplines in the study and how finely or broadly they are defined. A study of citation patterns in 1997, published by the National Science Foundation in 2000, across eleven broadly defined fields (physics, chemistry, earth and space sciences, mathematics, biology, biomedical research, clinical medicine, engineering and technology, psychology, social sciences, and miscellaneous other fields) found that among social science citations, 22.7 percent were from outside of the social sciences, mostly to articles in the health and professional fields, psychology, and clinical medicine. Among physics citations, only 18 percent were outside of the discipline, mostly to articles in chemistry and engineering and technology. It is, of course, not possible to state whether these figures are high or low, "good" or "bad," although it will be interesting to see how they change over time. National Science Foundation (2000: A412).

3. See Davis (1995: 35–42) for arguments in favor of interdisciplinarity in the classroom.

4. Klein (1990: 104).

5. "Instructive community" and "communication network": Davis (1995: 25–26), citing King and Brownell (1966: 67–95); "cultural system": Geertz (1983); personal identity: Becher (1987) and Abbot (2002: 206, 210); Geertz (1983); Becher (1987) and Abbott (2002: 206, 210).

6. See Klein (1990: 19–20); Davis (1995: 27); Swoboda (1979: 52); and Kockelmans (1979: 13–14). I present only a capsule version of the history of disciplines. For greater detail, see Klein (1990); Moran (2002); and Swoboda (1979).

7. Moran (2002: 3–4). Edward O. Wilson (1999: 4) argues that it was philosopher Thales of Miletus, in sixth-century B.C. Ionia, who put forth the idea of "the unity of the sciences . . . that the world is orderly and can be explained by a small number of

natural laws." Wilson notes that the physicist and historian of science Gerald Holton termed this idea the "Ionian Enchantment."

8. Descartes, Comte, and Kant all took this view of philosophy. See Moran (2002: 8–9).

9. See Davis (1995: 27) and Lattuca (2001: 5).

10. Swoboda (1979: 54–56).

11. Moran (2002: 6).

12. These were not universities (they had no students), but rather collections of prestigious scholars. The Royal Academy in England is an example of such a science academy. See Swoboda (1979: 58).

13. Moran (2002: 6–7).

14. Moran (2002: 11).

15. Davis (1995: 29).

16. Lisa Lattuca (2001: 5) notes that the first academic departments were formed at Harvard and the University of Virginia in the 1820s.

17. The power of the idea of disciplinary departments may be seen in the demise of several efforts to organize knowledge in a more interdisciplinary fashion: the Department of Social Relations at Harvard, which ended in 1970 after about twenty-five years; the University of California at Irvine's School of Social Sciences, which ended in 1990 after about thirty years; and the efforts of the University of California at Santa Cruz to organize around interdisciplinary colleges rather than departments, which ended in the 1990s, also after about thirty years. See Smelser (2004: 51–52). On the other hand, it would be wrong to conclude that disciplines map neatly into departments. Burton Clark (1995: 142) noted that "in one university . . . the subject area of 'biology' is spread across thirteen discipline-based departments and seventeen interdisciplinary programs" (quoted in Klein [2000: 17]).

18. Toward the end of his life, Nietzsche became concerned about the growth of disciplines and questioned whether by limiting the knowledge scholars pursued they would, in fact, achieve greater knowledge. He thought scholars seemed mostly interested in their own well-being rather than in the pursuit of knowledge. He also was sorry to see the decline of philosophy as an umbrella discipline. See Moran (2002: 11–12).

19. See Sá (2008: 539).

20. Neil Smelser (2004) quotes Christopher Jencks and David Riesman (1968: 523) as saying that "a discipline is at bottom nothing more than an administrative category." None of this should be taken to mean that disciplines do not change. They not only change from within, forming new subspecialties, but also proliferate. See Abbott (2001) and Smelser (2004).

21. Turner (2000: 51).

22. Tony Becher and Paul Trowler (2001: 41) also note that just because a department exists doesn't mean that its field is a discipline. Their added criterion is not the job market that Stephen Turner (2000) uses, but rather "international currency," which has a similar connotation.

23. Of course, socialization of doctoral students in any given discipline differs according to the particular department in which they receive their training and the particular disciplinary specialty they pursue. In economics, for example, those who trained at the University of Chicago and work in the field of monetary economics have had a quite different socialization from those educated at MIT or Harvard who work in the field of labor economics. Nonetheless, in both situations they will have read similar foundational materials and will have learned "to think like an economist." For an alternative view, see Amariglio, Resnick, and Wolff (1993), which argues that there is no unified discipline of economics.

24. Messer-Davidow, Shumway, and Sylvan (1993: 4).

25. Lenoir (1993: 72).

26. For more on these differences, see Lattuca (2001); Klein (2000); and Smelser (2004: 48–50).

27. Mansilla (2006: 18–19).

28. Joe Moran adds another element to the definition: "a radical questioning of the nature of knowledge itself and our attempts to organize and communicate it" (2002: 15). It is this definition that underlies Messer-Davidow, Shumway, and Sylvan (1993).

29. National Academy of Sciences (2005: 2).

30. In 1981, the European Centre for Higher Education (CPES) organized a symposium on interdisciplinarity in higher education in Europe and sought to define *interdisciplinarity, multidisciplinarity,* and *transdisciplinarity.* Earlier in that same year, UNESCO also sought to define the terms. Basically, they agree with the definitions I have given. See European Centre for Higher Education (1983: 21–22). However, not all authors agree with these definitions. For example, Stephen Jay Kline defines multidisciplinarity as the study of "the appropriate relationship of the disciplines to each other and to the larger intellectual terrain" (1995: 2).

31. Piaget (1972: 138).

32. Also see Julie Thompson Klein (1990: 66), which discusses transdisciplinarity as an unattainable "interconnectedness of all aspects of reality."

33. Stokols and Misra et al. (2008: S97).

34. See Gibbons et al. (1994) and Klein (2008: S117).

35. Lisa Lattuca notes another metaphor, created by F. A. Rossini and A. L. Porter (1984), to differentiate interdisciplinary and multidisciplinary work: "a seamless woven garment that stands in contrast to the patchwork quilt" (Lattuca 2001: 11).

36. For a history of the concept of transdisciplinarity in Europe and in the medical sciences, see Kessel and Rosenfield (2008).

37. For additional discussion, see Fuller (1988). Moreover, as Klein (2008) points out, a group may be cross-disciplinary, interdisciplinary, *and* transdisciplinary at various stages of its work.

38. Thomas Paxson (1996) distinguishes twenty-five different types of integration at four different levels. James Davis also provides detailed examples of the difference between serial team teaching with virtually no integration among faculty and courses

that are "both planned and delivered by a group of faculty working closely as a team" (1995: 7).

39. See DellaVigna (2009) for a review of these developments.

40. Klein (1996: 62) cites the use by chemists of mass-spectroscopy, originally developed by physicists.

41. English professor Diane Middlebrook and I taught an interdisciplinary course on women's choices at Stanford and used economic theory to examine several novels, including Jane Austen's *Pride and Prejudice,* Toni Morrison's *Beloved,* and Colette's *Cheri and the Last of Cheri.*

42. Jacobs and Frickel (2009: 45).

43. Stokols and Misra et al. (2008: S97).

44. See Paxson (1996), which makes this argument forcefully. But see also Sill (1996: 129), which notes that we know very little about *how* to teach students to integrate their knowledge over multiple disciplines.

45. Rogers, Scaife, and Rizzo (2005: 265–285).

46. See Lattuca (2001: 15). As a practitioner of both women's studies and feminist economics, I find these issues of particular interest. Ellen Messer-Davidow (2002) argues persuasively that women's studies has not become a discipline precisely because it has not integrated perspectives from multiple disciplines. Feminist economics does not seek to become a discipline, but it uses other disciplines (anthropology, history, sociology, philosophy, and psychology) to critique economics. See Ferber and Nelson (1993); Strober (1994); Kuiper and Sap (1995); and Ferber and Nelson (2003).

47. Lattuca (2001: 18).

48. Sill (1996: 130).

49. For example, James R. Davis (1995) confined his discussion of interdisciplinary courses to those that were team-taught.

50. When education historian David Tyack and I worked together, we used one another's disciplinary insights and published two joint articles (Strober and Tyack [1980] and Tyack and Strober [1981]), but mostly we wrote separately. All of our publications, however, benefited from our collaboration.

51. Abbott (2001: 131–136). Andrew Abbott argues that the interest in interdisciplinarity remained fairly constant during the last forty years of the twentieth century.

52. Rogers Hollingsworth and Ellen Jane Hollingsworth note that "from the very beginning, the Institute did not organize the production of knowledge around academic disciplines, as was increasingly the case in major universities" (2000: 223).

53. Klein (1990: 24) and Abbott (2002: 213).

54. Jacobs and Frickel (2009: 48). Also see Klein (1990:22–39); Davis (1995: 6); and Sherif and Sherif (1969). Hugh Petrie (1976) describes an interdisciplinary effort at the Sloan Program of the College of Engineering at the University of Illinois to look at how social sciences and humanities might best fit into the curriculum in engineering.

55. Klein (1990: 36–37).

56. Brint et al. (2009: 170). The major fields at colleges and universities that

were organized as interdisciplinary teaching programs (listed here by number of such programs) were non-Western cultural studies, race and ethnic studies, Western studies, environmental studies, international/global studies, women's studies, American studies, and brain and biomedical science (Brint et al., 2009: 164). As Brint notes, most of these programs were outside of the sciences, and many relate to underrepresented populations within the United States and to underrepresented areas of the world.

57. Jacobs and Frickel (2009: 44–45).

58. Brint et al. (2009: 45). Also see Brint (2005: 31); Stokols and Misra et al. (2008: S96); Kessel and Rosenfield (2008: S228); National Academy of Sciences (2005); and AAU (2005).

59. Sá (2008: 547).

60. Sá (2008: 545–46).

61. Brint (2005: 44) reports that 80 percent of the public and private research universities in his sample said they were developing interdisciplinary projects in the sciences and about two-thirds said they were doing so in the other fields.

62. Brint (2005: 46).

63. Jerry Jacobs and Scott Frickel (2009) argue strongly that the connection between interdisciplinarity and creativity needs empirical validation.

64. Irwin Feller (2006: 8) notes that some of this increase in interest may well have been a response by university administrators to the availability of new funding for interdisciplinarity. For example, in recent years, the National Institutes of Health and the National Science Foundation (NSF) have established several interdisciplinary center programs, including a program by the NSF, the Integrated Graduate and Education Research Training Program, to promote interdisciplinarity in graduate education.

65. See Brint (2005: 39–40).

66. Smelser also agrees with this assessment (2004: 64). And based on a large study of interdisciplinarity at research universities, Sá (2008: 550) concludes that it is highly unlikely that such institutions will give up their disciplinary structures, in large part because they are successful at creating complex interdisciplinary research structures that exist side by side with traditional departments.

67. In her study of faculty who engage in interdisciplinary work, Lattuca found that they continued to also work in their own disciplines. "Most individuals sought to balance disciplinary and interdisciplinary ways of knowing. . . . Many noted the lasting impact of their disciplinary training" (2001: 211, 223).

68. Klein (2005: 47). Jacobs and Frickel cite a study of more than thirteen hundred faculty, 70 percent of whom think that "interdisciplinary knowledge is better than knowledge obtained by a single discipline" (2009: 46). It appears that interdisciplinarity has taken on the aura of a fad in higher education, and some faculty who want to be seen as "up-to-date" therefore say they support it. In my view, it adds little to our understanding of knowledge production to compare the "goodness" of single-discipline versus multidiscipline knowledge, in the same way that it makes little sense to

ask whether qualitative or quantitative knowledge is "better." The kind of knowledge needed depends on the question (or questions) being asked.

69. As sources of funding for research from federal agencies have become more scarce since the middle of the first decade of the twenty-first century, these agencies, while continuing to laud interdisciplinary work, have begun to debate the proper percentage of funding that should go to it. Feller quotes the following from a National Research Council report: "In times of tight budgets, however, it is difficult to justify moving money away from already-squeezed disciplinary research programs that have consistently produced outstanding results" (2006: 7).

70. March (1991).

71. Wolfram Swoboda makes a similar point, arguing that pursuing disciplinary research or teaching is far more efficient than interdisciplinary work because "it is directed toward narrow goals promising short-term results," but that "efficiency is at best a secondary aim in education—that some things are done better inefficiently" (1979: 80). He notes that many of the great scientific discoveries were made not by using what March would call exploitation, but rather through exploration, including Darwin's voyage on the *Beagle*. Disciplines are also efficient in that they make it possible for a scholar to feel comfortable with only incomplete knowledge of a subject. As Abbott put it, "Disciplines . . . define what it is permissible not to know" (2002: 210).

72. None of this is to say that all new knowledge comes from interdisciplinary work. That is hardly the case. The exploitation/exploration dichotomy as well as the stock/bond dichotomy are merely metaphorical, and March's analysis is based on a nonempirical simulation. There exists no empirical validation of the relative roles of disciplinarity and interdisciplinarity in the creation of new knowledge and the solving of problems.

73. Adam Smith [1776] (1976: 539).

74. Mill [1848] (1957: 581).

75. Leigh Thompson (2000: 151).

76. It is interesting that at the same time that interdisciplinarity is heralded, collaboration in general, including within disciplines, is also increasing. In a study of almost 20 million papers and 2 million patents over the last five decades, Stefan Wuchty, Benjamin Jones, and Brian Uzzi (2007) found that the number of authors has increased in all fields and in almost all subfields. The authors report that in 2000, in mathematics, almost 60 percent of papers were written by a team, and in the social sciences slightly more than half of all papers were produced by teams. Only in the arts and humanities did single authorship remain the norm, with team authorship accounting for only 10 percent of published papers. Seeking to explain their findings, they note that one factor driving multiple authorship may be the increased specialization of scholars, which requires them to seek additional and more diverse collaborators. Also, the authors note that team-authored papers were more likely to be cited than were individually authored papers (even after correcting for self-citation, which is likely to be greater with more than one author). If frequent citation is a mark of a paper's creativity, team-authored papers appear to be more innovative on average than are single-authored papers.

77. David Sill (1996: 137) makes a similar argument. And he notes: "It is boundary crossing that makes possible the redefinition of the boundaries themselves" (1996: 142).

78. Leigh Thompson (2000: 154).

79. In some ways the case for interdisciplinarity is similar to the "integration and learning perspective" argument in favor of increasing racial and gender diversity in a work group. Robin Ely and David Thomas summarize that perspective as follows: "The insights, skills, and experiences employees have developed as members of various cultural identity groups are potentially valuable resources that the work group can use to rethink its primary tasks . . . in ways that will advance its mission" (2001: 240).

80. Burt (2004: 349–350).

81. Hollingsworth and Hollingsworth (2000: 226–228).

82. Caruso and Rhoten (2001: 15).

83. Dogan and Pahre (1990: 1). Using a more restrictive definition of innovation than Dogan and Pahre did, namely, "an advance that makes a substantial contribution," Karl Deutsch, John Platt, and Dieter Senghaas (1986: 414) observed that over a sixty-five-year period beginning in 1900, slightly more than half (55 percent) of social science innovations were interdisciplinary. As might be expected, the metrics Deutsch and his colleagues used to classify innovations in the social sciences did not go unquestioned. For example, Alex Inkeles argues that "their list stresses innovative thinking and seminal ideas more than the growth of knowledge" (1986: 14).

84. Page (2007: 303); Page (2007: 314).

85. Feller (2007: 46).

86. Abbott (2002: 215).

87. Lucy Shapiro's talk to my graduate seminar on interdisciplinarity, May 17, 2005.

88. Brint notes that institutions themselves have become an extremely important source of funds for faculty research. He estimates that they account for about 20 percent of total research funding (2005: 41). Sá discusses several strategies that research universities use to stimulate interdisciplinary work: competitions for seed money grants, "'steering structures' that oversee and coordinate resources in broad segments of the university, encompassing a multitude of academic units" (2008: 544), and new methods of recruiting and evaluating faculty.

89. See Derry and Schunn (2005: xv).

90. However, in one study youth appears to be a positive influence on the decision to pursue interdisciplinary work. In a study of researchers working on five interdisciplinary projects funded by the National Science Foundation, Rhoten and Parker (2004) found that young faculty and graduate students were much more likely to be involved in interdisciplinary work than were their senior colleagues.

91. In her study of faculty panels evaluating multidisciplinary projects, Michèle Lamont found that faculty used "existing disciplinary standards" to evaluate proposals and commented: "This may mean that at the end of the day, interdisciplinary scholarship is evaluated through several disciplinary lenses" (2009: 211).

92. See Mansilla and Gardner (2010).

93. See National Academy of Sciences (2005: chaps. 4 and 5).

94. See Mansilla and Gardner (2010) on faculty concerns about evaluating the quality of interdisciplinary work. See Amey and Brown (2004) on the disjuncture between the kinds of faculty behavior required for interdisciplinary work and the kind of behavior that research universities reward. One of the problems for young scientists is that interdisciplinary work must generally be submitted to center competitions that require monumental expenditures of time and effort; if federal agencies were to consider more small interdisciplinary proposals, young faculty might be more interested in submitting them (see Feller, 2006: 10).

95. Jacobs and Frickel (2009: 51) ask if there is a citation penalty for publishing in interdisciplinary journals and note that there is not much research on the question. Although one study points to the absence of a penalty, that result obtains only after quality of journal is accounted for. As they point out, since the quality of the journals for interdisciplinary work tends to be lower than those for work in single disciplines, holding quality of journal constant does not really answer the question posed.

96. For more on institutions' efforts to revise their institutional cultures as well as their hiring and promotion processes for interdisciplinary scholars, see Pfirman et al. (2005) and Derry and Schunn (2005: xvii). Also see Brint (2005); AAU (2005); National Academy of Sciences (2005); and Sá (2008).

97. Evaluation of interdisciplinary research is a complex problem that has only recently received systematic attention from researchers. In her study of interdisciplinary panel evaluations of research proposals, Lamont (2009) found that scholars accorded disciplinary deference to colleagues who came from the same discipline as the proposal writer. In 2006, the journal *Research Evaluation* devoted a special issue to the topic of evaluation of interdisciplinary work. For a summary of those papers, see Mansilla, Feller, and Gardner (2006). In another article in that special issue, Mansilla (2006: 17) pointed out that although some interdisciplinary research is evaluated according to the traditional outcome criteria of journal articles and citations, other such research is evaluated in terms of the degree to which it achieves integration. Also in that special issue, Feller (2006) discussed the role of the National Research Council ranking system for doctoral programs in constraining the development of interdisciplinarity in research universities. The National Academy of Sciences study *Facilitating Interdisciplinary Research* called for "the creation of journals that are dedicated to publishing research at the intersection of two or more fields" (2005: 140). In 2008, the *American Journal of Preventive Medicine* also published a special issue on the topic of interdisciplinary research with several articles on evaluation.

98. In the words of the National Academy of Sciences report, interdisciplinary research "is typically collaborative and involves people of disparate backgrounds. Thus, it may take extra time for building consensus and for learning new methods, languages, and cultures" (2005: 2–3).

99. Sharon Derry and Christina Schunn (2005: xviii) also note that funding for

interdisciplinary teaching programs is more unstable than for departmental programs and may well dry up in economically difficult periods.

100. Jacobs and Frickel (2009: 50–51) point to postmodernism, actor-network
theory, and the statistical technique of survival analysis as examples of such ideas and
methods.

101. Lattuca (2001).

102. See Boxer (1998; 2000); Rojas (2007); and Olzak and Kangas (2008).

Chapter 3

1. The proposal had also indicated that there would be a participant-observer
at the seminar who would keep notes of the proceedings. However, Adams did not
choose a faculty member to be a participant-observer or reporter, nor did Nancy or
seminar members assign such a person. Thus, Nancy's reports to Atlantic Philanthropies are the only written record of the Adams seminars.

2. The dean decided which departments would have postdocs, and particular
candidates were chosen by those departments. Participants were supposed to have at
least one course off whether or not they had a postdoc. In the science studies seminar,
the postdocs began meeting once a week by themselves and continued this all year.
The following year the postdocs in the ethics seminar continued this tradition.

3. Geertz (1983: 152–153).

4. Geertz (1983: 155).

5. Geertz (1983: 158).

6. Though not from an anthropological perspective, Edward Wilson (1999) also
provides a useful discussion of the difference among disciplines, particularly science
versus humanities, and social sciences with respect to crossing disciplinary boundaries. But Wilson is interested in consilience, a particular (and peculiar) kind of interdisciplinarity in which all knowledge is subsumed under the sciences.

7. Becher and Trowler (2001: 23).

8. Becher and Trowler (2001: 47).

9. Becher (1989: 23).

10. An interesting study by T. Gerholm (1985) from Linkoping University, cited by
Becher and Trowler (2001: 49–50), looks at how doctoral students are socialized and
argues that doctoral students need to learn not only the subject matter of their discipline but also its "tacit knowledge," ranging from how reports should look to how to
answer faculty questions about career goals and how to collaborate (or compete) with
fellow students. This tacit knowledge comes not through instruction, but through
interaction and observation.

11. For a critical review of this theoretical and empirical literature, see Braxton
and Hargens (1996).

12. The investigative category includes the sciences and engineering as well as
mathematics and economics. The artistic category includes the fine arts, architecture,
foreign languages, and English. The social category includes the humanities (includ-

ing philosophy), psychology, and all of the social sciences except anthropology. The enterprising category includes business and management, communications and journalism, computer and information science, law, and public affairs. See Smart, Feldman, and Ethington (2000: 59–60).

13. See Lattuca (2001).

14. Margolis (1993: 7). Also see O'Donnell and Derry (2005: 74), citing Sjölander, who outlined ten separate stages of development that individuals in interdisciplinary groups must go through before they can overcome their radically different perspectives and begin productive discussions.

15. Margolis (1993: 25).

16. Margolis (1993: 17).

17. Margolis (1993: 36).

18. It is important to recognize, however, that disciplines are not necessarily monolithic with respect to epistemologies and methods. For example, as we shall see in Chapter 6, there is a major split within sociology between quantitative and qualitative scholars and between those who do positive social science and those who are interested in action research. Still, most sociologists who do qualitative work have also been exposed to quantitative work in their training, and vice versa.

19. See Amey and Brown (2004: 100) for a list of terms and a summary of this literature.

20. Michèle Lamont also contrasts history and economics. "Unlike history . . . where the basis for unity is a shared sense of craftsmanship in research, economists' cohesion is grounded in a cognitive unification" (2009: 100).

21. See Klein (1990); Broome (2000); and Cronon (2006).

22. Cronon (2006: 331); Cronon (2006: 331–332).

23. Lamont (2009: 80).

24. Calhoun (1992: 186).

25. Bulick (1982: 124).

26. Lattuca (2001: 200).

27. Leijonhufvud (1973: 329).

28. Leijonhufvud (1973: 327–328).

29. In economics seminars I have attended throughout my career, the questioning is always sharp. The underlying theory behind aggressive questioning seems to be that if presenters know in advance that they will be questioned antagonistically, they will be more likely to prepare carefully, make sure there are no errors in their models and regressions, and refrain from unwarranted speculation beyond what the data and analyses support.

30. Also see Lamont (2009: 100–102).

31. Margolis (1993: 18).

32. Becher and Trowler (2001: 127).

33. Becher and Trowler (2001: 127).

34. Despite this, mathematician Robert Osserman (2004) argues that the public perception that mathematicians work alone is incorrect. "Usually mathematics is a

highly social activity, with collaboration between two or more individuals the rule rather than the exception." Becher and Trowler found mathematicians in their sample to be both social and solitary: "Many of the solitary-seeming mathematicians placed considerable stress on the need to talk over their problems with other people," but sometimes mathematical problems "can call for an intense, essentially individual effort of concentration" (2001: 125).

35. Hymes (1972).

36. Margolis (1993: 36).

37. Eisner (1982: 49).

38. The critical stance that troubled Jane is one of the new developments in literary studies that Michèle Lamont (2009: 72) discusses in her study, arguing that part of the process of decanonizing the canon has been "a critique of privileging the written text." Jane's desire to try on ideas rather than criticize them can be seen as a plea for returning to a privileging of the written text.

39. It is perhaps not accidental that it was a dramatist who held the "try it on" view. One of the first rules of improvisational acting is to always say "yes" to one's improv partner. If one's partner says, "Please sit down here," the only response that keeps the scene going is "Okay." Saying, "But there is no chair here," spoils the scene at once.

40. Coleridge [1817] (1968).

41. Elbow (1973: 149).

42. Elbow (1973: 161).

43. Elbow (1973: 163).

Chapter 4

1. Yankelovich (1999: 152–153).

2. Nancy had recommended that the number of postdocs be reduced in the second year so as to increase the ratio of senior faculty to postdocs, but with the inclusion of three junior faculty in the second year and leaving Nancy out of the ratio for both years, the ratio of senior to junior people in the second-year seminar was lower than it had been the first year (1.0 in the second year versus 1.6 in the first).

3. Although Peter used the male pronoun in speaking about the opportunity to fund a postdoc, in fact the postdoc he chose was a woman.

4. Peter was perhaps not aware that "speaking plainly" is not a universal norm among academics, and that, indeed, among postmodernists speaking plainly is not seen as desirable. Unraveling complexity, they believe, requires analysis that is not always clear at first reading or hearing.

5. Jerry Jacobs raises an interesting issue about disputes in general between English and philosophy and asks if perhaps Richard Whitley is right in asserting that one reason why "English and philosophy can maintain so much dissensus [is] because resources, though valuable and much sought after, are not indispensable" (2009: 4). In other words, when disciplinary proponents need to cooperate in order to get money for their research, they may be much more inclined to see one another's perspectives

than when, as in the case of English and philosophy, grant money is not really necessary to their projects.

6. See Mâsse et al. (2008: S151).

7. Lencioni (2003: 36).

8. Lencioni (2003: 36).

9. See Cozzens and Gieryn (1990).

10. Craig Calhoun cites several factors that he believes contribute to border patrolling, including the movement away from "scholarship (the mastery of traditional learning) towards research (production of 'new knowledge') [and] the growth and bureaucratization of funding sources" (1992: 139).

11. Derrida (1995: 419–420), as quoted in Moran (2002: 91).

12. Amariglio, Resnick, and Wolff (1993). What constitutes "real" economics according to mainstream economists is not subject matter but what Neil Smelser calls economics' "distinctive psychological postulates—such as optimization" (2004: 49).

13. Lamont (2009: 89, 88).

14. See Amariglio, Resnick, and Wolff (1993) concerning the efforts to keep economics "scientific." Steve Fuller notes that as compared to histories of other social sciences, "histories of economics seem to be most preoccupied with the scientific status of the discipline" (1993: 139). Fuller is suspicious of the science/nonscience dichotomy and argues that the attempt to find "properties common to all disciplines deemed scientific . . . may be an enterprise doomed to failure" (1993: 127).

15. Abbott (2001: 210).

16. Smith (1999: 68).

17. Yankelovich (1999: 41–43).

18. Studies of groups find it is common for individuals with low status to retreat from group discussions. See O'Donnell and Derry (2005: 64).

19. This same issue was at the root of the fight the year before between the postdoc from religious studies and the economist in the science studies seminar.

20. A quotation from a philosopher in Lamont's sample of academics on interdisciplinary evaluation panels makes a similar point. It is particularly interesting that this philosopher contrasts the norms of disputation for the discipline of philosophy with those of English, precisely the discipline from which Nabila came. "Philosophy differs from other disciplines because there's much more of a sense of argumentation or debate. . . . When you give a paper in philosophy, you give a paper and then you have an hour of people trying to find what's wrong with it. [The debates are] very clear, obvious, and not at all, so to speak, elegant." By contrast, "in English or in comparative literature . . . the discussion is, generally speaking, less ruthless" (Lamont, 2009: 65–66).

21. Based on their use of the term *dominant personality types,* one thinks, on first reading, that John Smart and his colleagues, in empirically testing Holland's theory of disciplinary differences, are testing whether there is an association between individual personality and disciplinary affect. Summarizing the results of their studies, they say that people choose fields of study "that parallel their dominant personality types"

(Smart, Feldman, and Ethington, 2000: 110). But a careful look at the construct they use to measure personality type indicates that it is a measure of abilities and interests, not affect. It is surely the case that different disciplines attract people with different abilities and interests. Whether they attract people with particular kinds of affect is not addressed in Smart's test of Holland's disciplinary categories.

22. Becher and Trowler (2001: xiii). In my own experience, many economists, especially women but not only women, including myself, have often noted that we don't use the ruthless style of seminar questioning that we see in many of our male colleagues. This is not to say, of course, that no women economists use a ruthless style of questioning or that all men economists do use it.

23. Hodgson (2004).

24. According to Becher and Trowler, "Merton (1973) canonizes the phenomenon as 'organized skepticism,' one of his four basic norms of scientific behaviour" (Becher and Trowler, 2001: 97).

25. For a recent review of the social psychology and sociology literature on the functioning of groups, see O'Donnell and Derry (2005: 54–58).

26. John Thompson (1991: 14).

27. John Thompson (1991: 14).

28. See Schwartzman (1989).

29. John Thompson (1991: 12).

30. Collins (1998: 76).

31. Leigh Thompson defines affective conflict as "personal, defensive, and resentful." Cognitive conflict is "largely depersonalized, . . . about the merits of ideas, plans, and projects" (2000: 132).

Chapter 5

1. Snow's idea is controversial. See Fuller (1993), which points out that efforts by philosophers of science to find criteria by which to distinguish science from non-science have been unproductive. Also, see the preface to the first edition of *Academic Tribes and Territories* (1989), in which Tony Becher says that it was his profound disagreement with Snow's thesis that led to his research on academic disciplines.

2. Also see Appendix Table A-1.

3. Pinch (2001). This is about twenty-five years earlier than most accounts of the origins of the science wars, which point to either the 1962 publication of Thomas Kuhn's *The Structure of Scientific Revolutions* or the development of science studies in the 1970s.

4. Wittgenstein, as quoted by Monk in Pinch (2001: 416, 418).

5. Science studies is different from science, technology, and society (STS). The latter is both a field of study and a movement of academics, and those outside of academia who are concerned with the relationships between science and technology on the one hand and society on the other. Commenting on STS, Susan Cozzens notes,

"We all know that science and technology are in society and that they do not sit very comfortably there" (2001: 53).

    6. Gould (2000: 253).

    7. Labinger (2001: 167).

    8. Fred is not alone among scientists who do not see competition in their field. Tony Becher and Paul Trowler quote a chemist in a study by B. C. Griffith and A. J. Miller who said: "Some people are quite competitive and secretive, but there are others who don't feel that they are in a rat race. They see themselves as being in competition with nature, not with other scientists. The race is only of secondary importance, because the job needs to be done" (Becher and Trowler, 2001: 119).

    9. See Gordon (1980: 115).

    10. Cozzens, in Cozzens and Gieryn (1990: 166–167).

    11. Cozzens and Gieryn (1990: 5).

    12. Smith (1999: 57).

    13. Smith (1999: 57–58).

    14. Smith (1999: 58).

    15. Before he left the seminar, the economist had not been bewildered but had also been a participant in the debates.

    16. Mermin (2001: 98).

    17. Wilson (1999: 8).

    18. In the seminar the following year, there was no proponent of visiting Evelyn's art studio, and such a visit never took place.

    19. In the *Chronicle of Higher Education*, Peter Monaghan (2002) reports on an interesting integration of art and science at the new Franklin W. Olin College of engineering in Needham, Massachusetts. Helen Donis-Keller, professor of both biology and art, is a visual, sound, and video artist but is also a biologist who worked on the human genome.

    20. Gould (2003: 259).

Chapter 6

    1. Sherif and Sherif (1969: x–xi).

    2. In order to provide time for faculty to do the required reading for the sessions, the plan was for them to have one of their courses each semester taught by a postdoc. However, there was not sufficient funding in the grant to provide postdocs for every seminar participant, and the provost decided which faculty would have one. Those who were not assigned a postdoc were advised to negotiate with their dean or department chair about postponing two of their elective courses to the following year. But in several cases, these negotiations did not work out, and at least two of the participants I interviewed were resentful about not having had any course relief.

    3. Gulbenkian Commission (1996: 80).

    4. Petrie (1976: 11).

    5. Frost and Jean (2003: 15).

6. Sherif and Sherif (1969: xi).

7. In Europe, interdisciplinarity, often termed Mode 2 knowledge, includes those who are being studied. See Gibbons et al. (1994).

8. For more on action research, see Nyden et al. (1997).

9. Cantor and Lavine (2006: B-20).

10. As in the social science seminar, the provost decided which faculty in the inequality seminar would have postdocs, and then they chose the particular people with whom they would work. Once more, all faculty participants were supposed to get at least one course off during the year, but several did not.

11. Sheila was constrained in her choice of participants because a faculty seminar on race was being planned at the same time she was choosing participants and it claimed several of the faculty that she had hoped to invite to the inequality seminar.

12. Sill (1996: 149).

13. Pieters and Baumgartner (2002) found that over the three years of the study, the rates of cross-disciplinary citation in the five top journals were 0 percent in both anthropology and psychology, 10 percent in economics (with most of those in finance, a discipline quite close to economics), and 13 and 15 percent in political science and sociology, respectively. In anthropology and psychology, the citation patterns with economics were symmetrical (zero going in both directions); but in political science and sociology, the relationships were asymmetric. Two-thirds of the interdisciplinary citations in political science were to economics, but only 15 percent of economics' interdisciplinary citations were to political science; in sociology, 22 percent of its interdisciplinary citations were to economics, but only 4 percent of economics' interdisciplinary citations were to sociology.

14. There were thirteen disciplines in the study: anthropology and archaeology, area studies, criminology, demography, economics, general social sciences, geography and regional science, international relations, planning and urban studies, political science and public administration, science studies, sociology, and miscellaneous social sciences. (National Science Foundation, 2000: Table A6–54, p. A415).

15. In the study of psychology citations, the other disciplines included physics, chemistry, earth and space sciences, mathematics, biology, biomedical research, clinical medicine, engineering and technology, social sciences, and miscellaneous other fields. Almost 20 percent of psychology's citations were to clinical medicine (National Science Foundation, 2000: Table A6–54, p. A412).

16. See Calhoun (1992), citing Rigney and Barnes.

17. Leijonhufvud (1973: 327).

18. Almond (1988: 830).

19. Michèle Lamont recounts the great surprise of one the cultural anthropologists she interviewed when he recalled that during his doctoral studies his adviser had not steered him to material in sociology that was quite relevant to his topic (2009: 88–89).

Chapter 7

1. See Amey and Brown (2004: 134) for a similar view on both the singular importance of effective leadership for the success of interdisciplinary work and the difficulty of providing it. Also see Stokols and Misra et al. (2008: S100) for a review of the literature on the importance of leadership to "collaborative processes and outcomes."

2. Citing her review of the literature, Barbara Gray argues that effective leaders of collaborative groups require both cognitive and process skills: an ability to provide intellectual stimulation by visioning and framing tasks and issues, thereby allowing participants to "unleash . . . their own curiosity and creativity" (2008: S125), and an ability to "ensure . . . that the interactions among team members are constructive and productive" (2008: S127).

3. Gadamer [1975] (2004: 385).

4. Amey and Brown (2004: S129).

5. Amey and Brown (2004: S129).

6. In the Luce seminars at Emory University, the leader structured the seminars more tightly than had any of the seminar leaders in this study. He chose a seminar theme and then solicited suggestions from faculty participants for readings several months before the seminar was set to begin. He then read their suggested books, chose a subset of their recommendations, and thereby put together a reading list for the seminar that was intellectually coherent. See Frost and Jean (2003). The problem with this much structuring is that it leaves little room for experimenting with presentation formats or helping participants to understand differences in habits of mind. These downsides of tight structuring were not problems for the Luce seminars because they did not aspire to have faculty participants engage with one another after the seminar to create interdisciplinary courses or research projects.

7. Several of these characteristics are related to those that Rogers Hollingsworth and Ellen Jane Hollingsworth noted among leaders at the Rockefeller Institute who were successful in creating and developing extraordinarily productive and high-quality interdisciplinary biomedical research: a "strategic vision" (related to communicating the purpose of the seminar); "the ability to provide rigorous criticism within a nurturing environment," and "the capacity to recruit sufficiently diverse personnel" (both related to having sufficient authority to lead and paying attention to group dynamics) (2000: 225).

8. Bennis (1997: 3).

9. In their study of high-performance teams, Carl Larson and Frank LaFasto (1989) note that such teams have a clear, elevating goal that is well communicated to participants.

10. Warren Bennis finds that successful leaders may have a variety of leadership styles, but they must "provide direction and meaning" and "generate and sustain trust" in order for the group to be successful (1997: 33).

11. Unlike the leaders of the seminars at Jefferson and the social science seminar at Washington, Nancy did not begin the first session of the science studies seminar with readings that she herself chose. Nor did she do what Sheila did in the inequality

seminar, which was to devote the first session to having participants get acquainted with one another and plan out the first few sessions. Instead, Nancy arranged to have the first session of the seminar be a presentation by Jack, an economist, on two of his own articles, one that he had coauthored with a seminar participant in literature and one of which he was the sole author. The respondent to the presentation was a faculty member from religious studies.

12. Klein (1990: 183).

13. Michèle Lamont notes that in the work of the interdisciplinary evaluative panels she studied, leaders and even nonleaders, did a great deal of emotion work: "Program officers, panel chairs, and some panelists engage in 'emotion work,' helping their colleagues save face even after defeat and reintegrating them into the group" (2009: 140). And in their study of an interdisciplinary group at Michigan State, Marilyn Amey and Dennis Brown found that "conflict management skills were required and the ability to create a safe environment for dialogue" (2004: 114). See also Stokols and Misra et al. (2008) for a review of the contribution that "sensitivity to members' emotional needs [makes] to effective leadership in team situations" (p. S100).

14. It may be that one reason why English professors "monopolized" the conversation with their disciplinary arguments is because there is so little agreement at the present time within the discipline of English. Lamont cites an unusual amount of disagreement in English about "standards, the practical meaning and reality of excellence, the merits of theory, the importance of disciplinary boundaries" (2009: 76).

15. Lencioni (2003: 36).

16. Lencioni (2003: 36).

17. Bennis (1997: 33). Gray's review (2008) of the literature on collaborative groups also points to the ability to create trust as a critical factor in successful group leadership.

18. Amey and Brown argue that effective leaders of interdisciplinary teams need to reach a neutral self and that, indeed, all members of an interdisciplinary group must find their neutral selves. They define a neutral self as "one where disciplinary presumptions about the world are suspended, where egos are left at the door, and where openness to new perspectives and learning can take place" (2004: 132). While I agree that interdisciplinary conversations require egos that are left at the door and openness to new perspectives, I am doubtful about the ability of senior faculty at research universities to suspend the disciplinary presumptions they have honed over decades. I think that successful leaders of interdisciplinary conversations and faculty engaged in interdisciplinary projects need not suspend their disciplinary presumptions so much as be keenly aware of them and be open to other views. But perhaps that is what Amey and Brown mean by suspension.

Chapter 8

1. Veronica Boix Mansilla (2006) notes that effects of interdisciplinarity often take some time to transpire.

2. Nachmanovitch (1990: 1).

3. Gadamer [1975] (2004: 102–103).

4. Fish (1989: 18).

5. Salter and Hearn (1996: 147).

Chapter 9

1. Moran (2002: 3).

2. Moran (2002: 3), citing Frank (1988: 100).

3. See Geertz (1983); Becher (1989); Becher and Trowler (2001); Margolis (1993); and Eisner (1982).

4. See John Thompson (1991) and Schwartzman (1989).

5. Some of Lisa Lattuca's subjects also pointed to giving only half credit for a team-taught course as an impediment to interdisciplinary teaching (2001: 194).

6. Gulbenkian Commission (1996: 97).

7. Davis (1995: chaps. 3 and 4).

8. Salter and Hearn (1996: 147).

9. Discussion with Lucy Shapiro, one of the founders of Bio X at Stanford University (May 17, 2005).

10. Michèle Lamont (2009: 18) makes a similar point about the need for panelists on cross-disciplinary evaluation teams to make their own norms, since they are unable to simply use the evaluative norms of their own disciplines.

11. Elbow (1973: 149).

12. The believing and doubting games are related to the concepts of Type I and Type II errors in statistical analysis. For example, the doubting game leads to insistence on a very low probability that a medication worked only by chance, so that Type I error is minimized and a patient will not be taking a medication that is in fact ineffective. But insisting on such a low probability may lead the researcher to commit at Type II error, to miss the possibility that the medication is in fact efficacious.

13. Yankelovich (1999: 43).

14. Discussion with Chris Miller, December 7, 2009.

15. Page (2007).

Bibliography

Abbott, Andrew. 2001. *Chaos of Disciplines.* Chicago: University of Chicago Press.

———. 2002. "The Disciplines and the Future." In Steven Brint (ed.). *The Future of the City of Intellect: The Changing American University.* Stanford, CA: Stanford University Press.

Almond, Gabriel A. 1988. "Separate Tables: Schools and Sects in Political Science." *PS: Political Science and Politics.* Fall: 828–842.

Amariglio, Jack, Stephen Resnick, and Richard Wolff. 1993. "Division and Difference in the 'Discipline' of Economics." In Ellen Messer-Davidow, David R. Shumway, and David J. Sylvan (eds.). *Knowledges: Historical and Critical Studies in Disciplinarity.* Charlottesville: University Press of Virginia, 150–184.

Amey, Marilyn J., and Dennis F. Brown. 2004. *Breaking Out of the Box: Interdisciplinary Collaboration and Faculty Work.* Greenwich, CN: Information Age Publishing.

Association of American Universities (AAU). 2005. *Report of the Interdisciplinarity Task Force.* Washington, DC: Association of American Universities.

Becher, Tony. 1987. "The Disciplinary Shaping of the Profession." In Burton R. Clark (ed.). *The Academic Profession: National, Disciplinary, and Institutional Settings.* Berkeley and Los Angeles: University of California Press, 271–303.

———. 1989. *Academic Tribes and Territories: Intellectual Enquiry and the Cultures of Disciplines.* Milton Keynes, UK: Society for Research into Higher Education and Open University Press.

Becher, Tony, and Paul R. Trowler. 2001. *Academic Tribes and Territories: Intellectual Enquiry and the Cultures of Disciplines.* Milton Keynes, UK: Society for Research into Higher Education and Open University Press.

Bennis, Warren. 1997. "The Secrets of Great Groups." *Leader to Leader* 3: 29–33.

Bourdieu, Pierre. 1991. *Language and Symbolic Power.* Cambridge, MA: Harvard University Press.

Boxer, Marilyn. 1998. *When Women Ask the Questions: Creating Women's Studies in America*. Baltimore: Johns Hopkins University Press.

———. 2000. "Unruly Knowledge: Women's Studies and the Problem of Disciplinarity." *NWSA Journal* 12(2): 119–129.

Boyer, Ernest L. 1990. *Scholarship Reconsidered: Priorities of the Professoriate*. Princeton, NJ: Carnegie Foundation for the Advancement of Teaching.

Brainard, Jeffrey. 2003. "NIH Needs Change, but Not Administrative Overhaul, Says U.S. Report." *Chronicle of Higher Education*. July 30.

Braxton, John M., and Lowell L. Hargens. 1996. "Variation Among Academic Disciplines: Analytical Frameworks and Research." In John C. Smart (ed.). *Higher Education: Handbook of Theory and Research* 11. New York: Agathon Press, 1–46.

Brint, Steven. 2005."Creating the Future: 'New Directions' in American Universities." *Minerva* 43: 23–50.

Brint, Steven, Lori Turk-Bicakci, Kristopher Proctor, and Scott Patrick Murphy. 2009. "Expanding the Social Frame of Knowledge: Interdisciplinary Degree-Granting Fields in American Colleges and Universities, 1975–2000." *Review of Higher Education* 32(2): 155–183.

Broome, Ranier. 2000. "Beyond One's Own Perspective: The Psychology of Cognitive Interdisciplinarity." In Peter Weingart and Nico Stehr (eds.). *Practising Interdisciplinarity*. Toronto: University of Toronto Press.

Bulick, Stephen. 1982. *Structure and Subject Interaction: Toward a Sociology of Knowledge in the Social Sciences*. New York: Marcel Kekker.

Burt, Ronald S. 2004. "Structural Holes and Good Ideas." *American Journal of Sociology* 110(2):349–399.

Calhoun, Craig. 1992. "Sociology, Other Disciplines, and the Project of a General Understanding of Social Life." In Terrence C. Halliday and Morris Janowitz (eds.). *Sociology and Its Publics: The Forms and Fates of Disciplinary Organization*. Chicago: University of Chicago Press, 137–196.

Cantor, Nancy, and Steven D. Lavine. 2006. "Taking Public Scholarship Seriously." *Chronicle of Higher Education*. June 9: B20.

Carnegie Foundation for the Advancement of Teaching. 1978. *Missions of the College Curriculum*. San Francisco: Jossey-Bass.

Caruso, Denise, and Diana Rhoten. 2001. "Lead, Follow, Get Out of the Way: Sidestepping the Barriers to Effective Practice of Interdisciplinarity. A New Mechanism for Knowledge Production and Re-Integration in the Age of Information." The Hybrid Vigor Institute.

Clark, Burton. 1995. *Places of Inquiry*. Berkeley and Los Angeles: University of California Press.

Coleridge, Samuel Taylor. 1968 [1817]. *Biographia Literaria*. Oxford: Oxford University Press.

Collins, Randall. 1998. *The Sociology of Philosophies*. Cambridge, MA: Harvard University Press.

Cozzens, Susan. 2001. "Making Disciplines Disappear in STS." In Stephen H. Cutcliffe and Carl Mitcham (eds.). *Visions of STS: Counterpoints in Science, Technology, and Science Studies*. Albany: State University of New York Press, 51–66.

———. 1990. "Autonomy and Power in Science." In Susan Cozzens and Thomas Gieryn (eds.). *Theories of Science in Society*. Bloomington: Indiana University Press, 164–184. Cozzens, Susan, and Thomas Gieryn. 1990. "Introduction: Putting Science Back in Society." In Susan Cozzens and Thomas Gieryn (eds.). *Theories of Science in Society*. Bloomington: Indiana University Press, 1–14.

Cronon, William. 2006. "Getting Ready to Do History." In Chris M. Golde, George E. Walker, and Associates (eds.). *Envisioning the Future of Doctoral Education, Preparing Stewards of the Discipline, Carnegie Essays on the Doctorate*. San Francisco: Jossey-Bass, 327–349.

Davis, James R. 1995. *Interdisciplinary Courses and Team Teaching: New Arrangements for Learning*. Phoenix, AZ: American Council on Education and Oryx Press.

DellaVigna, Stefano. 2009. "Psychology and Economics: Evidence from the Field." *Journal of Economic Literature* 47(2): 313–372.

Derrida, Jacques. 1995. *Points...: Interviews, 1974–1994*, ed. Elisabeth Weber, trans. Peggy Kamuf and others. Stanford, CA: Stanford University Press.

Derry, Sharon J., and Christina D. Schunn. 2005. "Interdisciplinarity: A Beautiful but Dangerous Beast." In Sharon J. Derry, Christina D. Schunn, and Morton Ann Gernsbacher (eds.). *Interdisciplinary Collaboration: An Emerging Cognitive Science*. Matwah, NJ: Lawrence Erlbaum Associates, xviii–xx.

Deutsch, Karl W., John Platt, and Dieter Senghaas. 1986. "Major Advances in the Social Sciences Since 1900: An Analysis of Conditions and Effects of Creativity." In Karl W. Deutsch, Andrei S. Markovits, and John Platt (eds.). *Advances in the Social Sciences, 1900–1980. What, Who, Where, How?* Cambridge, MA: University Press of America, 373–420.

Dewey, John. 1966 [1916]. *Democracy and Education*. New York: Free Press.

Dogan, Mattei, and Robert Pahre. 1990. *Creative Marginality*. Boulder, CO: Westview Press.

Eisner, Elliot. 1982. *Cognition and Curriculum: A Basis for Deciding What to Teach*. New York: Longman.

Elbow, Peter. 1973. *Writing Without Teachers*. New York: Oxford University Press.

Ely, Robin J., and David A. Thomas. 2001. "Cultural Diversity at Work: The Effects of Diversity Perspectives on Work Group Processes and Outcomes." *Administrative Science Quarterly* 46(2): 229–273.

European Centre for Higher Education. 1983. *Interdisciplinarity in Higher Education*. Bucharest: European Centre for Higher Education.

Feller, Irwin. 2002. "Performance Measurement Redux." *American Journal of Evaluation* 23: 435–452.

———. 2005. "Who Races with Whom; Who Is Likely to Win (or Survive); Why?" Paper presented to the symposium "The Future of the American Public Research University," Pennsylvania State University, February 26.

———. 2006. "Multiple Actors, Multiple Settings, Multiple Criteria: Issues in Assessing Interdisciplinary Research." *Research Evaluation* 15(1): 5–15.

———. 2007. " Interdisciplinarity: Paths Taken and Not Taken." *Change* November/December: 46–51.

Ferber, Marianne, and Julie Nelson (eds.). 1993. *Beyond Economic Man: Feminist Theory and Economics*. Chicago: University of Chicago Press.

———. 2003. *Feminist Economics Today: Beyond Economic Man*. Chicago: University of Chicago Press.

Fish, Stanley. 1989. "Being Interdisciplinary Is So Very Hard to Do." *Profession 89.* New York: MLA, 15–22.

Frank, Roberta. 1988. "'Interdisciplinarity': The First Half Century." In E. G. Stanley and T. F. Hoad (eds.). *Words for Robert Burchfield's Sixty-Fifth Birthday.* Cambridge: D. S. Brewer, 91–101.

Frost, Susan H., and Paul M. Jean. 2003. "Bridging the Disciplines: Interdisciplinary Discourse and Faculty Scholarship." *Journal of Higher Education* 74(2): 119–143.

Fuller, Steve. 1988. *Social Epistemology*. Bloomington: Indiana University Press.

———. 1993. "Rhetoric of the Social Sciences." In Ellen Messer-Davidow, David R. Shumway, and David J. Sylvan (eds.). *Knowledges: Historical and Critical Studies in Disciplinarity*. Charlottesville: University Press of Virginia, 125–149.

Gadamer, Hans-Georg. 2004 [1975]. *Truth and Method*. London: Continuum.

Geertz, Clifford. 1983. "The Way We Think Now: Toward an Ethnography of Modern Thought." In *Local Knowledge: Further Essays in Interpretive Anthropology*. New York: Basic Books, chap. 7.

Gibbons, Michael, Camille Limoges, Helga Nowotny, Simon Schwartzman, Peter Scott, and Martin Trow. 1994. *The New Production of Knowledge: The Dynamics of Science and Research in Contemporary Societies*. London: Sage Publications.

Gordon, Colin (ed.). 1980. *Power/Knowledge, Selected Interviews and Other Writings, 1972–77, with Michel Foucault*. New York: Pantheon Books.

Gould, Stephen Jay. 2000. "Deconstructing the 'Science Wars' by Reconstructing an Old Mold." *Science Magazine*, January 14: 253.

———. 2003. *The Hedgehog, the Fox, and the Magister's Pox*. New York: Harmony Books.

Gray, Barbara. 2008. "Enhancing Transdisciplinary Research Through Collaborative Leadership." *American Journal of Preventive Medicine* 35(2S): S124–S132.

Gregorian, Vartan. 2004. "Colleges Must Reconstruct the Unity of Knowledge," *Chronicle of Higher Education*. June 4.

Gulbenkian Commission on the Restructuring of the Social Sciences. 1996. *Open the Social Sciences*. Stanford, CA: Stanford University Press.

Hodgson, Geoffrey M. 2004. "Reclaiming Habit for Institutional Economics." *Journal of Economic Psychology* 25: 651–660.

Hollingsworth, Rogers, and Ellen Jane Hollingsworth. 2000. "Major Discoveries and Biomedical Research Organizations: Perspectives on Interdisciplinarity, Nurturing Leadership, and Integrated Structure and Cultures." In Peter Weingart and

Nico Stehr (eds.). *Practising Interdisciplinarity*. Toronto: University of Toronto Press.

Hymes, Dell. 1972. "Models of the Interaction of Language and Social Life." In *Directions in Sociolinguistics: The Ethnography of Communication*. New York: Holt, Rinehart and Winston.

Inkeles, Alex. 1986. "Advances in Sociology—A Critique." In Karl W. Deutsch, Andrei S. Markovits, and John Platt (eds.). *Advances in the Social Sciences, 1900–1980. What, Who, Where, How?* Cambridge, MA: University Press of America, 13–20.

Jacobs, Jerry A. 2009. *Chronicle Review*. November 22.

Jacobs, Jerry, and Scott Frickel. 2009. "Interdisciplinarity: A Critical Assessment." *Annual Review of Sociology* 35: 43–65.

Jaschik, Scott. 2005. "Ph.D. Education—Beyond Disciplines." *Inside Higher Ed News*. April 14. http://www.insidehighered.com/news/2005/04/14/grad.

Jencks, Christopher, and David Riesman. 1968. *The Academic Revolution*. Garden City, NY: Doubleday.

Kessel, Frank, and Patricia L. Rosenfield. 2008. "Toward Transdisciplinary Research: Historical and Contemporary Perspectives." *American Journal of Preventive Medicine* 35(2S): S225–S234.

King, Arthur, and John Brownell. 1966. *The Curriculum and the Disciplines of Knowledge*. New York: John Wiley & Sons.

Klein, Julie Thompson. 1990. *Interdisciplinarity: History, Theory, and Practice*. Detroit: Wayne State University Press.

———. 1996. *Crossing Boundaries: Knowledge, Disciplinarities, and Interdisciplinarities*. Charlottesville: University Press of Virginia.

———. 2000. "A Conceptual Vocabulary of Interdisciplinary Science." In Peter Weingart and Nico Stehr (eds.). *Practising Interdisciplinarity*. Toronto: University of Toronto Press.

———. 2005. "Interdisciplinary Teamwork: The Dynamics of Collaboration and Integration." In Sharon J. Derry, Christina D. Schunn, and Morton Ann Gernsbacher (eds.). *Interdisciplinary Collaboration: An Emerging Cognitive Science*. Matwah, NJ: Lawrence Erlbaum Associates, 23–50.

———. 2008. "Evaluation of Interdisciplinarity and Transdisciplinarity Research: A Literature Review." *American Journal of Preventive Medicine* 35 (2S): S116–S123.

Kline, Stephen Jay. 1995. *Conceptual Foundations for Multdisciplinary Thinking*. Stanford, CA: Stanford University Press.

Knapp, Susan. 2006. "Complex Problems Don't Respect Disciplinary Boundaries." *Focus on Faculty: A Supplement to Dartmouth Life*. December 1 and 3.

Kockelmans, Joseph J. 1979. "Science and Discipline: Some Historical and Critical Reflections." In Joseph J. Kockelmans (ed.). *Interdisciplinarity and Higher Education*. University Park: Pennsylvania State University Press.

Kuhn, Thomas S. 1962. *The Structure of Scientific Revolutions*. Chicago: University of Chicago Press.

Kuiper, Edith, and Jolande Sap (eds.). 1995. *Out of the Margin: Feminist Perspectives in Economics.* London: Routledge.

Labinger, Jay A. 2001. "Awakening a Sleeping Giant." In Jay A. Labinger and Harry Collins (eds.). *The One Culture? A Conversation about Science.* Chicago: University of Chicago Press.

Lamont, Michèle. 2009. *How Professors Think: Inside the Curious World of Academic Judgment.* Cambridge, MA: Harvard University Press.

Larson, Carl E., and Frank M. J. LaFasto. 1989. *Teamwork: What Must Go Right/What Can Go Wrong.* Newbury Park, CA: Sage Publications.

Lattuca, Lisa R. 2001. *Creating Interdisciplinarity: Interdisciplinary Research and Teaching among College and University Faculty.* Nashville: Vanderbilt University Press.

Leijonhufvud, Axel. 1973. "Life Among the Econ." *Western Economic Journal* 11(3): 327–337.

Lencioni, Patrick M. 2003. "The Trouble with Teamwork." *Leader to Leader* 29 (Summer): 35–40.

Lenoir, Timothy. 1993. "The Discipline of Nature and the Nature of Disciplines." In Messer-Davidow, Ellen, David R. Shumway, and David J. Sylvan (eds.). *Knowledges: Historical and Critical Studies in Disciplinarity.* Charlottesville: University Press of Virginia, 70–102.

Lynch, Michael. 2001. "Is a Science Peace Process Necessary?" In Jay A. Labinger and Harry Collins (eds.). *The One Culture? A Conversation about Science.* Chicago: University of Chicago Press.

Mansilla, Veronica Boix. 2006. "Assessing Expert Interdisciplinary Work at the Frontier: An Empirical Exploration." *Research Evaluation* 15(1): 17–29.

Mansilla, Veronica Boix, Irwin Feller, and Howard Gardner. 2006. "Quality Assessment in Interdisciplinary Research and Education." *Research Evaluation* 15(1): 69–74.

Mansilla, Veronica Boix, and Howard Gardner. 2010. "Assessing Interdisciplinary Work at the Frontier: An Empirical Exploration of 'Symptoms of Quality.'" http://www.interdisciplines.org/interdisciplinarity/papers/6.

March, James G. 1991. "Exploration and Exploitation in Organizational Learning." *Organization Science* [Special Issue: Organizational Learning Papers in Honor of (and by) James G. March] 2(1): 71–87.

Margolis, Howard. 1993. *Paradigms and Barriers: How Habits of Mind Govern Scientific Beliefs.* Chicago: University of Chicago Press.

Mâsse, Louise C., Richard P. Moser, Daniel Stokols, Brandie K. Taylor, Stephen E. Marcus, Glen D. Morgan, Kara L. Hall, Robert T. Croyle, and William M. Trochim. 2008. "Measuring Collaboration and Transdisciplinary Integration in Team Science." *American Journal of Preventive Medicine* 35(2S): S151–S160.

Mermin, N. David. 2001. "Conversing Seriously with Sociologists." In Jay A. Labinger and Harry Collins (eds.). *The One Culture? A Conversation about Science.* Chicago: University of Chicago Press.

Messer-Davidow, Ellen. 2002. *Disciplining Feminism: From Social Activism to Academic Discourse*. Durham, NC: Duke University Press.

Messer-Davidow, Ellen, David R. Shumway, and David J. Sylvan. 1993. "Introduction: Disciplinary Ways of Knowing." In Ellen Messer-Davidow, David R. Shumway, and David J. Sylvan (eds.). *Knowledges: Historical and Critical Studies in Disciplinarity*. Charlottesville: University Press of Virginia, 1–24.

Mill, John Stuart. 1957 [1848]. *Principles of Political Economy*. Fairchild, NJ: Augustus M. Kelley.

Monaghan, Peter. 2002. "The Fine Art of Engineering." *Chronicle of Higher Education* August 2: A40.

Moran, Joe. 2002. *Interdisciplinarity*. London: Routledge.

Nachmanovitch, Stephen. 1990. *Free Play: Improvisation in Life and Art*. New York: Tarcher/Putnam.

National Academy of Sciences, National Academy of Engineering, and Institute of Medicine. 2005. *Facilitating Interdisciplinary Research*. Washington, DC: National Academies Press.

National Institute of Medicine. 2003. *Enhancing the Vitality of the National Institutes of Health: Organizational Change to Meet New Challenges*. Washington, DC: National Academies Press.

National Science Foundation. 2000. *Science and Engineering Indicators—2000*. Arlington, VA: National Science Foundation. http://www.nsf.gov/statistics/seind00/pdfstart.htm.

Nyden, Philip N., Anne Figert, Mark Shibley, and Darryl Burrows. 1997. *Building Community: Social Science in Action*. Thousand Oaks, CA: Pine Forge Press.

O'Donnell, Angela M., and Sharon J. Derry. 2005. "Cognitive Processes in Interdisciplinary Groups: Problems and Possibilities." In Sharon J. Derry, Christina D. Schunn, and Morton Ann Gernsbacher (eds.). *Interdisciplinary Collaboration: An Emerging Cognitive Science*. Matwah, NJ: Lawrence Erlbaum Associates, 51–82.

Olzak, Susan, and Nicole Kangas. 2008. "Organizational Innovation: Establishing Racial, Ethnic, and Women's Studies Majors in the U.S." *Sociology of Education* 81: 163–188.

Organization for Economic Cooperation and Development. 1972. *Interdisciplinarity: Problems of Teaching and Research in Universities*. Paris: Organization for Economic Cooperation and Development.

Osserman, Robert. 2004. "Mathematics with a Moral." *Chronicle of Higher Education*. April 23.

Page, Scott E. 2007. *The Difference: How the Power of Diversity Creates Better Groups, Firms, Schools, and Societies*. Princeton, NJ: Princeton University Press.

Paxson, Thomas D., Jr. 1996. "Modes of Interaction Between Disciplines." *Journal of Education* 45(2): 79–95.

Petrie, Hugh G. 1976. "Do You See What I See?: The Epistemology of Interdisciplinary Inquiry." *Educational Researcher* 5(2): 9–15.

Pfirman, Stephanie L., James P. Collins, Susan Lowes, and Anthony F. Michaels. 2005.

"Collaborative Efforts: Promoting Interdisciplinary Scholars." *Chronicle of Higher Education.* February 11: B.15.

Piaget, Jean. 1972. "The Epistemology of Interdisciplinary Relationships." In OECD, *Interdisciplinarity: Problems of Teaching and Research in Universities.* Paris: OECD, 127–139.

Pieters, Rik, and Hans Baumgartner. 2002. "Who Talks to Whom? Intra- and Interdisciplinary Communication of Economics Journals." *Journal of Economic Literature* 40 (June): 483–509.

Pinch, Trevor. 2001. "Does Science Studies Undermine Science? Wittgenstein, Turing, and Polanyi as Precursors for Science Studies and the Science Wars." In Jay A. Labinger and Harry Collins (eds.). *The One Culture? A Conversation about Science.* Chicago: University of Chicago Press.

Rhoten, Diana, and Andrew Parker. 2004. "Risks and Rewards of an Interdisciplinary Research Path." *Science* 306 (December 17): 2046.

Rhoten, Diana, Andrew Parker, and Stephanie Pfirman. 2006. "Women in Interdisciplinary Science: Exploring Preferences and Consequences." *Research Policy* 36: 56–75.

Richards, Donald G. 1996. "The Meaning and Relevance of 'Synthesis' in Interdisciplinary Studies." *Journal of General Education* 45(2): 114–128.

Rogers, Yvonne, Mike Scaife, and Antonio Rizzo. 2005. "Interdisciplinarity: An Emergent of Engineered Process." In Sharon J. Derry, Christina D. Schunn, and Morton Ann Gernsbacher (eds.). *Interdisciplinary Collaboration: An Emerging Cognitive Science.* Matwah, NJ: Lawrence Erlbaum Associates, 265–285.

Rojas, Fabio. 2007. *From Black Power to Black Studies: How a Radical Social Movement Became an Academic Discipline.* Baltimore: Johns Hopkins University Press.

Rossini, F. A., and A. L. Porter. 1984. "Interdisciplinary Research: Performance and Policy Issues." In R. Jurkovich and J. H. P. Paelinck (eds.). *Problems in Interdisciplinary Studies.* Brookfield, VT: Gower Publishing, 26–45.

Sá, Creso M. 2008. "Interdisciplinary Strategies' in U.S. Research Universities." *Higher Education* 55: 537–552.

Salter, Liora, and Alison Hearn. 1996. *Outside the Lines: Issues in Interdisciplinary Research.* Montreal: McGill-Queens University Press.

Scerri, Eric. 2000. "Interdisciplinary Research at the Caltech Beckman Institute." In Peter Weingart and Nico Stehr (eds.). *Practising Interdisciplinarity.* Toronto: University of Toronto Press.

Schwartzman, Helen B. 1989. *The Meeting.* New York: Plenum Press.

Shapiro, Lucy. 2005. Presentation to Education 353X, "Interdisciplinarity in Higher Education." Stanford University, Stanford, CA, May 17.

Sill, David J. 1996. "Integrative Thinking, Synthesis, and Creativity in Interdisciplinary Studies." *Journal of General Education* 45(2): 129–151.

Sherif, Muzafer, and Carolyn Sherif. 1969. *Interdisciplinary Relationships in the Social Sciences.* Chicago: Aldine Publishing.

Sjölander, S. 1985. "Long-term and Short-term Interdisciplinary Work: Difficulties,

Pitfalls, and Built-in Failures." In L. Levin and I. Lind (eds.). *Interdisciplinarity Revisited.* Stockholm: OECD, SNBC, Linköping University.

Smart, John C., Kenneth A. Feldman, and Corinna Ethington. 2000. *Academic Disciplines: Holland's Theory and the Study of College Students and Faculty.* Nashville: Vanderbilt University Press.

Smelser, Neil J. 2004. "Interdisciplinarity in Theory and Practice." In Charles Camic and Hans Joas (eds.). *The Dialogical Turn: New Roles for Sociology in the Postdisciplinary Age.* Lanham, MD: Rowman & Littlefield, 43–64.

Smith, Adam. 1976 [1776]. *An Inquiry into the Nature and Causes of the Wealth of Nations.* Chicago: University of Chicago Press.

Smith, Barbara Herrnstein. 1999. "Microdynamics of Incommensurability: Philosophy of Science Meets Science Studies." In Diederik Aerts, Jan Broedkaert, and Ernest Mathijs (eds.). *Einstein Meets Magritte: An Interdisciplinary Reflection (The White Book of Einstein Meets Magritte).* Dordrecht, Netherlands: Kluwer Academic Publishers.

———. 2001. "The Sciences and the Humanities: Is There a War Going On?" Paper presented at the symposium "The Two Cultures Revisited," University of Dayton, February 14.

Snow, C. P. 1998 [1959]. *The Two Cultures.* Cambridge: Cambridge University Press.

Steiner, I. D. 1972. *Processes and Productivity.* New York: Academic Press.

Stokols, Daniel, K. L. Hall, B. K. Taylor, and R. P. Moser. 2008. "The Science of Team Science: Overview of the Field and Introduction to the Supplement." *American Journal of Preventive Medicine* 35(2S): S77–S89.

Stokols, Daniel, S. Misra, R. P. Moser, K. L. Hall, and B. K. Taylor. 2008. "The Ecology of Team Science: Understanding Contextual Influences on Transdisciplinary Collaboration." *American Journal of Preventive Medicine* 35(2S): S96–S115.

Strober, Myra H. 1994. "Rethinking Economics Through a Feminist Lens." *American Economic Review* 84(2): 143–147.

———. 2006. "Habits of the Mind: Challenges for Multidisciplinarity." *Social Epistemology* 20(3–4): 315–331.

Strober, Myra H., and David B. Tyack. 1980. "Why Women Teach While Men Manage: A Report on Research in Progress." *Signs: Journal of Women in Culture and Society.* Spring, 494–503.

Swoboda, Wolfram W. 1979. "Disciplines and Interdisciplinarity." In Joseph J. Kockelmans (ed). *Interdisciplinarity and Higher Education.* University Park: Pennsylvania State University Press, 49–92.

Taylor, Mark C. 2009. "End the University as We Know It." *New York Times,* April 27.

Thompson, John B. 1991. Introduction to Pierre Bourdieu, *Language and Symbolic Power.* Cambridge, MA: Harvard University Press.

Thompson, Leigh. 2000. *Making the Team: A Guide for Managers.* Upper Saddle River, NJ: Prentice Hall.

Turner, Stephen. 2000. "What Are Disciplines? And How Is Interdisciplinarity Different?" In Peter Weingart and Nico Stehr, (eds.). *Practising Interdisciplinarity*. Toronto: University of Toronto Press.

Tyack, David B., and Myra H. Strober. 1981. "Jobs and Gender: A History of the Structuring of Educational Employment by Sex." In P. Schmuck, W. Charters, and R. Carlson (eds.). *Education Policy and Management: Sex Differentials*. New York: Academic Press.

Warner, Michael. 1999. *The Trouble with Normal: Sex, Politics, and the Ethics of Queer Life*. Cambridge, MA: Harvard University Press.

Wilson, Edward O. 1999. *Consilience: The Unity of Knowledge*. New York: Vintage Books.

Wuchty, Stefan, Benjamin F. Jones, and Brian Uzzi. 2007. "The Increasing Dominance of Teams in the Production of Knowledge." *Science* 316 (May 18): 1036–1039.

Yankelovich, Daniel. 1999. *The Magic of Dialogue: Transforming Conflict into Cooperation*. New York: Simon & Schuster.

Index

Abbott, Andrew, 24, 62, 178n51, 180n71
academia and academic structure:
    barriers to team teaching in, 138–40,
    151, 192n5; disciplinary knowledge
    in, 14–15, 176n17; disciplinary
    mold of, 173n2; doubting game
    emphasized in, 9–10, 47–48,
    164–66, 185n39, 192n12; example
    of non-departmental structure,
    14; funding possibilities and, 20,
    179n64; interdisciplinary research
    evaluations and, 25–26, 181n91;
    making room for interdisciplinary
    courses in, 151–52; purpose of
    meetings in, 68–70; reward
    system of, 2; routines embedded
    in, 136; subcultures (gated
    communities) in, 50; support
    for social sciences seminar and,
    101–2. *See also* administrators;
    academic departments; academic
    journals; faculty; funding sources;
    universities
academic departments: demise of
    interdisciplinary, 176n17; disciplines
    in relation to, 14–15, 176n22; earliest

formation of, 14, 176n16. *See also*
    disciplines
academic journals: approaches
    to writing for, 178n50; book-
    borrowing patterns and, 37; call for
    interdisciplinary, 182n97; citation
    patterns in, 109, 175n2, 189nn13–15;
    citations and assertions of power
    in, 76; increase in collaboration
    evidenced in, 180n76; prestige
    of interdisciplinary vs. single
    discipline, 182n95; renewed interest
    in interdisciplinarity in, 20
Adams (pseud.) faculty seminars:
    collegiality increased due to, 141–42;
    details about, 169, 170; focus of,
    7; funding for, 6; insights about
    interdisciplinarity gained in, 146–49;
    leadership style in, 118, 123–24, 126,
    190–91n11; participants chosen for,
    155; purpose of, 119, 121, 149–50, 159–
    60; team teaching and, 157, 158. *See
    also* ethics seminar (Adams); science
    studies seminar (Adams)
administrators: cross-disciplinary
    discussion and, 94–98; faculty

Acknowledgments

I ACKNOWLEDGE, WITH SPECIAL THANKS, SEMINAR PARTICI-
pants and administrators for their candid interviews and the Ford
Foundation for its financial support.

Several Stanford colleagues helped me to conceptualize the study and interpret the data: Patricia Gumport, with whom I cotaught a doctoral seminar on interdisciplinarity; several speakers in that seminar who helped me
to understand interdisciplinarity in science; John Hennessey, Jeffrey Kosek,
Bernard Roth, and Lucy Shapiro; and two students in the seminar, Michah
Landsman and Christopher Tilghman. Stanford colleagues Deborah Gru-
enfeld, James March, and Deborah Meyerson pointed me to sources from
the organization behavior literature, and Stanford mathematicians Donald
Ornstein and Solomon Pfeferman, were helpful in corroborating the habits
of mind of mathematicians and the practices in mathematics seminars explained by "Barry" in the representation seminar at "Jefferson."

The Ford Foundation International Working Group on Universities organized by Davydd Greenwood provided interesting ideas and sources at an
early stage of the project, especially Jorge Balan, Donald Brenneis, Dolores
Byrnes, Davydd Greenwood, and Maresi Nerad.

Cecile Andrews, Jerry Burger, Lena Chu, Carol Muller, Wenda O'Reilly,
Carter Schwonke, Jason Scott, and two anonymous reviewers read the entire
manuscript and suggested changes. Kate Wahl, my editor at the Stanford University Press, also offered numerous helpful suggestions.

An interdisciplinary "team" of two colleagues and three family members went far beyond the calls of friendship and kinship throughout this project, believing in the importance of the study, offering interpretations of data, and suggesting changes in the manuscript: economist Clair Brown, historians Mary Felstiner and Rashi Jackman, anthropologist Elizabeth Strober, and psychiatrist Jay Jackman.